# The Cavern-Mystery Transmission

*Asian Studies at Hawaii, No. 38*

# The Cavern-Mystery Transmission

## A Taoist Ordination Rite of A.D. 711

Charles D. Benn

ASIAN STUDIES AT HAWAII

UNIVERSITY OF HAWAII

UNIVERSITY OF HAWAII PRESS

HONOLULU

**Library of Congress Cataloging-in-Publication Data**

Benn, Charles D., 1943–

The cavern-mystery transmission : a Taoist ordination rite of

A.D. 711 / Charles D. Benn.

p.   cm. — (Asian studies at Hawaii ; no. 38)

Revision of the author's thesis (doctoral)—University of Hawaii, 1977.

Includes bibliographical references and index.

ISBN 0–8248–1359–6 (alk. paper)

1. Ordination of women—Taoism. 2. Taoism—Rituals.

3. Ordination (Liturgy) 4. Yü-chen, Princess, daughter of T'ang

Jui-tsung, Emperor of China, 690–762 or 3. 5. Chin-hsien,

Princess, daughter of T'ang Jui-tsung, Emperor of China, 688–732.

I. Title. II. Series.

DS3.A2A82    no. 38

[BL1940.4]

950 s—dc20

[299'.51438]            91–13926

CIP

# CONTENTS

*Preface*                                                                    vii

*Abbreviations*                                                               ix

*Prelude*                                                                      1

Chapter One
*Dramatis Personae*                                                            5

Chapter Two
*The Stage*                                                                    21

Chapter Three
*The Drama*                                                                    39

Chapter Four
*Denouements*                                                                  72

*Finale*                                                                       99

*Appendix One:*
*Chang Wan-fu's Account of the Princesses' Ling-pao Investiture*              115

*Appendix Two:*
*A Synopsis of the Ordination Rite for the Ling-pao Canon*                    121

*Appendix Three:*
*The Works of Chang Wan-fu*                                                   137

CONTENTS

| | |
|---|---|
| *Notes* | 153 |
| *Glossary* | 189 |
| *Bibliography* | 201 |
| *Index* | 211 |

*Illustrations follow page 106*

# PREFACE

THIS STUDY BEGAN as a sketch, several pages long, in a doctoral dissertation completed in 1977. The sketch was devoted to T'ang princesses who took vows as Taoist nuns and was based mainly on secular sources. Subsequently, I discovered in the *Repository of the Taoist Canon* an account of the Ling-pao investiture, "The Transmission of the Cavern-Mystery," for Princesses Gold-Immortal and Jade-Perfected, which the prelate Shih Ch'ung-hsüan conducted in A.D. 711. Chang Wan-fu, a cleric who witnessed the event and who may have been one of its officiants, wrote the report (see Chapter One on the lives and works of the Princesses and priests). Although Chang was one of the foremost liturgists in his day, no biography of him has survived and virtually all information about him derives from those of his writings still extant in the *Repository of the Taoist Canon* (a detailed analysis of the texts has been supplied in Appendix Three).

What impressed Chang most was the munificence of the trappings which the ladies or their father supplied for the ordination. His description focuses on the altar, its furnishings, and the pledges that the ladies offered (the account is analyzed in Chapter Two and translated in Appendix One). He provides only fleeting glimpses of the rite itself. What transpired during the proceedings can only be reconstructed from other sources, especially from the oldest surviving manual for performing the liturgy of the Ling-pao investiture, which Lu Hsiu-ching compiled in the fifth century. Although it is somewhat hazardous to apply Lu's regulations to an ordination which took place more than two and a half centuries later, his manual enjoyed great esteem with later Taoists, and many of his protocols undoubtedly survived in the rite conducted for the Princesses (Lu's work is the basis for Chapter Three and the core of the synopsis in Appendix Two).

With the exception of the initial administration of vows, Taoist ordinations were not rites that marked the passage of novices into the priesthood. The higher levels of investiture were ceremonial transmissions of increasingly prestigious scriptural corpora whose bestowal afforded aspirants access to more mysterious and powerful secrets. Since these canons occupied ranks of differing esteem in the scheme of things, ordinations were also devices for assigning status within the Taoist clergy. Consequently, the investiture of Princesses Gold-Immortal and Jade-Perfected cannot be understood without reference to the ecclesiastical hierarchy of orders which Chin-ming Ch'i-chen (ca. A.D. 550) and Chang Wan-fu defined for medieval Taoism (Chapter Four).

With some notable exceptions, Chinese, Japanese, French, and American specialists in Taoism have focused their attention on dating and analyzing scriptures and related texts, on investigating various religious ideas or theories such as meditation and alchemy, or on defining Buddhist influences on Taoism. No modern authority has dealt with the institutional framework of the Taoist priesthood in medieval China. This study attempts to fill that vacuum by examining in depth a specific case of investiture and by describing in general the hierarchical structure of the clergy into which that ordination fit.

I would like to thank the American Council of Learned Societies for supplying me with a grant some years ago to revise my dissertation for publication. This study is a product of that endeavor. I would also like to thank Professors Brian McKnight, David Chappell, and Michael Saso as well as Patricia Crosby of the University of Hawaii Press for their invaluable assistance during the research and preparation for publication of this work.

# ABBREVIATIONS

CSTP     Chin-shih ts'ui-pien

CTS     Chiu T'ang shu

CTW     Ch'üan T'ang wen

HTS     Hsin T'ang shu

HY     Harvard-Yenching index to the Cheng-t'ung Tao-tsang (Repository of the Taoist Canon compiled in the Cheng-t'ung era, 1436–1450)

P     Pelliot collection of Tun-huang manuscripts, Bibliothèque Nationale, Paris

S     Stein collection of Tun-huang manuscripts, British Museum

TCTC     Tzu-chih t'ung-chien

TFYK     Ts'e-fu yüan-kuei

THY     T'ang hui-yao

TLCCFK     T'ang liang-ching ch'eng-fang k'ao

TTLT     Ta T'ang liu-tien

# *Prelude*

Tucked away in an obscure corner of the *Repository of the Taoist Canon (Tao-tsang)*, appended almost as an afterthought to a text on the ordination of Taoist priests, is a rare document written by Chang Wan-fu which describes the transmission of the Ling-pao canon at a rite of investiture during the T'ang dynasty (618–907). It is rare, not only because eyewitness accounts of such proceedings are virtually nonexistent, but also because the recipients of the scriptures were ladies of royal blood, the daughters of Emperor Jui-tsung (r. 684–690 and 710–713). The passage begins:

On the tenth of February, 711, I witnessed Princess Gold-Immortal and Princess Jade-Perfected visit Reverend Preceptor Shih—
   Grand Canon Preceptor of the Three Caverns;
   Abbot of the Supreme Purity Abbey;
   Grandee of Illustrious Noble Rank, Gold Signet and Purple Ribbon [grade three, step two];
   Chief of the Service for Stentorian Annunciation [grade three, step two];
   Principality-Founding Duke, Ho-nei Commandery [grade two, step one];
   Pillar of State, First Class [grade two, step one]
—to receive investiture as Taoist priests [*shou-tao;* literally, receive the Tao], rend
   the Self-Generated Tally of the Numinous Treasure,
and secure
   the Canon of the Central Covenant in Eight Satchels, forty-seven chapters,

I

two True-Writ Registers,
Belt Talismans, and
Staffs

in the Abbey of Refuge in Perfection (Kuei-chen kuan) at the Great Inner
Palace (Ta-nei).

The text then proceeds to give a detailed description of the altar, ritual
paraphernalia, and pledges that pertained to the rite.[1]

Taoist ordination was a highly formalized and esoteric ritual, sanctified and legitimized by protocols from divine codes, for a preceptor's
transmission of a scriptural corpus to students. The Ling-pao canon,
especially a body of key writs within it, was sacred because it formed
itself spontaneously from ethers before the creation of the universe and
was therefore a pristine manifestation of primeval cosmic forces. After
genesis, the highest deity had the holy texts cast in gold tablets and
engraved on jade slats. Then he authorized the bestowal of them upon
the most eminent deities under his command and had them deposited in
celestial archives where they remained undisturbed for eons. When the
proper moment arrived, he released them from the repository, and the
Perfected revealed them to an annointed mortal worthy. Ordination was
the mundane analogue to the celestial conferral of the canon and to its
terrestrial revelation. However, although the function of Ling-pao
investiture was the awarding of the entire corpus to ordinands, it is
quite clear from the oldest manual for conducting the rite that the transmission of the canon as a whole was less important than the transmission of its parts, that is, certain writs, registers, talismans, and injunctions therein. These written documents, often cast in celestial scripts
undecipherable to the uninitiated, possessed immense magical power,
which the priest activated through visualizations, invocations, and
other techniques to alter his own destiny and the destinies of his parish-
ioners, secure peace and prosperity for the empire, and prevent or dispel natural calamities. In short, ordination was a rite of empowerment
during which the officiant conferred on students the instruments which
would thereafter enable them to discharge their offices as priests,
namely, the six major Ling-pao retreats as well as other, lesser rites.
The power of the writs, registers, and talismans was of such a magni-
tude that great care was taken to ensure that they did not fall into the
wrong hands. Should the uninitiated or unscrupulous acquire them,
they might employ them for malevolent or mean rather than benevolent
and altruistic ends. Consequently, in the course of the investiture the
preceptor conferred sets of injunctions that defined the standards of
behavior and mental attitudes to which those privileged to receive the

scriptures were expected to adhere. On their part the ordinands established covenants and swore oaths which enjoined them to maintain the absolute secrecy of the canon and guaranteed their eternal fidelity to their overlords, their teachers and the gods. In addition, they furnished bonds, in the form of pledges, to secure their pacts and vows and were warned that they would suffer certain punishment in the afterlife should they fail to honor their word. Ordinations had all the character of juridical proceedings. Finally, although the officiant presented the canon to students during the investiture, they were not unversed in the scriptures before they undertook this momentous step. They could not have performed the roles assigned them at the ordination rite nor could they have conducted the retreats which investiture entitled them to execute without having previously studied the texts and having undergone extensive training in certain meditative and liturgical acts. Ordination was only the final phase of education for the priesthood, during which an initiate received a master's last instructions and approbation.

There was no single investiture for the priesthood in Taoism because there was no single corpus of scripture. Seven distinct canons emerged in the most creative period of the religion between A.D. 150 and 500, all but one of which claimed legitimacy by virtue of a revelatory tradition (see Chapter Four, numbers 5 through 11). Those aspiring to a clerical vocation could request instruction in any one or, after A.D. 578, several of these from a master and, on satisfying their preceptors that they were worthy, receive the sacred texts through a ritual of transmission. The seven corpora, and the clerical orders which they generated, did not enjoy equal prestige, and by the middle of the sixth century they had been arranged in a hierarchy. Those sacred texts which enjoyed the highest repute rose to the top, and the remainder assumed positions in lower ranks of lesser honor. There is some inconclusive evidence that Princesses Gold-Immortal and Jade-Perfected received one or more of the lower-ranking canons, but it is the transmission to them of the two most esteemed sets that is best documented. The Ling-pao scriptures occupied the second highest rung of the ladder, but, in terms of their social role, they were actually more important than any other sets during medieval times. The Ling-pao retreats, constructed from elements in the canon, were the most common forms of religious service offered by Taoism to the family, the community, and the state during the late Nan-pei ch'ao (317–589), Sui (581–618), and T'ang periods. So when Shih Ch'ung-hsüan administered vows to the Princesses at their ordination in 711, he was effectively admitting them to the working priesthood. The Shang-ch'ing order held the supreme rank in the priesthood based on its claim to having access to a corpus of scripture superior to all others, a claim which other orders appear to have accepted without much objection. That corpus was, of course, the object of esoteric transmission during its investitures. Although membership in it did not preclude officiating at public rites, including the Ling-pao retreats, it was an elite that concentrated mainly on individual spiritual perfection. In that respect it resembled the Ch'an (Zen) school, whose adherents devoted themselves to what was generally considered a higher state of spiritual discipline and accomplishment. Princesses Gold-Immortal and Jade-Perfected also sought initiation into the mysteries of the Shang-ch'ing canon. Some twenty-two months after their Ling-pao ordinations they received these sacred texts at a rite of investiture, thereby attaining the highest honor and status possible within the Taoist priesthood.

In attaining these lofty ranks in the ecclesiastical hierarchy the ladies followed the same route and enjoyed the same powers, prerogatives, and duties as their male counterparts. There is no evidence that they were the objects of discrimination based on their sex. The discrimination, if it can be called that, to which they were subject was the consequence of their social status as members of the royal family. In their demands for pledges, liturgical protocols imposed a greater burden upon the Princesses than upon commoners. It appears that Taoism accorded women equality with men during medieval times.

# CHAPTER ONE

# *Dramatis Personae*

PRINCESSES GOLD-IMMORTAL (Chin-hsien kung-chu) and Jade-Perfected (Yü-chen kung-chu) were the daughters of Lady Tou, Jui-tsung's third consort, who was also the mother of Emperor Hsüan-tsung (r. 713–756). They were born between 688 and 690.[1]

On February 27, 684, Empress Wu Tse-t'ien (r. 690–705) seated their father on the throne, the day after deposing his elder brother, Chung-tsung (r. 684 and 705–710). Jui-tsung ruled in name only. His mother denied him the right to occupy the royal apartments in the palace and to participate in decision-making. The Empress actually wielded the power of the monarchy. However, unlike dowagers of earlier epochs, she was not content to govern behind the façade of her son's throne. On October 16, 690, she overthrew the T'ang dynasty and proclaimed the founding of the Chou dynasty. Three days later she deposed Jui-tsung and assumed the throne in her own right, the first and only woman to do so in Chinese history. Jui-tsung was reduced to the status of "Imperial Successor," shorn of any semblance of power and isolated in the forbidden precincts of the palace at Lo-yang. His position at court deteriorated to such a degree that he became vulnerable to attacks from the lowest quarters. Wei T'uan-erh, a household slave in the palace, developed a deep animosity toward him because he had rejected her advances. She concocted a plot to devastate him by eliminating two of his wives, Lady Liu and Lady Tou, and secretly buried a doll in their courtyard. Then she went to Empress Wu, whose favor and trust she enjoyed, and falsely accused the women of practicing sorcery, a crime classified as depravity, one of the Ten Abominations or most heinous offenses in the T'ang law code. On the morning of December 15, 692, Lady Liu and Lady Tou attended an audience with Wu Tse-t'ien. After they had withdrawn, the Empress' agents, probably eunuchs, murdered them and buried their corpses at a secret location on the palace grounds. Alarmed by the disappearance of his wives, Jui-tsung nevertheless maintained his composure and did not mention the matter. Shortly thereafter, T'uan-erh made another attempt to bring him to ruin, but apparently strained her credibility. The Empress was not convinced that her allegations were true and had her put to death. Jui-tsung escaped unscathed.[2]

A remarkably astute and ruthless infighter, Wu Tse-t'ien seized and maintained power, in part, through a reign of terror the objective of which was to eradicate all resistance to her authority, especially any opposition that originated from or focused on that branch of the Li clan that constituted the royal house of the T'ang. Her suspicions about the loyalty of his family placed Jui-tsung and his immediate family in constant peril. On March 6, 693, the Empress had two officials cut in two at the waist in the market of Loyang for having visited the deposed monarch privately—that is, for having visited him without first notifying the throne. Thereafter neither nobles nor officials were able to call upon him. Subsequently, some informant accused Jui-tsung of secretly plotting rebellion. Empress Wu assigned responsibility for investigating this charge to Lai Chün-ch'en, the infamous head of her secret police. Lai rounded up a group of suspects that he claimed were involved in the conspiracy. All save a man named An Chin-ts'ang, who was a menial in the Service of the Grand Standard-Bearer (T'ai-ch'ang ssu), falsely confessed to participating in the alleged plot when confronted with torture. Chin-ts'ang alone steadfastly maintained the innocence of the Imperial Successor. While being interrogated, he somehow managed to seize a knife and ripped open his stomach to demonstrate his sincerity. On learning of this development, Wu Tse-t'ien dispatched a litter to move the poor man into the palace where an imperial physician restored the internal organs to his abdominal cavity and sutured the wound with white mulberry-bark thread. With the aid of medicine prescribed by the doctor, Chin-ts'ang survived the ordeal. His heroic sacrifice discredited the testimony of the suspects who had confessed, and the case against Jui-tsung was dropped. Nevertheless, the effect of the incident was to further isolate Jui-tsung from contact with the outside world. He became a prisoner in his own apartments. For a time he was spared further harassment, but in 697 Lai Chün-ch'en lodged false charges against him, alleging that he had conspired to rebel against the throne in collusion with Chung-tsung, Princess T'ai-p'ing, and the Wu princes (paternal nephews of Empress Wu). However, Lai, like Wei T'uan-erh, had gone too far. The princes and the Princess aggressively pursued a countersuit which effectively foiled his machination. The accused were exonerated, and this automatically inculpated the accuser. Lai was arrested for fabricating legal complaints, imprisoned, and executed on June 26 of the same year.[3]

In 698 the fortunes of the Li house began to improve somewhat when Empress Wu recalled Chung-tsung from exile. Several months later Jui-tsung petitioned his mother requesting permission to cede his right to the throne to his elder brother, and on October 24 she installed the latter as heir-apparent. This rehabilitation of Chung-tsung was an act to appease popular sentiment, which had turned against the Empress' military policies. At the time, she was having great difficulty recruiting troops to repel a Turkish invasion. The elevation of Chung-tsung restored public confidence, and she was able to raise another army. The Turks withdrew to the steppes in the face of forces superior to their own. In making this concession to the royal house of the T'ang, Wu Tse-t'ien did not intend to surrender her authority or to undermine her newly established dynasty. On January 31, 699, she conferred her surname, Wu, on the Crown Prince, thereby making him heir to the Chou, not the T'ang, throne. Furthermore, she continued to use terror as an instrument for intimidating the royal Li family. On October 8, 701, Chung-tsung's eldest son, his daughter Princess Yung-t'ai, and her husband perished on the orders of the Empress when Chung-tsung's second son revealed that they had criticized two of her favorites. She was not about to tolerate opposition of any sort from the Li clan.[4]

On February 20, 705, the T'ang was finally freed from Wu Tse-t'ien's tyranny when a cabal of T'ang loyalists overthrew her. Two days later, Chung-tsung reclaimed the throne and restored the T'ang dynasty. Although the Empress was stripped of all power and died soon afterward (December 16), her influence persisted. She had succeeded in concentrating power in her own hands by severely weakening the authority of the Li clan as well as the confidence of her sons, and by skillfully manipulating the appointments and dismissals of high-ranking ministers to prevent the formation of organized resistance to her governance. When she died, she left as a legacy two feeble successors; a bureaucracy dominated by factionalism, incompetence, and corruption; and an inner court controlled by mothers, wives, and daughters. Moreover, the climate of intrigue which she had fostered while on the throne persisted unabated, and conspiracy was the rule of politics for nearly a decade after her deposition. At some point between 705 and 710 Jui-tsung, who was Prince Hsiang at the time, nearly fell victim to one of these conspiracies when three officials accused him of plotting rebellion with his sister, Princess T'ai-p'ing. Fortunately for him, a censor pointed out that he had voluntarily ceded his right to the throne in 698. It seemed highly improbable that a man of such character would be involved in a conspiracy to foment rebellion, and the case was dropped. On July 3, 710, Chung-tsung himself succumbed to the machinations of his wife, Empress Wei, who had poison introduced into his food. After his demise the Empress made preparations to establish a regime patterned after that of Wu Tse-t'ien's, but Hsüan-tsung, Jui-tsung's third son, moved quickly to thwart her ambitions. On the night of July 22 he staged a coup d'etat, during which the Empress and her supporters were put to the sword. Even this was insufficient, however, to restore normalcy to the court. Princess T'ai-p'ing, the direct heir to Empress Wu's style of politics, built her own clique at court and made plans to seize power. On July 29, 713, Hsüan-tsung again took command of the palace by force of arms and exterminated her partisans. The Princess committed suicide at imperial order three days later. Only then were the last vestiges of Wu Tse-t'ien's influence eradicated. Political stability finally returned to the empire.[5]

Such was the less than salubrious environment in which Princesses Gold-Immortal and Jade-Perfected spent their formative years. For fifteen years or so they lived in the inner palace where a climate of suspicion and fear prevailed, where their mother was murdered, where their father was repeatedly attacked, and where their own safety could not be guaranteed. It is impossible to determine from existing documents how they reacted emotionally to these circumstances, but they clearly developed a deep interest in Taoism. As a philosophy, Taoism had supplied the conventional rationale for withdrawal from the life of engagement, especially political engagement, since at least Chuang Tzu's time (ca. 370–301 B.C.). Hermits, who by nature favored retirement from society, and officials, who not infrequently resigned from posts or rejected offers of employment in the government during troubled times, were in the habit of undertaking the study of the *Tao-te ching* and the *Chuang Tzu* because they found in the doctrine of non-action expounded in these works a justification for repudiating the activism of service to society or the state. Furthermore, the quietism advocated in the texts created a kind of psychological armor that protected the practitioner from stress. These notions may have struck sympathetic chords in the minds of the Princesses, who may have been introduced to the works early in their lives. Their father wrote a commentary on the *Tao-te ching*. Unfortunately, it is not known when he completed the annotation or if his interests influenced the thinking of his daughters.[6]

As a religion, Taoism, like Buddhism, offered women the only socially acceptable alternative to matrimony in medieval China. Customarily princesses remained in the forbidden precincts or their fathers' mansions until marriages had been arranged for them. Then they left to join the households of their husbands. All seven of Jui-tsung's elder daughters were duly wed. Only Princesses Gold-Immortal and Jade-Perfected, the Emperor's youngest, entered the priesthood. The Princesses were certainly aware that Princess Yung-t'ai's marriage had conferred no special immunity from accusations or executions. Wedlock offered them a way out of the palace, but not out of politics. They also understood that taking vows to become a nun—Buddhist or Taoist—entailed a departure from the family and secular life *(ch'u-chia* and *ch'u-su)*. As will be seen in the case of Jade-Perfected, this departure by no means totally insulated members of the royal house from involvement in the political and familial affairs of the dynasty. However, it did ensure that the women would not become candidates for marriage alliances, and thus afforded them a measure of detachment that appears to have made engagement in court politics a matter of choice on their part. The cloister offered the two Princesses a haven which the family could not. As nuns they were less likely to be implicated in the strife, stress, and reprisals that prevailed at court during their youth.[7]

According to her epitaph, Princess Gold-Immortal was ordained in 706, the year following the overthrow of Wu Tse-t'ien and approximately three years after she reached the marriageable age of fourteen. Another inscription contends that the ordination of Jade-Perfected occurred in 710 or 711, when she received the Tao from Yeh Fa-shan (616–July 12, 720). On the surface, these statements seem to contradict Chang Wan-fu's account of the Ling-pao investiture at the Kuei-chen Abbey in 711. This is probably not the case. There were at least three levels of initiation and ordination which served as preliminary steps to the conferral of the Ling-pao scriptures (see Chapter Four, numbers 3, 4, 5, 7, and 8): a ritual for taking vows (oaths sworn which bound the professor to maintain the Injunctions for the Beginning of Perfection, *Ch'u-chen chieh*, and to remain celibate), the transmission of the *Tao-te ching* and related matter, and the bestowal of the canon based on the *San-huang wen* (Writ of the Three Sovereigns). These documents may be referring to two of these stages. Furthermore, since the ladies were ordained at a single rite on the same altar in later investitures, it is quite possible that they took vows and received the *Tao-te ching* and the San-huang canons together as well.[8]

Whatever the case, the fall of Empress Wu appears to have influenced the Princesses' decision. After founding the Chou dynasty in 690, the

Empress abolished the Taoist ideology of the T'ang and inaugurated her own ideology based on Buddhism. Although she was not hostile to Taoism, she did not foster or patronize it much either. Under the circumstances it seems unlikely that the Empress would have permitted members of her family to take vows as Taoist priests during that period even if they had wanted or had been old enough to do so. On March 3, 705, Chung-tsung, in turn, abolished the Empress' Buddhist ideology and restored the Taoist ideology of the early T'ang. This act removed the bias against Taoism that existed at court and paved the way for the Princesses to pursue their ambitions. Moreover, the overthrow of Empress Wu altered Jui-tsung's status. As previously indicated, his mother had controlled virtually all of his affairs while she was on the throne. After the T'ang restoration, Jui-tsung gained a measure of independence, which meant that he had greater control over his family's affairs. He also acquired a modicum of leverage at court which he could have used to lobby for his youngest daughters' plans to become nuns and to thwart efforts to arrange marriages for them. In this respect, Princesses Gold-Immortal and Jade-Perfected seem to have been more fortunate than their elder sisters, all of whom were married out probably before Empress Wu's fall.[9]

There was one case which established a precedent, of sorts, for permitting princesses to take vows as Taoist priests. On October 12, 670, ten days after the death of her mother, Lady Yang, Wu Tse-t'ien requested authorization to have her most beloved child ordained as a means of ensuring bliss for Lady Yang in the afterlife. In medieval China it was common for descendants to undertake pious acts of this nature to accrue merit for an ancestor so that the soul of the deceased would obtain release from hell and enter the Elysian Fields *(Fu-t'ien* or *Fu-ti).* Taoism borrowed the notion of hell and this particular mechanism of salvation from Buddhism. Empress Wu chose a Taoist ordination for her daughter because, as the wife of Emperor Kao-tsung (r. 650–684) at the time, she fully supported the T'ang Taoist ideology. The daughter, who was about six years of age, was given the Taoist sobriquet T'ai-p'ing, and an abbey was established for her. Later, in 677, Tibetan emissaries arrived in the capital and submitted a petition requesting a marriage alliance with the throne. In it they specifically asked for the hand of Princess T'ai-p'ing, who was then about thirteen, almost the marriageable age. The court rejected the petition and immediately installed the Princess as abbess of the convent which it had earlier founded for her.[10]

Princess T'ai-p'ing's ordination laid the foundation for subsequent investitures of princesses. She took vows, received a Taoist sobriquet, and had a temple built for her. Later Jui-tsung honored Princesses Gold-Immortal and Jade-Perfected in the same manner when they were ordained. However, the precedent rested on shaky grounds because Princess T'ai-p'ing's ordination was spurious. It is highly improbable that she was ever seriously inducted into the priesthood, actually performed any sort of liturgical or administrative duties in the abbey, or even left the palace.

In the first place she was too young for ordination. According to Taoist regulations, six or seven (seven or eight *sui*) was the proper age for the transmission of the first Taoist register. But that conferral marked confirmation, the formal recognition of a child as a member of the religious community, not ordination, the formal acknowledgment of an individual's admission to or advancement in the priesthood. Investiture required a relatively high level of literacy, a well-developed memory, and intellectual maturity. The meager evidence that exists with regard to the age of those who underwent the ordination involving the transmission of the *Tao-te ching,* one of the lowest levels, suggests that the mid-teens to mid-twenties was the appropriate period for such an undertaking. As Princess T'ai-p'ing was only about six years old when she took her vows, she was clearly too young to have understood the texts transmitted to her or the duties that devolved upon her as a consequence of receiving them. In the second place, had she been a nun sworn to chastity, the Tibetans would not have been so bold as to ask for her hand. The citizens of the capital, and therefore the emissaries, were undoubtedly aware that she had not left the palace to assume her place in the abbey. In the third place, the court overreacted in its response to the Tibetans' petition. If Princess T'ai-p'ing was really a nun, it had only to remind the emissaries of the fact. Instead, the throne felt compelled to strengthen her claim by promoting her to abbess. The Princess was a nun in name only. Her investiture and promotion to abbess were devices employed to accomplish the court's ends: in the first instance, to provide a formal expression of Empress Wu's filial devotion for her mother and, in the second, to avoid a diplomatic incident as well as to prevent the daughter's separation from her mother. The pretense that Princess T'ai-p'ing was a Taoist priest was finally dropped when the Princess was wed between July 26 and August 23 of 681.[11]

The use of Taoist ordination as an expedient for satisfying imperial whims proved to be a useful example nearly a century later. When Emperor Hsüan-tsung took a liking to one of his sons' wives, he had the lady ordained as a Taoist nun and lodged her in an abbey of the inner palace, between October 25 and November 23 of 740. After the son acquired a new consort, the Emperor defrocked the object of his affec-

tion and installed her in his harem during August of 745. She was, of
course, none other than the renowned beauty Yang Yü-huan, better
known as Yang Kuei-fei, and her investiture was nothing more than a
device for dissolving her first marriage.[12]

The ordination of Princesses Gold-Immortal and Jade-Perfected was
of a different order from those of Princess T'ai-p'ing and Yang Kuei-fei.
Chang Wan-fu's account of the events at the Kuei-chen Abbey testifies
to the fact that their investiture fully conformed to Taoist protocols governing the transmission of the Ling-pao canon. Furthermore, the Princesses subsequently resided in abbeys at the capital and remained celibate throughout the rest of their lives.[13]

Aside from the note on Princess Gold-Immortal's ordination in 706,
little else is known of the early lives of the Princesses. Only after the
enthronement of their father on July 25, 710, did officials and historians
begin to devote serious attention to their affairs. For a brief time a flurry
of decrees, memorials, and notices concerning them appeared in dynastic annals and documentary collections. One of the first of these reads:
"On December 31, 710, His Majesty installed his two daughters Princess Hsi-ning [later Gold-Immortal] and Princess Lung-ch'ang [or
Ch'ang-lung, later Jade-Perfected] as Taoist nuns in order to provide
bliss for the Grand Empress, the Celestial August [Empress Wu]. For
this reason He wished to establish temples for them in the western part
of the capital." This passage was written without careful scrutiny of the
original documents in question. The Emperor was not empowered to
ordain Taoist priests. Moreover, Princess Gold-Immortal, and probably Jade-Perfected as well, had completed one or more stages of investiture by this time and consequently were already ordained. Finally, the
decree which Jui-tsung issued on this day called for the establishment of
an abbey for Princess Jade-Perfected only. The original author of this
statement took some liberties with the facts. Nevertheless, the passage is
important because it indicates that the Emperor may have given his
blessings to the forthcoming investiture of his daughters as a pious act of
filial devotion to his deceased mother (Empress Wu) in a fashion similar
to her effort to promote the salvation of her mother.[14]

To understand better the ordination of the Princesses, the key events
pertaining to it are chronicled here.

*December 31, 710:* Jui-tsung issued a decree calling for the establishment of an abbey for Princess Ch'ang-lung in Ch'ang-an.

*January 10, 711:* Jui-tsung issued a decree calling for the establishment of an abbey for Princess Hsi-ning in Ch'ang-an.

*February 10, 711:* The ritual of investiture for the transmission of the Ling-pao canon began.

*February 19–20, 711:* The *Su-ch'i* (Nocturnal Annunciation) rite was performed during the night and the ordination completed the next day.

*May 2, 711:* The throne bestowed the title Yü-chen (Jade-Perfected) on Princess Ch'ang-lung as well as on the abbey being readied for her.

*May 6, 711:* The throne bestowed the title Chin-hsien (Gold-Immortal) on Princess Hsi-ning as well as on the abbey being readied for her.

*May 26, 712:* Pressure from the bureaucracy forced Jui-tsung to suspend construction on the abbeys for his daughters. The Emperor ordered that the abbeys and the unused building materials be surrendered to the managers of the Princesses' fiefs.

*December 1, 712:* The Princesses received the Shang-ch'ing canon and attained the highest possible level in the priestly hierarchy on earth.

It is quite evident from these events and acts that Jui-tsung's enthronement altered circumstances for his daughters. He had attained a position which enabled him to dispense substantial funds from the imperial treasury for endowments to support their ambitions for a clerical career.[15]

However, Jui-tsung's rise to power also worked to the disadvantage of the Princesses. As Emperor he was the embodiment of the state and guardian of the commonweal. As such even the management of his family's affairs was open to public scrutiny. Officials could and did raise questions about his use of public moneys to build abbeys for his daughters. The intensity of their censure was greater than usual because they were thoroughly familiar with the corrupt practices that had prevailed under his predecessor. After the deposition of Empress Wu in 705, Chung-tsung bestowed appanages of unprecedented size on imperial princesses and created administrative apparatuses for them which had previously been reserved only for princes. Following his demise and the overthrow of Empress Wei in 710, many of those privileges were withdrawn, but the bureaucracy remained acutely attuned to any abuses which suggested deviance from standards established at the beginning of the T'ang before the advent of Empress Wu. For nearly a year and a half Jui-tsung suffered repeated rebukes from high-ranking officials for undertaking the construction of the abbeys. The pressure finally became too great, and the Emperor caved in to the demands of his officials. Imperial funding was terminated. The temples were eventually completed, but apparently at the Princesses' own expense.[16]

Not much is known of Princess Gold-Immortal's life after 712. Although she entered a cloister, she retained an appanage which entitled her to two-thirds of the state's revenue from 1,400 households. In 717 she moved into an abbey at Ch'ang-an which was renamed Yüan-tu kuan in 722. In late 731 the Princess accompanied the court on a progress to Loyang, and on June 6, 732, she died in that city's K'ai-yüan Abbey at the age of forty-three. Gold-Immortal was buried at Ch'iao-ling, Jui-tsung's tumulus northeast of Ch'ang-an. Her tomb inscription was engraved in stone from a facsimile which Emperor Hsüan-tsung drafted in running grass script.[17]

Princess Jade-Perfected was far more active than her elder sister. In 722 she moved into the An-kuo Abbey at Ch'ang-an and shortly thereafter became involved in the affairs of the royal house. On the death of his father (Emperor Kao-tsung's third son, who committed suicide around August 22, 690, because he feared that Empress Wu's agents were about to murder him), Li I-hsin fled to the far south (ling-wai) and became a servant to conceal his identity. After the restoration of the T'ang in 705 he returned to the capital and received an appointment as successor to his father, with the title of prince. Soon after, a cousin, who coveted his title and appanage, falsely accused him of having fraudulently claimed that he was the legitimate heir, and as a result I-hsin was stripped of his title and revenues. Later Princess Jade-Perfected learned the true facts, and in 724 she submitted a memorial to the throne requesting that the injustice be corrected. After reviewing the case Hsüan-tsung restored I-hsin's legacy. On October 20, 729, the Princess again came to the defense of a clansman and threw her support to a great-grandson of Emperor T'ai-tsung (r. 627–650) whom a powerful minister had attacked by urging a censor to impeach him. Her sense of fair play was not limited to her own family. At some point she interceded with the throne on behalf of a distant descendant of Wei Cheng (580–February 11, 643), the most eminent minister of the early T'ang. The descendant had been condemned to death, but as a consequence of her intervention, the man's sentence was commuted. Jade-Perfected appears to have had a strong sense of justice, perhaps engendered by her familiarity with the legal travesties committed against her kin and others during her youth.[18]

On at least two occasions in Hsüan-tsung's reign the throne enlisted the Princess' services as a Taoist priest to perform rites for the benefit of the state. In early 735 she received a mandate ordering her to proceed to the Yang-t'ai Abbey, which was the residence of the eminent Shang-ch'ing Patriarch Ssu-ma Ch'eng-chen (646–July 12, 735), on Mt. Wang-wu (northwest of Loyang), and to conduct the Retreat of the Gold Register with the prelate. According to contemporary Taoist liturgies, the performance of this ritual protected the nation and ensured the salvation of the monarch. As officially interpreted at the time, the rite had the power to harmonize the forces of nature, prevent natural calamities and disasters, prolong the life of the emperor, and guarantee prosperity for the empire.[19]

On April 23, 753, the Emperor again ordered her to perform a task for the throne, dispatching her to Ch'iao-chün (Po-chou, on the border of Honan and Anhwei Provinces) to conduct a Taoist rite at the Chen-yüan kung, a temple complex which had been erected at what was purportedly Lao Tzu's birthplace. Hsüan-tsung commissioned this act as an expression of his gratitude to Lao Tzu, who had revealed the location of a Heavenly Treasure *(T'ien-pao)* in an epiphany that had occurred the previous year. In the fourth month (April 29 to May 27) she accomplished her mission, and the rite was blessed with auspicious portents that appeared at the shrines dedicated to Lao Tzu and his mother. On her return, Jade-Perfected visited Mt. Sung east of Loyang and stopped at Mt. Wang-wu. A certain Master Hu from the Tung-ling kung on Mt. Heng (east of Ta-t'ung in Shansi Province) rushed to meet her there. The Princess asked him to transmit the Eight Registers *(Pa-lu)* and the Numinous Text of the Three Caverns in Purple Writ *(San-tung tzu-wen ling-shu)* to her. This investiture began on the night of May 23, 743, when the altar was established. In the course of the next ten days Jade-Perfected performed the Nocturnal Annunciation *(Lu chen-wen)*, on the night of May 30, and received oral instructions. The rite came to a close on June 2, when the gods departed in the smoke of the incense rising from the center of the altar.[20]

Like her elder sister, Jade-Perfected retained her secular property after her ordination. For some time she maintained a country estate *(shan-chuang)* outside of Ch'ang-an. At some point Hsüan-tsung and his court visited the villa, and the Emperor wrote a poem to commemorate the occasion. His verses have not survived, but a poem that Wang Wei (701–d. between August 5 and September 3, 761) wrote at imperial command to rhyme *(feng-ho)* with it has. Eventually her wealth and her title, Princess Jade-Perfected, became an embarrassment to her. In 744 she petitioned her elder brother to have the title revoked, her appanage abolished, and her revenues and manors returned to the throne. Hsüan-tsung rejected her first request, but honored the second. He bestowed a new title, T'e-ying, on her, a title by which she was known thereafter.[21]

On December 18, 755, An Lu-shan rebelled and marched on the capitals. Imperial forces collapsed, forcing Hsüan-tsung to abandon Ch'ang-an on July 14, 756, and flee to Szechuan where he retired in favor of his son Su-tsung (r. 756–763). A royal army recaptured Ch'ang-an in the autumn of 757. Hsüan-tsung returned to the city in the early part of the next year and was lodged in the Hsing-ch'ing Palace. T'e-ying joined his entourage there. No longer involved in political affairs, the retired Emperor occupied his free time by throwing parties for his friends at which the entertainers of the Pear Garden *(Li-yüan ti-tzu)*, a troupe which he had formed early in his reign, performed. On at least one occasion his younger sister even served wine to his guests at her brother's request. In the course of events the coterie managed to offend a powerful eunuch by treating him like an upstart. Feeling slighted, the eunuch went to Su-tsung, whose favor he enjoyed, and cast aspersions on the group, hinting that a conspiracy was brewing which might pose a threat to the throne. On September 3, 760, the Emperor had his father moved into the Great Inner Palace, ordered T'e-ying to take up residence in the cloister named after her (Yü-chen kuan), and banished many of the other members in the coterie. Ironically, in her declining years the former princess fell victim to the same sort of intrigue which she had known all too well in her youth. She died between May 14, 762, and August 24, 763, in her early seventies.[22]

Shih Ch'ung-hsüan became the third actor in the drama of the Princesses' investiture by virtue of an imperial appointment which designated him preceptor for the ladies, an appointment probably made soon after Jui-tsung's accession in 710. Originally Shih was a boot stitcher in Ho-nei, the seat of prefectural government in Huai-chou (modern Ch'in-yang hsien, just northeast of Loyang in Honan Province). At some point he took vows as a Taoist priest and, as his title Grand Canon Preceptor of the Three Caverns reflects, subsequently rose to the highest level of the clerical hierarchy. The Three Caverns refers to the original, major divisions of the *Tao-tsang,* which, in pre-T'ang and T'ang times, were based on the *San-huang wen (Tung-shen* corpus), the Ling-pao canon, and the Shang-ch'ing corpus of scripture. It also refers to the most important stages of ordination, which involved the transmission of those texts (see Chapter Four, numbers 8, 10, and 11). Shih's title indicates that he had received all three sets of texts in a rite or rites of investiture, ascending from the *Tung-shen* canon to the Shang-ch'ing corpus. He made his first and only mark in secular annals on April 9, 706, when he was promoted to the honorary rank of fifth grade, appointed to the office of Libationer for the Directorate of the Sons of State (Kuo-tzu chi-chiu, grade three, step two), and had conferred on him the title of

Duke. The Directorate managed the affairs of six schools in the capitals which provided education for sons and grandsons of the nobility and high-ranking officials. As Duke of Ho-nei, his native district, Shih held an appanage entitling him to two-thirds of the state's revenues from two thousand households. Ironically, he received those honors as a reward for his contribution to the establishment of the Sheng-shan ssu, a Buddhist monastery in Loyang which Chung-tsung renovated and rededicated to the memory of Wu Tse-t'ien after her demise.[23]

Actually, Shih Ch'ung-hsüan's rise to eminence had less to do with that project than with the influence of Princess T'ai-p'ing, to whose clique he was attached. He probably acquired most of the bureaucratic and aristocratic offices and titles ascribed to him in the account of the investiture of the two Princesses through the application of Princess T'ai-p'ing's leverage at court. For example, he occupied the post of Libationer by virtue of a supernumerary appointment. During Chung-tsung's reign, princesses employed this device to build parties of supporters within the imperial bureaucracy. It is doubtful that Shih actually managed the affairs of the Directorate since, as a priest, he had neither the secular administrative expertise nor the high degree of education in the Confucian canon that would have qualified him for that office. By the beginning of 711 he had been transferred from the post of Libationer for the Directorate of the Sons of State to that of Chief of the Service for Stentorian Annunciations. This latter office supervised the activities of two bureaus, which handled protocol for visiting emissaries from foreign lands and the funeral and burial rites for high-ranking officials in the capitals. Since, at the time, the service was also responsible for administering the state's policy toward Buddhist and Taoist clergies and monasteries, the appointment of a prelate to the post was somewhat less incongruous than it sounds. Again, however, Shih may not have had any real responsibility for running the service. During Jui-tsung's reign some appointments to that office appear to have been titular only. In 713 the throne elevated the priest Yeh Fa-shan to the post. Yeh had no administrative experience in government, either, and undoubtedly held the post as a sinecure. Ch'ung-hsüan's two remaining titles—Grandee of Illustrious Noble Rank, Gold Signet and Purple Ribbon; and Pillar of State, First Class—fixed his rank and seniority in the civil service. That rank placed him at the apex of officialdom. In addition to these honors, he enjoyed special favor because he was given extraordinary rights of passage in and out of the palace and was the frequent recipient of liberal gifts from the imperial coffers.[24]

Despite his prominent political position within the imperial government, Shih Ch'ung-hsüan's real value to the throne was his leadership

of the Taoist community. Shortly after his accession, Jui-tsung appoint-
ed Shih Abbot of the Supreme Purity Abbey, T'ai-ch'ing kuan, in
Ch'ang-an. Furthermore, the Emperor, perhaps at the instigation of
Princess T'ai-p'ing, dispensed a disproportionate share of patronage to
the temple which provoked a comment in one official's remonstrance.
This abbey became the most important Taoist community in the capital
at the time, and its abbot played a major role in the T'ang promotion of
Taoism as a dynastic ideology.[25]

At some point in this period Hsüan-tsung established a commission
to compile a reference work for the *Tao-tsang* and appointed Shih its
director. Hsüan-tsung, who was disturbed by the errors and omissions
which had crept into Taoist scriptures as a result of repeated hand-copy-
ing over the centuries, ordered this body to assemble a glossary to correct these deficiencies and supply definitions and pronunciations for
obsolete, obscure, and arcane terminology in the texts. Ch'ung-hsüan
appears to have used his position as head of the commission to influence
the process for selecting its members, because a disproportionate number of seats on it were assigned to his subordinates. Of forty-two members, not including Shih himself, twenty-four were officials (all but two
were imperial academicians) and eighteen were clerics. Of the latter,
eleven, or sixty-one percent, were priests from the T'ai-ch'ing kuan. In
the course of executing their mandate the scholars and priests consulted
texts of more than two thousand chapters *(chüan)* that were extant in the
libraries of the capital. They probably completed the compendium in
713. Its title was *I-ch'ieh Tao-ching yin-i* (The Sound and Sense to the
Complete Taoist Canon), and it had two parts: a glossary in 140 chapters and a catalog of ancient scriptures with an annotated bibliography
of texts in 113 chapters. Aside from two prefaces, one by Hsüan-tsung
and the other by Shih Ch'ung-hsüan; an introductory treatise on Taoism, the *Miao-men yu-ch'i*, written by Shih; a contribution by Chang
Wan-fu; and some citations in two Sung (960–1279) texts, nothing else
remains from the 253 chapters of this compendium. However, it was a
pioneering work which must have quickly become an indispensable aid
to anyone interested in the canon. It also laid the foundation for Hsüan-
tsung's later efforts to assemble a complete Taoist library and dissemi-
nate it throughout the empire.[26]

Shih's biographers characterized him as haughty, but his status as a
priest seems to have been a greater source of trouble for him. The sec-
tarian rivalry between Buddhists and Taoists which prevailed in the
early years of the T'ang persisted to a degree at the beginning of the
eighth century. Shih's rise to eminence and the favoritism which he
enjoyed at court irritated Buddhists in the capital. In a fit of jealously a

group of them set about the task of bringing him to ruin by concocting a bizarre plot. They expended tens of thousands of cash to bribe a character named Tuan Wan-hsien, who was mentally unbalanced. Sometime between March 1 and June 21 of 712, Tuan snuck through the Ch'eng-t'ien Gate of the Great Inner Palace, dashed into the Hall of the Great Bourne (T'ai-chi tien), sat himself upon the throne, and proclaimed himself emperor. So ensconced he declared: "I am Li An-kuo. A physiognomist told me that I would become the Son of Heaven (emperor) when I reached the age of thirty-one." After his arrest, Tuan tried to implicate Shih in this crime of high treason, falsely claiming that Shih (the physiognomist?) had sent him (to seize the throne?). The authorities apparently uncovered the real facts of the conspiracy, however, because the prelate escaped unscathed. The throne banished Tuan to the far reaches of the south (Ling-nan) and issued a decree forbidding contention between Buddhists and Taoists. Ch'ung-hsüan's position at court was not in the least undermined by the incident.[27]

The last member of the cast at the Princesses' ordination was Chang Wan-fu, the witness and author of the text that describes the rite. Little is known of him. None of the ancient histories for the T'ang period mention him. No account of his life survives in the biographical or hagiographical compendia of the *Tao-tsang* or in the collections of commemorative inscriptions customarily written at the death of eminent individuals during the T'ang. He left no poetry and, if any was addressed to him by the poets of his day, it has perished. Finally, none of his writings appears in the *Complete T'ang Prose* or its two supplements.

The sparse information that exists about Chang Wan-fu derives almost entirely from his writings, eight in number, which survive in the *Tao-tsang* (see Appendix Three). Seven of them address subjects dealing with rituals, ordination, precepts, and vestments—matters of pragmatic concern to the priesthood. The signatures to four of these (Appendix Three, numbers 2, 3, 5, and 8) designate him a Priest of the Supreme Purity Abbey. In his introduction to the *I-ch'ieh Tao-ching yin-i,* Shih Ch'ung-hsüan lists Wan-fu as a collaborator in the compilation of the text and assigns him the title of Grand-Worthy *(Ta-te)* of the Supreme Purity Abbey in the capital. One of Chang's contributions to that project is still extant, a short treatise (or part of it) on the *Tu-jen ching* (Appendix Three, number 1), which was one of the most important texts in the Ling-pao canon. Obviously, Wan-fu was Ch'ung-hsüan's subordinate at the abbey during Jui-tsung's reign. That temple had formerly been the mansion of Princess An-lo (daughter of Empress Wei and coconspirator in her mother's plot to seize the throne), who had taken possession of it in 707. After her execution on the night of July 21,

710, the throne seized the property, converted it into an abbey, entitled it Supreme Purity, and ordered Shih to occupy it. On July 29, 713, or immediately thereafter, the prelate was executed along with other partisans of Princess T'ai-p'ing, and the abbey was abolished. Consequently, all of the works that Chang Wan-fu signed as a priest of that temple were written before the middle of 713 and most probably between 710 and 713.[28]

It is clear from these texts that he had not yet attained the highest rank in the clerical hierarchy. In the first chapter of the *Ch'uan-shou san-tung ching-chieh fa-lu lüeh-shuo,* the work to which he appended his description of the Princesses' ordination and a colophon dated January 13, 713, the final stage, the transmission of the Shang-ch'ing corpus, is conspicuously missing from his inventories of the items conferred on ordinands at various levels of investiture. Furthermore, although his account of the Ling-pao ordination for Princesses Gold-Immortal and Jade-Perfected is rich in detail about the physical aspects of the altar and mentions some of the events that took place during the rite, his notes on the Shang-ch'ing investiture for the ladies, which occurred almost two years later, is very short and vague. It is safe to assume that he did not personally observe the second rite. As with other canon, the transmission of the Shang-ch'ing scriptures was an esoteric ritual. Consequently, if Chang had not received the corpus himself, he would not have been entitled to participate in its ordination rite.

The signature affixed to another text (Appendix Three, number 4), which provides protocols for the performance of the Nocturnal Annunciation, gives his title as Canon Preceptor of the Three Caverns *(San-tung fa-shih)* from the Pure Capital Abbey (Ch'ing-tu kuan) of the Great T'ang. This indicates that sometime after 713 Chang completed the final stage of investiture involving the transmission of the Shang-ch'ing scriptures and that he moved into the Pure Capital Abbey, also located in Ch'ang-an, when the Supreme Purity Abbey was closed. In the prologue to a text, which is an almanac for selecting the proper days to conduct investiture rites, and which Chang signed as Student of the Three Caverns *(San-tung ti-tzu)* from the Ch'ing-tu Abbey (Appendix Three, number 7), he said that he had been a Taoist *(sheng Ching-yü,* ascended to the Pure Territory) for more than fifty years and a priest *(ts'ung-shih chieh-shih,* pledged his oath with his preceptor) for more than forty. This must have been one of the last texts that he wrote, compiled when he was probably in his seventies and close to the end of his life.[29]

# CHAPTER TWO

# *The Stage*

THE INVESTITURE of Princesses Gold-Immortal and Jade-Perfected took place at the Abbey of Refuge in Perfection (Kuei-chen kuan), which was apparently a kind of imperial Taoist chapel located in the Great Inner Palace, an enormous compound constructed during the Sui dynasty (581–618) in Ch'ang-an. In this precinct were the residential quarters for the emperor, the seat of dynastic government, and the center for state ceremonies in the early T'ang. According to Chang Wan-fu it was at the Kuei-chen Abbey, probably in its front cloister, that

> earth was excavated to form an altar in three tiers which was about 3.54 meters (or 11.6 feet) high. Gold lotus-blossom poles *(chin-lien hua-tsuan)*, purple and gold title-tablets *(chin-tzu t'i-pang)*, and a blue-green silk cordon *(ch'ing-ssu)* encircled the altar.

Three-tiered altars were common fixtures in ancient Chinese rituals, Taoist and non-Taoist. As the citation indicates, workmen employed a construction technique *(hang-t'u)* now known in Western circles as tamped earth, stamped earth, or terre pisée, which had been used in China for more than two thousand years. They built a caisson of wooden planks and then proceeded to fill it with thin layers of dirt. They compacted each of these layers tightly by tamping. When the workmen reached the top of the caisson, they dismantled the frame. This left a free-standing platform, on which they constructed the next tier in the same manner as the first. When finished, the altar resembled a miniature ziggurat with three tiers, each 1.2 meters or nearly four feet tall.[1]

During the T'ang dynasty Buddhists staged their ordinations on platforms (*chieh-t'an,* precept platforms) somewhat similar to those used by
Taoists. In his diary, Ennin, the well-known Japanese monk who made
a pilgrimage to China in the middle of the ninth century, describes two
of them that he encountered in the course of his visits to various monasteries. Unlike the structures at the Princesses' investiture, however, the
altars that Ennin depicts were permanent structures. They were made
of brick and stone and housed in separate buildings. The altar at the
Kuei-chen kuan was a temporary fixture, probably intended for use
only at the Ling-pao investiture of the Princesses, since it does not
appear to have had a masonry facing or flooring and was open to the
elements. Wind and rain would have quickly destroyed it. It was constructed outdoors because the officiant at most, if not all, Taoist retreats
invited various celestial and terrestrial spirits to participate in the rites.
Their progress to the stage would have been impeded had the altar been
enclosed in a building.[2]

Chang Wan-fu's description of the Princesses' altar leaves a great
deal to be desired. One of the oldest diagrams for such fixtures appears
in a text that he wrote, but unfortunately it does not depict the arrangement for the altar employed at this level of investiture. However, details
about the altars used at the rites for transmission of the Ling-pao canon
can be found in the scriptures of the corpus, which was brought together
about A.D. 400; the *T'ai-shang tung-hsüan ling-pao shou-tu i* (HY 528), a
manual for conducting the ordination compiled by Lu Hsiu-ching (406–
March 31, 477), who appears to have been the first to undertake the
task of formulating a liturgy for Ling-pao investitures; and the *Wu-shang
pi-yao,* a compendium of excerpts from Taoist scriptures and texts compiled under imperial auspices by a commission between 577 and 578. In
addition, a series of illustrations, which is helpful in reconstructing the
scene of the Princesses' ordination, survives in the *Wu-shang huang-lu ta-
chai li-ch'eng i* (HY 508), a compendium of protocols for conducting the
Yellow Register Retreat that Liu Yung-kuang (1134–1206) collected
and his pupil Chiang Shu-yü (1156–1217) edited early in the thirteenth
century. There is a certain amount of danger in attempting to recreate
from these texts the physical environment and procedures of the transmission at the investiture in 711, because ritual regulations underwent a
great deal of change between 400 and 1300, and this, in turn, engendered diversity in the versions of the liturgy written by different authors
in different periods. Nevertheless, it is difficult to visualize what transpired at the Kuei-chen Abbey without some reference to them.[3]

Chang gave a figure for the height of the altar, but neglected to mention the length and breadth. The *Wu-shang pi-yao* offers two different

sets for these dimensions: 6.5 meters (or 21 feet, 4 inches) and 9 meters
(or 31 feet) for each side. The choice between these alternatives was
supposed to be made on the basis of the number of people who participated in the rite. These measurements refer to the size of the altar's lowest tier or outer perimeter. They yield, respectively, 42 square meters
(or 458 square feet) and 89 square meters (or 961 square feet) for the
total area occupied by the altar. Naturally, the actual space, the top tier
or Inner Altar, where most of the rite was performed, was smaller.[4]

A blue-green silk cordon encircled the altar, joining the title-tablets
that hung above its gates, which were formed by erecting blossom-
poles. Pre-T'ang sources provide at least three different schemes for the
arrangement of gates and placards. When Lu Hsiu-ching formulated
his liturgy for the investiture, he adopted the regulations for the plan of
the altar from the *T'ai-shang tung-hsüan ling-pao yü-chüeh* (now entitled
*T'ai-shang tung-hsüan ling-pao ch'ih-shu yü-chüeh miao-ching;* HY 352), one
of the original scriptures in the Ling-pao canon. The protocols which
Lu cited were not specifically designed for ordination. Called the "Sacrifice to the Five Sovereigns [the Gods of the Five Directions] of the
Numinous Treasure from the Primordial-Commencement for Summoning the Perfected" *(Yüan-shih ling-pao wu-ti chiao-chi chao-chen),* they
appear to have been formulas for conducting a primitive version of the
*Su-ch'i* (Nocturnal Annunciation) that was supposed to be performed on
a sacred marchmount and which utilized the True Writs and the Five
Talismans. These regulations instructed the officiant to erect four gates
on the altar, one for each of the four cardinal directions of the compass.
Placards, which had long inscriptions addressed to the deities who presided over the particular regions which they represented, were then
hung above the gates. The tablet for the fifth direction, the center, and
another dedicated to the Perfected were suspended to the right and to
the left of the main gate. The main portal was probably the gate which
represented the season in which the ordination took place. For example,
if the investiture occurred in the summer, the south gate became the
main portal. Though Lu does not say so, it is evident from his directions for the movements of the officiant and the ordinands that a second
enclosure had to have been erected outside the first or Inner Altar *(Nei-
t'an).* This area was called the Capital Altar *(Tu-t'an)* and had at least
two gates: the Celestial Gate *(T'ien-men)* in the northwest corner and the
Terrestrial Portal *(Ti-hu)* in the southeast corner. Most likely this enclosure was identical to the four-gate tier of the ten-gate altar described
below (also see Figure 1).[5]

By the third quarter of the sixth century, a variant of Lu Hsiu-ching's
scheme had emerged. This plan, calling for six gates, was incorporated

into the *Wu-shang pi-yao* and labeled "The Procedure for Establishing an Altar to Perform the *Su-lu* [Nocturnal Revelation, that is, *Su-ch'i*] Rite" *(She-t'an su-lu fa)*. It was basically the same as Lu's, but seems to have been devised to account for the two extra placards in his scheme. In addition to the gates for the four seasons, the *Wu-shang pi-yao* instructs the officiant to erect separate gates for the center and the Perfected *(Chung-chen men)*. The gate representing the season in which the investiture occurred was designated the Regal Gate. The gates for the center and the Perfected were located to the left and to the right of the Regal Gate, respectively, rotating as the Regal Gate rotated around the altar as the year progressed (see Table 1). Since the ordination for Princesses Gold-Immortal and Jade-Perfected took place in the spring, the Regal Gate would have been placed in the east, the Central Gate in the north-northeast and the Gate of the Perfected in the south-southeast if these regulations were applied in 711. According to the *Wu-shang pi-yao,* the gates on this altar were formed with poles 2.66 meters or 8.7 feet in length; this would have left openings 1.48 meters (4.8 feet) or 1.18 meters (3.9 feet) in width. The poles that were used to enclose the rest of the altar were two meters or 6.77 feet in length. Blue-green cordons *(ch'ing-sheng)* were strung in two courses around the altar, joining title-tablets 8.85 by 7.84 centimeters (3.87 by 3.38 inches), which hung above the gates. All comings and goings, meaning all ritual entrances and retreats, were supposed to proceed through the Gate of the Perfected.[6]

The third form of altar was employed in exceptional circumstances. Lu Hsiu-ching stipulates that "if the number of ordinands *(ti-tzu)* is small, then one should use the retreat altar according to the standard regulations for the Yellow Register Retreat." The *Wu-shang pi-yao* suggests opting for the same alternative to the six-gate altar, specifically calling for "a layered altar of ten gates *(ch'ung-t'an shih-men)*" arrayed according to the protocols given in the *Huang-lu ching* (Scripture of the Yellow Register), a text from the original Ling-pao canon which is now

**Table 1.** The Seasonal Rotation of Altar Gates according to the
　　　　　*Wu-shang pi-yao*

| Season | Regal Gate | Central Gate | The Perfected |
|---|---|---|---|
| Spring | East | North-northeast | South-southeast |
| Summer | South | East-southeast | West-southwest |
| Fall | West | South-southwest | North-northwest |
| Winter | North | West-northwest | East-northeast |

lost except for excerpts cited in the *Wu-shang pi-yao* and other compendia. Fortunately, four illustrations depicting the arrangement of the altar and its lanterns have survived in the *Wu-shang huang-lu ta-chai li-ch'eng i*. The scheme for this altar had three separate enclosures (layers?), the innermost sector or highest tier of which was punctuated by ten gates (see Figure 2). The second or middle had four gates and the outermost, or lowest, one. The number of gates in the enclosure for the inner or upper altar corresponded to the Ten Heavens or Directions, a notion which the authors of the Ling-pao scriptures adopted from Buddhism. Eighteen long and ten short poles were used to form the gates and sides of the innermost or top barrier of the altar. The wooden poles were carved with finials in the shape of lotus blossoms, painted with lacquer, and planted in the earth of the altar. These instructions explain Chang Wan-fu's use of the term gold lotus-blossom poles. Three courses of blue-green or deep-red cordons ran around the altar: the first directly beneath the finials of the tallest poles, the second immediately under the finials of the shortest, and the last two 59 centimeters (1.95 feet) below the second cordon. These cordons served as bars or fencing *(lan)* for the spaces between the gates, but not for the gates themselves.[7]

It is possible that none of the altars just described had tiers or steps at all. They may well have been constructed simply by tracing the outlines of the enclosures, one within the other, on the ground. The poles would then have been erected along the lines forming these squares. There is evidence to support such an interpretation. This simpler scheme may have been employed during hard times such as periods of religious persecution or occasions when at investitures the ordinands did not have the wherewithal to pay for the construction of a tamped-earth altar. However, such accommodations must have been a far less desirable alternative, because the altar was nothing less than a substitute for the sacred mountain. Failure to provide elevation weakened the symbolism and power of the structure, making it less worthy than a tiered altar. Whatever the case, the ordination of Princesses Gold-Immortal and Jade-Perfected unquestionably took place on a ziggurat-like altar of three tiers.[8]

According to Chang Wan-fu, the title-tablets that hung from the blue-green cordon above the gates were purple and gold in color. This statement does not square with the regulations governing investiture rites in pre-T'ang sources. Those rules called for scripts or tablets to be written or painted with the symbolic hues of the directions that the gates represented: blue-green for the east, red for the south, white for the west, black for the north, and yellow for the center. However, as Table 2 shows, these sources do not agree with one another on the proper

**Table 2.** Color Schemes for Title-Tablets on Ling-pao Altars

| Gate | HY 352 | HY 528 | HY 1130 |
| --- | --- | --- | --- |
| East | Blue-green script | Blue-green script on a red field | Vermilion script on a blue-green tablet |
| South | Red script | Red script on a yellow field | Yellow script on a red tablet |
| West | White script | White script on a black field | Black script on a white tablet |
| North | Black script | Black script on a blue-green field | Blue-green script on a black tablet |
| Center | Yellow script | Yellow script on a white field | White script on a yellow tablet |
| The Perfected | Purple script | Purple script on a yellow field | Purple script on a yellow tablet |

color scheme. On the altar for the ordination of Princesses Gold-Immortal and Jade-Perfected, none of these formulas were employed. Instead all of the placards had the color scheme reserved for the Gate of the Perfected, purple script on a gold tablet. An exception may have been made in this instance because the women were members of the imperial clan. Purple and gold were, after all, royal colors as well.[9]

It is impossible to determine with total certainty, from Chang Wan-fu's two-sentence description, which plan was employed in the arrangement of the Princesses' altar. However, given the conditions specified in Lu Hsiu-ching's manual and in the *Wu-shang pi-yao,* it was probably constructed according to the regulations for the Yellow Register Retreat. There were, after all, only two ordinands. This means it had three enclosures, composed of blossom-poles and blue-green cordons, with an inner altar punctuated by a series of ten portals marked by title-tablets. These boundaries defined the consecrated precincts in which various elements of the rite were conducted. They were also lines of defense which protected the interior against the intrusions of unwanted influences. Since the officiant invited or summoned various spirits, immortals, and Perfected to participate in the investiture, the perimeter was deliberately weakened by the creation of gates that were not barred and which permitted the entrance of the unseen powers as well as the mortal congregation to the sacred arena. The protocols recognized that the portals were vulnerable points in the altar's structure of defense, which had to be secured in a way that appeased the gods so that no disasters would occur during the rite. This form of protection involved other aspects of the altar's array, namely, paraphernalia and pledges.

The spaces between the poles of the altar's enclosure at the Kuei-chen Abbey were partially filled with bunting suspended from all four sides of its structure, attached either to the poles and cordons of the enclosures or to individual poles erected outside them. Chang Wan-fu lists nine types of such trappings (Appendix One: Pennons). This number was one of the most sacrosanct in Taoist cosmology. Its components—one, two, three, four, five, six, seven, eight, and nine—were the units that formed the magic square *(lo shu)*, which was widely used to structure consecrated altars and rituals in Taoism. It is not clear what purpose banners served at Taoist retreats. Liturgical protocols directed the faithful to raise them at temples for the Celestial Venerables, at places having scriptures or statues, at homes, or for the dead and for the ill. Whatever significance they had for Taoist rites, the fluttering pennons supplied an element of motion and vitality to the altar's static and inert structure of earth, poles, and cordons. Their ornamentation—motifs of ethereal beings, sacred beasts and birds, numinous flora, radiant suns, flying clouds, precious metals and stones, and landscapes—enlivened an otherwise essentially stark stage by adding colorful images appealing to the eye.[10]

The floors of the Princesses' altar, which were nothing more than bare earth, were also the objects of embellishments. They were covered with cushions of layered cloth made from brocades dyed in the colors of the five directions (Appendix One: Floor Coverings). Doubtlessly, these articles, fabricated from one of the most expensive textiles available, were placed at the gates corresponding to their colors according to the cosmic symbolism of the altar (blue-green for the east, red for the south, white for the west, black or purple for the north, and yellow for the center). In addition, dragon whisker, phoenix pinion, and other types of mats were laid out on the ground. During the T'ang the Chinese had not yet accustomed themselves to the chair and normally sat on mats placed on the floor, in much the same manner as Japanese still do, or on low couches. Mats and cushions served to protect clothing and the body from the dirt on the ground or, in this case, on the altar.[11]

Chang Wan-fu also says that "chiliads and myriads of lamp trees *(hua-shu,* literally blossom-trees) were arrayed on and below the altar as well as within the cloister of the abbey. The illumination of their beams pierced and penetrated the dark (Appendix One: Lighting Accoutrements)." He lists four types of these appurtenances: gold lotus, silver lotus, Seven Treasure, and polychrome (literally, five-colored). The lamp trees burned oil and clearly did not supply enough light, because candles and lanterns were also supplied. Chang described seventeen types of lanterns and four sorts of candles, categorized according to their decorations, which were similar to those on the banners except that some of the lanterns had patterns—such as the purple flaming orchids, blue-green beam magic mushrooms, thousand moonbeams, five stars (the five planets visible to the naked eye), seven luminaries (sun, moon, and five planets), and twenty-eight asterisms—which depicted magical or astronomical light sources. Undoubtedly the arrangement of the lamp trees formed some symbolic pattern relevant to Taoist ritual, but Chang offers little assistance in this regard.

The *Ming-chen k'o,* one of the scriptures in the original Ling-pao corpus, has a set of protocols for conducting a rite for lighting lanterns to dispel natural calamities and to pacify the nation and people; it specifies that the number of lanterns should be fixed according to the numbers associated with the regions in which the disaster occurred: nine for the east, three for the south, twelve for the center, seven for the west, and five for the north. More importantly, the *Chin-lu chien-wen,* another text from the corpus that is now lost except for excerpts in other works, contained instructions for a more elaborate lighting arrangement, an illustration of which survives in the *Wu-shang huang-lu ta-chai li-ch'eng i.* This diagram depicts the order of the lanterns as deployed on the ten-gate altar for the Yellow Register Retreat, a plan which, as has been noted, may have been employed at the Princesses' investiture. It shows the positions for most of 159 lanterns in sixteen groups (no lamp trees or candles are listed) that were deployed around the perimeter of the altar. These groups represented the seven generations of ancestors, nine sectors of hell, twenty-four segmental energies, eight trigrams, nine celestial palaces, ten directions, twenty-eight asterisms, thirty-six heavens, five marchmounts, and the like. Each lantern was hung from a separate pole, and a card on which its name was written was placed beneath it. In two instances, the titles of lantern clusters—the twenty-eight asterisms and thirty-six heavens—correspond to those given in Chang Wan-fu's enumeration. Consequently, Chang may well have been referring in those cases and others, when their titles contain numbers, to groups of lanterns and not to the motifs on them. Such clusters may have occupied positions of cosmological import to the altar's structure at the Kuei-chen kuan. The *Wu-shang huang-lu ta-chai li-ch'eng i* also states that lanterns were positioned at regular intervals around the inside of the enclosure for the Inner Altar. This provision was essential for the performance of the investiture liturgy. The *Su-ch'i* (Nocturnal Annunciation), which was the core of both Ling-pao ordination and the Yellow

Register Retreat, was conducted at night, and the officiant depended on light from the lanterns to move about the altar and to read the offices from the liturgical texts. Undoubtedly a number of the appurtenances listed by Chang Wan-fu, perhaps some of those whose titles contain no reference to Taoist numerology, were not part of the symbolic array on the perimeter of the altar, but occupied positions around the Inner Altar.[12]

Tables were the most important pieces of furniture on the altar. They supported the incense burners and served as stations where the officiants and ordinands stopped during tours of the Inner Altar to pay homage to the gods of the five directions. They were placed in each of the five directions and other locations on the stage. No expense was spared for the Princesses. The tables on their altar were manufactured from jade, gold, and aromatic woods. They had reliefs of "soaring simurghs, dancing phoenixes, gold blossoms, and jade leaves" carved or incised on them (Appendix One: Tables) and were probably fairly low to the ground (see Figure 3). The tables were covered with brocade kerchiefs whose colors corresponded to the directions which they represented and whose designs depicted "matched cranes and paired simurghs, flying dragons, and bowing phoenixes" (Appendix One: Table Cloths). Curly gold dragon plaques and jade disks were, in turn, placed on the cloths, where they purportedly pacified (*chen*, literally, suppressed), the gods of the five directions (Appendix One: Table Settings).[13]

According to the *Wu-shang pi-yao,* each of these tables was to have an incense fire (censer), a dragon (plaque), and a piece of silk corresponding in color to the hue of the direction which it represented. Presumably, the braziers that Chang mentions in his text rested on the tables in accordance with this rule, though he does not say so. He lists six types of them, apparently categorizing them by the nature of their decorations (Appendix One: Braziers). These braziers were supplied with incense caskets and incense chests of pure gold and silver. The protocols for the primitive version of the *Su-ch'i* in the Ling-pao canon instruct officiants to place placards with inscriptions written in vermilion ink on white ginkgo wood (*pai-yin mu*) beneath each of six braziers, one for each of the five directions and one for the Perfected, at the six gates.[14]

In his notes on ordination rites, which appear just before his account of the Princesses' investiture, Chang lists the ingredients of the incense under the title "The Five Aromatics" (*wu-hsiang*):

1. Aloeswood, 1,
2. Frankincense, 2,
3. White sandalwood, 3,

4. Putchuk, 4,
5. Cloves, 5,
6. Borneo camphor, 7,
7. Cinnabar *(sha)*, 3,
8. Realgar *(hsiung)*, 4.

One of the original Ling-pao scriptures calls for an incense made from a mixture of the Five Aromatics, and Lu Hsiu-ching adds that five *tou,* two *sheng* (nearly five liters or five and a half quarts) of this compound were needed to conduct the ritual of ordination. It is noteworthy that all of the aromatics, numbers one through six, were imported products; this testifies to the influence of foreign cultures in the T'ang and pre-T'ang periods.[15]

The five aromatics—both the notion and the substances—appear to have been adopted from Buddhism, and this explains the foreign origin of the aromatics. Given this fact, the inclusion of the last three items in Chang's list is something of a mystery. Their addition brings the total number to eight, exceeding the figure specified in the subtitle. Furthermore, the appended numbers are out of sequence with those for the previous five items, and the meaning of the latter is not clear. They do not appear to have any numerological connection with the five directions nor do they seem to refer to the proportions of the aromatics used in mixing the incense. Just as confusing is the fact that the last two substances were mineral compounds not known for their aromatic properties. It is possible that these last two, cinnabar and realgar, were used as constituents in the base for the incense because they had time-honored associations with alchemical elixirs. In T'ang and pre-T'ang times the elixir had a symbolic meaning in Taoist liturgy, if not a real role in the priest's endeavors to attain immortality. The interrelationship between alchemy and ritual was so strong that Joseph Needham has suggested that the incense burner was a precursor of the alchemical furnace. More importantly, alchemical symbolism played a part in most Taoist retreats, including that conducted for Ling-pao ordinations. Toward the end of these rituals the officiant performed a sub-rite called the "Return to the Censer" *(Fu-lu),* during which he called for "the spontaneous production of liquid gold, cinnabar's red and jade's green, and the magic mushroom's blossom" while standing or sitting in front of a censer from which incense smoke rose heavenward.[16]

The seductive power that aromatics exerted over the spirits made incense an essential element for the proper execution of virtually all religious acts (liturgical, meditative, alchemical, and so forth) in Taoism. Chang Wan-fu says that "broadcasting the vapors of the Five Aromatics brings down the Powers *(Ling)* of the five directions." Here Chang is referring to the "Lighting of the Censer" *(Fa-lu)*, a ritual performed at the beginning of investitures and other retreats during which the officiant not only enticed the gods of the macrocosm to descend to the consecrated altar by igniting incense, but also called forth the spirits of the microcosm (the gods within his own body) by means of visualization. Incense was the instrument which the priest employed to start the proceedings, but also the agent which he used to conclude them. If it could attract, it could also dispatch. At the end of various retreats, during the *Fu-lu,* the officiant entrusted his message to the smoke of the burning incense and its guardian spirits so that it could be conveyed to the gods in Heaven.[17]

Although Chang Wan-fu does not give the total for the number of tables placed on the Princesses' altar, the regulations governing the arrangement of such furniture that were set forth in the *Wu-shang pi-yao* called for three more above and beyond those for the five directions. The first of these was to be placed in front of a venerable icon and was reserved for the scriptures that were to be transmitted to the ordinands. According to one of the original Ling-pao scriptures, the True Writs in Five Slats and Five Talismans of the Numinous Treasure *(Tung-hsüan wu-p'ien chen-wen wu-fu)* should rest on a scarlet kerchief 147.5 centimeters (57.5 inches) in length and be covered with a blue-green cloth of the same length. The kerchief was considered a worthy substitute for smearing blood on the lips *(sha-hsüeh)* and the cover a substitute for the cutting of hair *(tuan-fa),* both of which were older methods for sealing oaths. The treatment of the scriptures at ordinations had become somewhat more elaborate by the early eighth century. Chang says that embroidered wrappers were provided for the texts presented to the Princesses (Appendix One: Canon Wrappers). Their designs depicted Divine Diamond Kings, Immortal Lads and Divine Maids, smoky clouds, mountains and rivers, grasses and trees, insects and fishes, sacred beasts and holy birds, ornamented marvels, and precious objects. The scriptures enclosed in wrappers were placed in Seven Treasure, Nine Immortal, yellow-gold, and white-jade cases (Appendix One: Canon Cases). In addition, blue-green, scarlet, plain white, purple, yellow, and cloud-brocade as well as polychrome (five-color) embroidered bags (Appendix One: Satchels) were supplied to encase the liturgical registers. The second table served as a lectern for the chief officiant, who knelt before it while sending forth his petitions to the gods. It was probably there that the True Writs were unrolled, that is, exposed, and the officiant performed a key rite of the investiture by reading them in order to transmit them to his ordinands. The third table, which was also located in front of an icon, was the seat for various pledges.[18]

Liturgical pledges *(fa-hsin)* were offerings made, among other reasons, to suppress or appease the gods who oversaw investitures and other retreats at the request of the officiant. The first type was an essential instrument for the defense of the vulnerable gates in the precinct's perimeter, bribes of a sort which insured that the rite would proceed without untoward incident. But they were also thought of as collateral for the ordinands' oaths sworn to the gods of the five directions. If an ordinand neglected to provide these items at his ordination, the Five Sovereigns *(Wu-ti)* would not receive his name for entry into their ledgers, and the Five Demon Monarchs *(Wu mo-wang)* would ruin him. Chang labels these offerings *fang-ts'ai* (colored silks of the directions), and he states that they were employed to "appease *(an)* [the gods of] the five directions." In 711 Princesses Gold-Immortal and Jade-Perfected presented eighteen lengths of blue-green net, six lengths of scarlet silk net, fourteen lengths of white silk net, ten lengths of black silk net, and twenty-four lengths of yellow silk net—a total of 850 meters (or 928 yards) of this kind of fabric—for that purpose (Appendix One: Articles of Appeasement). The unit of measure for the Princesses was the bolt *(p'i,* a strip of cloth 53 centimeters by 11.80 meters, or 21 inches by 12.90 yards), which ritual regulations reserved for the emperor and, presumably by extention, his family. According to Lu Hsiu-ching, these stuffs were placed under the tables of the five directions, the cloths' colors matching the directions they represented.[19]

According to the liturgies for performing the Nocturnal Annunciation, east, south, west, and north had nine, three, seven, and five energies *(ch'i),* respectively, while the center had one. Since two ordinands were to receive the Ling-pao scriptures at the investiture in 711, the quantities of cloth, fixed by the numbers associated with these energies, was doubled for the first four directions. The measure of the cloth supplied for the center was determined not by the number of the energy which it was supposed to possess, but by adding the figures for the energies of east and south (or those for west and north) and again doubling the sum. The total so calculated, twenty-four, represented the twenty-four segmental energies of the year (two for each month), which was also the sum of the energies associated with the primary Celestial Master parishes. The cloth and other elements of the altar's array were expressions of the Taoist passion for and belief in the magic power of cosmic numerology.[20]

A second category of pledges was far more extensive. These articles were "all employed to ward off *(chen)* malign influences within the altar and to serve as bonds to the numinous bureaucrats *(Ling-kuan)."* Chang lists thirteen varieties (Appendix One: Pledges).

*Purple Silk Net, 240 lengths (2,832 meters or 3,096 yards).* In Taoist liturgy this form of gage was labeled "Destiny Silk *(Ming-tseng)"* or "Basic Destiny Silk *(Pen ming tseng)."* The amount required for Princesses Gold-Immortal and Jade-Perfected was fixed according to a regulation from a scripture in the original Ling-pao canon which, in turn, was based on a fundamental Taoist notion about mortality or destiny. At birth, Heaven assigns every person an optimum longevity of 120 years. If one has not attained that age at the time of his death, it is because the Three Officials *(San-kuan),* the gods who keep the ledgers in which everyone's transgressions are entered, have deducted days or years from the original allocation for failures to observe the injunctions, rebellions against the preceptors, violations of covenants, and the like. Since few if any were presumed to have led a perfectly sinless life, few if any were thought to be capable of conserving the original allotment of 120 years. Consequently, at investitures an ordinand should present 120 bolts of cloth and beg the celestial bureaucracy to extend the calculation for his destiny (that is, restore his birthright). In actuality, however, only emperors, empresses, crown princes, and presumably princesses were required to supply this quantity of material. Patterned silk of a purple hue was also reserved for people of this rank. An ordinand of inferior status was supposed to provide plain, unpatterned cloth *(man-tseng)* and calculate the yardage of the stuff according to his age (for example, if an aspirant were twenty-five years old he would be required to submit twenty-five units). The units of measure also varied according to social status. According to Chang Wan-fu, the ordinands were supposed to turn the purple net over to their Scriptural Preceptors *(Ching-shih)* for use in making liturgical vestments.[21]

*Pongee (coarse silk), 480 lengths (5,664 meters or 6,192 yards).* Chang does not explain the function of this item. Judging by the number of units submitted, it was somehow linked to the twenty-four segmental energies of the cosmos. There is no evidence that this kind of coarse silk was used in pre-T'ang times as a gage for Ling-pao ordinations, but it was employed at the investitures for the *Tung-shen ching* and at the transmissions of three Shang-ch'ing scriptures, one of which asserts that it served as a substitute for smearing blood on the lips in oath-taking.[22]

*Cash, 240 strings (240,000 coins).* The regulations for the primitive version of the Nocturnal Annunciation in the original Ling-pao canon required an offering of 24,000 gold coins as a pledge to the officials of the twenty-four life vapors *(ch'i,* energies) which inhabit the body and give it life. If gold coins were not available, copper could be substituted.

Should the ordinands fail to supply this gage, their names would not be moved to the Ledger of Destiny *(Ming-chi)*, that is, they would not be saved from hell or become immortals, and their cases would be turned over to the Office of the Capital Spirits *(Tu-shen ts'ao)* for investigation. The amount of money provided for the Princesses was not twice, but five times that required in the protocols.[23]

*Gold, 200 liang or ounces (7,920 grams or 255 troy ounces).* One of the rules governing the performance of the Nocturnal Annunciation in the Ling-pao canon required an offering of five ounces of superior gold as a pledge to the gods of the Five Marchmounts. A regulation in another text from the canon called for a bond of nine ounces as a surety to the gods of the Nine Heavens. The gods of the Five Marchmounts and the Numinous Mountains would deny those who failed to supply this gage the opportunity of studying their ledgers. The cases of those poor ordinands would also be turned over to the Office of the Bureaucrats of the Shades *(Yin-kuan ts'ao)* for investigation. In his notes on ordination rites, Chang Wan-fu says that twenty-four ounces of silver and gold were required as a pledge to the twenty-four life vapors *(sheng-ch'i)* and nine ounces as a gage to the Nine Heavens. The figure for the quantity supplied by the Princesses has no basis in Ling-pao protocols, but the number may be related to the number of gods for the Ten Directions. It is possible that each woman offered ten ounces to each of these deities.[24]

*Five-color Cloud Brocade, 25 lengths (295 meters or 322.5 yards).* According to Chang, brocade *(chin)* is synonymous with interdiction *(chin)* and the five colors with the five desires. The cloth, thus, symbolizes the students' endeavors to suppress or overcome desire in their minds. This is accomplished by observing the religious injunctions. These stuffs appear to have been a pledge offered as a guarantee that the ordinands would not violate their vows to maintain the precepts conferred upon them.[25]

*Incense, 120 catties (76 kilograms or 166 pounds).* Incense, especially that manufactured from aloeswood, played a role as a gage in the transmission of Shang-ch'ing scriptures. The motivation for the presentation of this quantity on the Princesses' part as well as for their submission of writing materials and implements (mentioned below) was probably pragmatic in nature. That is to say, the protocols required these offerings in order to provide for materials that could be used by the ordinands or their preceptors to perform subsequent retreats, which were the offices they performed as Ling-pao priests.[26]

*Continuous (?) Blue-Green Seven Treasure Thread, 500 liang or ounces (19.8 kilograms or 43.5 pounds).* In his notes on ordination, Chang Wan-fu discusses a pledge of plain thread in 123 centimeters (4 feet) in length, or 5

and 10 *liang* (66 and 132 grams, or 2.3 and 4.6 ounces) in weight if mea-
sured in hundred-foot lengths. The amount of thread presented by the
Princesses seems to have been calculated according to a variation of this
formula. The weight, 5 *liang*, was multiplied by the length, 100 *ch'ih*
(feet). Chang also describes the blue-green thread in symbolic terms. It
represents man's endeavor "to implement the Tao *(hsing Tao)* like
Heaven and compassionately to nurture living things."[27]

*Memorial Paper, 24,000 sheets. Writing Brushes and Inksticks, 240 each.*
Chang assigns no role for writing materials and implements as guarantees of the ordinands' oaths. He does note that they were the instruments by which officiants conveyed their petitions to the celestial
bureaucrats, who, though distant spirits, nevertheless communicated
with the world. During the investiture rite for the *Tao-te ching*, the recipients of the scriptures were required to make fair copies of the texts
transmitted to them, but this does not seem to have been the case for
Ling-pao ordinations.[28]

*Knives for Straightening (?) Documents, 12.* Book knives were originally
used to prepare or scrape errors off bamboo slips. By the T'ang, however, most writing was done on paper. These implements appear to
have served some function in the preparation of paper for writing.[29]

*Knives and Kerchiefs for Preserving Injunctions, 38 each.* The title for these
tools suggests that they were linked in some fashion to the precepts,
three sets of which were presented to ordinands in conjunction with
Ling-pao investitures. Knives were used in some investitures to divide
or rend tallies *(ch'üan)* and split rings. They also served as gages for the
transmission of the *Tung-shen ching (San-huang wen)*, but not, in pre-
T'ang times, for transmission of the Ling-pao canon. The number of
knives presented by the Princesses, a figure of no cosmological significance, betrays their purpose. They were gifts to the thirty-eight officiants who participated in the ordination, and they seem to have played a
very small role as sureties.[30]

*Gold Dragon Plaques, 6.* As previously noted these items were used in
the first instance as defensive devices to protect the tables placed on the
altar. In the second instance they served temporarily as pledges of the
ordinands' oaths. But most importantly, they were paraphernalia for
accomplishing the Casting of the Dragon Tablets *(T'ou lung-chien)*, a rite
which was performed as the final act of the investiture. The plaques
(three for each of the Princesses) may have been set on the altar in order
to consecrate them in preparation for the performance of the rite later.[31]

*Gold Knobs (or buttons), 54.* The original Ling-pao canon stipulates
that nine of these items are to be joined to each of three wooden tablets
that were cast or buried with the gold dragon plaques. Hence a total of

twenty-seven knobs (here doubled because there were two ordinands) was required to accomplish the rite of Casting the Dragon Tablets. Chang Wan-fu says that these instruments were bits for controlling the wild dragons that carried the messages of the tablets to the gods. The word *niu* literally refers to the knob on a seal which enables the user to grasp the signet and impress it on a document. Perhaps Taoists adopted the term because it had strong connotations linking it to the verification of official papers by means of seals. In one sense their investiture rites were nothing more than complex ceremonies for establishing covenants and oaths with the gods, similar in many respects to imperial bureaucratic procedures for certification of government documents.[32]

The protocols are somewhat ambivalent about pledges. On the one hand, they favor them because they are superior to previous procedures for swearing oaths: the smearing of blood on the lips and the cutting of hair. The former was still practiced by Taoists as late as the early fourth century A.D. Ko Hung (283–343) mentions the smearing of blood on the lips as part of a rite for the transmission of the *San-huang wen* and the *Wu-yüeh chen-hsing t'u* (Illustrations of the Five Marchmounts' True Forms). When the Ling-pao lineage established itself at the end of the fourth century A.D., it found that practice not to its liking and abandoned it along with the cutting of hair. It substituted pledges as guarantees of vows. On the other hand, its scriptures treated the gages as inferior to the practices of the halcyon epochs of high antiquity. In the golden ages of the past, people followed the Tao in their hearts naturally, and consequently sureties were unnecessary. But the revelation of the Ling-pao canon occurred in a degenerate age when humankind was corrupt and pursued wealth only. Under such circumstances the gods had no other option but to compel ordinands to part with some of their worldly goods as a condition for the conferral of the scriptures.[33]

Pledges were not only material sacrifices made to demonstrate the sincerity of the ordinand's vows. Some were also gifts presented to influence the decisions and actions of the numinous rulers, ministers, and functionaries who administered the unseen government of the cosmos. Like their worldly counterparts, these otherworldly bureaucrats exercised control over the governed by virtue of powers enabling them to collect intelligence about the behavior of the faithful, to record violations of the ethical codes (sins) or virtuous deeds (merit), and to impose penalties on offenders or bestow rewards on the upright. The ledgers they kept were critical to the destinies of all Taoists since a negative accounting (more sins than merits) could shorten their lifespans or condemn them to an afterlife of torment. Conversely, a positive accounting would guarantee a longer life or blissful existence after death. However, this system of retribution did not operate with machine-like precision. The ethereal officials were as venal as the mundane. Consequently, pledges also possessed the character of bribes and were utilized to induce the keepers of the otherworldly records to expunge and alter the information about the ordinands contained in their books. Should the ordinands fail to render the proper gratuity, various bureaus (the Office of Capital Spirits, Office of the Bureaucrats of the Shades, and the like) took their cases under review and punctiliously scrutinized their entries on the ledgers in search of any and all infractions, large or small, with an eye to imposing punishments for any breach of the rules.

When the ordination rite was completed, the pledges ceased to have the numinous legal value that they had possessed during the rite and were distributed. The protocols required that 20 percent of them be turned over to the preceptor(s) who was (were) not permitted to use the gages for his (their) own private needs. Another 20 percent went to the begging poor and to priests who had retired to the mountains. The last stipulation concerning donations to mountain-dwelling priests is very interesting because it explains in part how these hermits were able to survive without a livelihood. The remaining 60 percent was reserved for sponsoring rituals—burning incense and lighting lanterns—which would establish the ordinands' merit and thereby contribute to their salvation. The cases of those who violated the rules on distribution of pledges would be turned over to the Three Officials for investigation and punishment.[34]

As indicated above, social status was a determinant of the quality and quantity of pledges presented. In its notes on "Destiny Silk" presented during the rites of investiture for the Tung-shen, Ling-pao, and Shang-ch'ing scriptures, the *Wu-shang pi-yao* establishes discriminatory regulations. In every case the emperor (and presumably his family) is required to submit the cloth in *p'i* (bolts), nobles (and the wealthy?) in *chang* (a unit of ten feet), and commoners in *ch'ih* (feet). Allowances are made on the basis of rank and wealth. Those with few resources are excused from expending large sums on their ordinations while those with plenty are expected—required—to draw amply on their stores to put on an impressive show. The Princesses obviously belonged to the latter category, and the gages for their investiture vastly exceeded anything specified in the protocols.[35]

The opulence of the altar, its paraphernalia, and the pledges left the greatest impression on Chang Wan-fu. He devotes 81 percent of his account of the Princesses' investiture to describing the stage and its accoutrements. Obviously, it was not the normal fixture or array for the ordination of an ordinary ordinand. In the conclusion to his description

(Appendix One), Chang estimates the value of the musical instruments, secular clothing (500 sets fabricated from coarse silk were provided for each woman), 10,000 lengths of brocade and net (obviously the quantity has been exaggerated), cash, colored silk, and liturgical paraphernalia at 10,000 strings of cash. And this figure did not include the worth of the objects (cloth and pledges) employed to defend the sacred precincts. One gage alone, the 200 *liang* of gold, was worth $103,275 at January 1989 prices. This munificence testifies to Jui-tsung's favoritism toward his daughters and explains the strong, persistent censure that his officials delivered on the question of his expenditures for the construction of their abbeys. If he authorized the issuance of these huge sums just for their ordination, then the outlays which he approved for building their temples must truly have been stupendous.[36]

The altar for the Princesses' ordination was a simulacrum of the sacred mountain, which held a position of immense importance in various Taoist scriptural traditions. On such lofty prominences, especially in their caves, the Gods, Perfected, and Immortals hid the precious canon, and there they revealed those holy texts to anointed mortal worthies at appropriate times (Chapter Four, numbers 5, 8, and 10). In fact, had Gold-Immortal and Jade-Perfected strictly observed the dictates of the Ling-pao scriptures, they would have traveled to one of the marchmounts and taken their vows there. However, long before their time, expense and inconvenience had compelled Taoists to resort to the expedient of erecting altars in urban abbeys as substitutes for mountains in the performance of their liturgies. When they built these artificial alternatives, they imbued the mounds with a symbolism that represented much more than the sacred mountain. Their altars were calculated recreations of the structure of the cosmos in miniature. The configuration of the gates at cardinal points of the compass replicated the order of nature, celestial and terrestrial, and established invisible channels through which the ethers *(ch'i)* from the distant nodes of the east, south, center, west, and north flowed into the platform. The numbers and hues of the altar's trappings, furniture, and pledges conformed to those associated with the forms of ether residing in the five directions and, like magnets, attracted streams of those energies to the sacred precincts. Any deviation from the time-honored pattern of order and symbolism in this array disrupted the rhythm of nature and vitiated the ordination. Thus, the well-tempered altar was a primitive engine, fueled by cosmic gases, which, when ignited by the officiants, endowed the ritual of ordination with the magic aura that sanctified the transmission of the canon.

# CHAPTER THREE

# *The Drama*

UNFORTUNATELY, aside from some desultory comments devoted mainly to auspicious portents and an epiphany, Chang Wan-fu neglected to describe what transpired during the liturgy of investiture for the Princesses' ordination in A.D. 711. Perhaps he felt constrained to hold back because regulations in the protocols forbade disclosure of the rite's innermost secrets to the uninitiated, or perhaps he assumed that anyone interested in such minutiae could consult the appropriate manuals on the subject. None of the latter dating from his time are extant, but Lu Hsiu-ching's detailed collection of protocols, the *T'ai-shang tung-hsüan ling-pao shou-tu i,* is. Its survival testifies not only to the reverence with which later Taoists regarded it and its author but also to its continuous popularity and use as a guide for the performance of Ling-pao ordinations. In certain respects Lu's text is defective, but passages from the original Ling-pao scriptures, a short set of directions in the *Wu-shang pi-yao,* and other liturgical works can be used to fill lacunae, clarify obscure points, and amplify insufficient directives in his text.[1]

Before the investiture could commence, Princesses Gold-Immortal and Jade-Perfected had to purify themselves by ablutions, fasting, and burning incense. Ablution involved bathing in scented waters—one scripture recommends mixing the Five Aromatics in the bath—and was a religious act accompanied by visualizations and invocations. In the Ling-pao tradition, fasting was a prerequisite for receiving, copying, and reciting scripture; drafting registers and talismans; worshiping; visiting a preceptor to make inquiries; and concocting elixirs. Fasting probably took place in an oratory—an isolated, quiet chamber that had been a standard fixture of the faith since the third century A.D.—set aside and equipped for private devotions. During these periods of abstinence it was customary for the priest to burn incense, read scripture, and meditate.[2]

In theory, ordinations were supposed to be scheduled on a small number of auspicious days fixed by the canon itself. Those designated for the performance of Ling-pao investitures during the spring were the fifty-first (chia-yin) and fifty-second (i-mao) days of the sixty-day cycle. Neither date, January 31 and February 1 of 711, was selected for the Princesses' ordination. Instead, those in charge chose the first day (chia-tzu) of the cycle: this, though uncanonical, was the most propitious day of all. This violation of the protocols is difficult to explain, since Taoists were normally punctilious about such matters. Perhaps it was the will of the royal house, whose power was sometimes greater than precedent, that forced the clergy to deviate from the norm.[3]

One of the original Ling-pao scriptures calls for six officiants in all (one for each of the categories listed below) to preside at ordination rites. By the middle of the fifth century A.D. this figure had grown considerably, and in the time of Princesses Gold-Immortal and Jade Perfected the total was fixed at thirty-eight for the transmissions of all canons.

1. *Three Canon Preceptors* (Fa-shih). These were the Preceptor of Initiation *(Tu-shih),* Preceptor of Registration *(Chi-shih),* and Preceptor of Scripture *(Ching-shih).* According to the Ling-pao scriptures, the Preceptors should be men of eminent virtue who are capable of interpreting the mysterious and abstruse meaning of scripture. At investitures these men were the chief officials who executed the critical offices of the esoteric rite.[4]

2. *Five Cantors* (Tu-chiang). Those selected should be men of talent and wisdom who are perspicuous, who can understand the marvelous principles, and who are conversant with the liturgical regulations. The cantors established the schedule for the rite, struck the bells and the drums at appropriate times during the course of the investiture (a task involving timing), and, most importantly, led the congregation's responses. They were penalized forty prostrations for neglecting to make a response, fifty for failing to praise the gods in their responses, and sixty for striking the bell too early or too late.[5]

3. *Six Directors of the Retreat* (Chien-chai). The directors were charged with the responsibility of inspecting the execution of the ordination rite to determine if any violations of the protocols occurred.

They were supposed to impeach those guilty of such infractions and correct their errors or omissions. The directors were penalized sixty prostrations for finding a fault but not impeaching the offender so that the congregation could correct it. They apparently also served as liaisons between the clergy and the lay sponsors of the rite, and were instrumental in guaranteeing that these patrons properly furnished the altar for the investitures or other rites. During the T'ang, abbeys had permanent posts for Directors of the Retreats.[6]

4. *Seven Attendants of the Scripture* (Shih-ching). These attendants managed the scriptures and the writs, and arranged the kerchiefs and the wrappers for them.[7]

5. *Eight Attendants of the Incense* (Shih-hsiang). These officiants deployed the braziers and were charged with ensuring that the smoke of the incense was never interrupted. They were penalized thirty prostrations for permitting the extinction of the fire and seventy for allowing a censer to be overturned.[8]

6. *Nine Attendants of the Lanterns* (Shih-teng). These men were responsible for guaranteeing that light radiated to all points *(ssu-fang)* of the altar as well as for the care of all lighting appurtenances. They were penalized twenty prostrations for permitting the flame of a lantern to die.[9]

Chang Wan-fu says that the preceptor should choose priests of eminent virtue, who had been fellow students with him and with whom he was personally acquainted, to fill these posts. Otherwise he should select students of sufficient spirituality *(shen-tsu ti-tzu?)* who were exceptionally accomplished and talented.[10]

The first formality that Princesses Gold-Immortal and Jade-Perfected were required to undergo at their ordination was called "Visiting the Preceptor and Submitting the Statement" (see Appendix Two, section I). They discharged this obligation on February 11, when they went to the Kuei-chen Abbey and met with Shih Ch'ung-hsüan. According to the *Wu-shang pi-yao*, the ordinands appeared before their preceptors to make three obeisances, striking their foreheads on the ground, and to perform "long kneelings *(ch'ang-kuei)*." The "long kneeling" was a formal sitting posture intended to convey respect to a host or superior. It involved placing the knees on a mat, pressing legs and ankles together, resting the buttocks on the heels, and straightening the back. It can still be seen at performances of the Japanese tea ceremony. In this position the students submitted statements *(ts'u-wen)* providing particulars about their native places (hamlets or wards, villages, subprefectures, and prefectures) and ages. They called themselves by the title *Tung-shen ti-tzu* (Students of the Cavern-Divine), appropriate to their status as aspirants to the Ling-pao canon, and supplied the name of the corpus that they wished to receive—in this instance, the *Ling-pao chen-wen fu t'u yü-tzu* (The True Writs, Talismans, Illustrations, and Jade Graphs of Ling-pao). The statements were then dated and handed to the preceptor.[11]

According to the *Huang-lu chien-wen* (a text from the original Ling-pao canon which is now lost except for excerpts in other works), the ordination was to take seven days, presumably beginning with the Visitation to the Preceptor and concluding with the performance of the Nocturnal Annunciation. The elapse of time between these two events at the Princesses' ordination was actually ten days. This discrepancy is easily explained. The *Huang-lu chien-wen* also stipulated that the Nocturnal Annunciation could not take place if a wind was blowing which might disturb the True Writs. Under those circumstances, the participants in the rite were to withdraw and fast *(t'ui-chai)* for three days before they could make another attempt. Apparently just such a wind rose on February 16, 711, forcing the postponement of the Princesses' Nocturnal Annunciation for three days.[12]

The Princesses probably spent the time between their first visit with Shih Ch'ung-hsüan and the day of their investiture fasting as prescribed in the protocols. Fasts were required preliminaries for most Taoist rituals as well as those of the state religion. The ladies also may have undergone the first phase of initiation in the Ling-pao investiture during that period. In their time the transmission of the Ling-pao canon consisted of three stages called the Three Covenants *(San-meng),* for each of which the preceptor conferred a different set of injunctions. The Initial Covenant *(Ch'u-meng)* appears to have entailed a separate ritual during which the Spontaneously Generated Tally was split or divided and the officiant presented the ordinands with the Injunctions for Arresting (literally, Closing and Blockading) the Six Emotions (Appendix Two, section II, parts A and B). As Chang Wan-fu notes, the rite was part of the Princesses' ordination, and Abbot Shih probably conducted it for Gold-Immortal and Jade-Perfected at some point during the ten days preceding the Nocturnal Annunciation. The breaking, rending, or dividing of tallies *(ch'üan, ch'i, fu)* was an ancient procedure for establishing binding contracts. The state continued to use it in the T'ang dynasty to assign commissions to officials; to confirm bureaucratic and military appointments; and to mark aristocratic, bureaucratic, and military status, among other things. The superior (emperor, official, officer) retained one half and the subordinate the other. Should an occasion arise later when the commission, appointment, or status required validation, the two halves were mated, the joining of the uniquely split parts authenticating the original division and compact.[13]

At its inception, religious Taoism adopted the tallies *(ch'üan* and *ch'i)* and the method for employing them. These items appear in the inventories of materials transmitted to ordinands at all but one of the levels of ordination (see Chapter Four, numbers 5, 6, 8, 9, 10, and 11). The *Tung-hsüan ling-pao tzu-jan ch'üan i* (HY 522), a text of unknown date, is a liturgical guide for performing the rite of Rending the Self-Generating Tally. Its format (see Appendix Two, section II, part A) is very similar to that given in Lu Hsiu-ching's manual for the Ling-pao investiture. In fact, it contains provisions for "Receiving the Canon" and "Transmission of the Ten Injunctions." This evidence indicates that the text was a simplified version of the liturgy for Ling-pao ordination which combined the rituals of Rending the Tally with the transmission of the canon. Regrettably, although its directives call for "Rending the Tally" and "Transmission of the Tally," they offer no descriptions of these acts. However, a manual for conducting the rite of transmission for the *Tung-shen ching,* probably dating from the T'ang, provides a good description of the manner in which such tallies were split. The preceptor ordered the ordinand to seize the handle of a knife and place the blade directly above the graph *t'ung* in the text of the tally. Then the student pulled the knife while the officiant pushed it to cut the document. The preceptor retained one half and the ordinand the other half. Thereafter the newly ordained priest was fully established as his preceptor's subordinate.[14]

Despite its title, the purpose of the Injunctions for Arresting the Six Emotions was not to control the emotions alone, but the senses, desires, mind, and hand as well.

1. Do not permit your eyes to observe widely or be disturbed by the glorious colors, because they will destroy your pupils and you will lose your sight. Your light will be indistinct and undiscerning.
2. Do not permit your ears to hear the cacophony or be muddled by the five musical notes. You will injure your spirits and defeat the proper. Evil sounds howl and wail.
3. Do not permit your nose to smell widely the various odors which are rank stenches. It is easy to become muddled and fouled, and your body *(hsing)* will not be pure or proper.
4. Do not permit your mouth to covet oily or fragrant things. You will foul the flow to the regal spirits, and the spirits of your viscera will flee in anger.

5. Do not permit your hand to violate the law or commit abominations by stealing other's things or coveting profit for yourself. There are disasters of which you are unaware.

6. Do not permit your mind to love or desire because these emotions agitate and shake the Five Spirits, injuring the vital secretions *(ching)* and destroying the energies *(ch'i)*. Your core *(t'i)* will be bewildered and confused.

The objective of these injunctions is to restrict the flow of sense data to the mind and to eradicate desire and sin. The precepts are the foundations for cultivating a physical and spiritual discipline that is capable of developing true perception, maintaining inner quiescence and purity, preventing harm to the body and soul, and establishing mental stability and tranquility. The underlying premises for these notions are that man is endowed with a perfect nature spiritually and physically; that senses and desires can defile, disrupt, and damage that nature; and that self-control enables the adept to preserve its pristine state.[15]

The Central Covenant *(Chung-meng)* was the second stage of the ordination. During this phase the officiant transmitted the canon in forty-seven scrolls and the Great Injunctions, Superior Grade, of Wisdom at what Lu Hsiu-ching labeled "The Annunciation and Report of the Nocturnal Revelation *(Su-lu)* for the True Writs under the Great Covenant *(Ta-meng)* of the Numinous Treasure by Externalizing the Officials and Worshiping the Memorial *(Pai-piao)*." Actually the Central Covenant consisted of two or three separate rites, the first of which was called "The Reading of the Petition on Yellow Silk (see Appendix Two, section III, part A)." This reading was supposed to take place the day before the performance of the *Su-ch'i;* in the Princesses' case, this was February 18, 711.[16]

As the title of the rite indicates, its core was the recitation of a document that the officiant had previously written on yellow silk (Appendix Two, section III, part A, number 4). The petition would be addressed to the Superior Sovereigns, the Five Elders of the Primordial Commencement (the gods of the five directions), and other ethereal beings. In it the officiant identifies himself by name and titles and tenders his credentials, that is, he recalls the name of the preceptor from whom, and the date when, he received the canon. This is followed by a statement informing the gods that he has superior students of certain ages who have been very diligent and who have supplied pledges as collateral for their oaths. He continues by stating that these ordinands wish to receive the "Scriptures, Talismans, Illustrations, and Jade Graphs of the Numinous Treasure and Cavern-Mystery *(Ling-pao tung-hsüan ching*

*fu t'u yü-tzu)"* in so many chapters. The officiant concludes by announcing that he is going to transmit the canon according to the protocols for
exposing the writs contained in the Bright Code *(Ming-k'o)*. He then
asks that his petition be forwarded to the deities of the Nine Heavens.
Afterward the preceptor signs the document, giving his name and
native district, dates it, and supplies the names of the districts in which
the rite has been taking place.[17]

Following the Reading of the Yellow Silk Petition, the officiant recites
the Rescript for Revering the Compact (Appendix Two, section III,
part A, number 5). This is a decree which respectfully orders certain
spirits of the officiant's body to grasp the petition for revealing the True
Writs and proceed to the Most Exalted Bureaus *(T'ai-shang ts'ao)* on
high, where they are to submit it. The preceptor also asks these spirits to
correct errors and supply omissions in his text. Moreover, he warns
them not to permit superior officials, the demons of the Six Heavens, or
the inferior officials of the stale emanations to interfere with the execution of their task or to damage the document which they are carrying.[18]

Then the officiant rises, clacks his teeth nine times (to alert the Nine
Heavens), and utters an invocation in which he announces that on this
auspicious day . . ., superior students, by virtue of their karma and
their encounter with the scripture, the Treasure Slats of the Supreme
Sovereign *(Shang-huang pao-p'ien)*, have reverently established a covenant (the Initial Covenant?) with the Nine Heavens on the Mysterious
Marchmount (the altar) and declared it to the Five Sovereigns and the
sources of the twelve rivers, imploring them to record it. Next he
requests that His Eminence the Dawn *(Kao-ch'en)* order the myriad
powers to array themselves on the altar, form a guard, and wait for the
announcement of the ordination the next day (Appendix Two, section
III, part A, number 6).[19]

Through this rite the preceptor supplied the gods of the five directions
and others with formal written notification that he was about to transmit the Ling-pao canon to his students. In the course of it he acted as
guarantor for the ordinands, assuring the gods that they were worthy of
receiving the gift of scriptures by virtue of their diligence and that they
had provided pledges and established covenants as required. To ensure
that his declaration reached his numinous superiors in proper form, he
requested that the functionaries in the ethereal bureaus review and
amend it where it was deficient.

The second part of the Middle Covenant, the Nocturnal Annunciation as adapted for ordination, took place on the night of February 19,
711. Although there appears to have been no wind, auspicious snow-
flakes fluttered down like flowers at the altar just as the officiants began

to chant the retreat of annunciation for Princesses Gold-Immortal and Jade-Perfected. One can only reconstruct what transpired thereafter from conjectures based on the contents of the protocols for investiture, mainly those in Lu Hsiu-ching's manual.[20]

Lu's liturgy for the Ling-pao ordination is a pastiche of discrete elements which he assembled from the original canon. On the one hand, he derived the general framework for it from the primitive version of the *Su-ch'i* as he found it in the scriptures. Incidentally, he also revised the protocols for the *Su-ch'i* and constructed the first manual for its performance (chapter 16 of HY 508; see Appendix Three, number 4). On the other hand, he adapted that rite by adding acts designed specifically for conferring the writs, slips, registers, injunctions, and vows—acts that had not previously been elements of the Nocturnal Annunciation.

Those elements in his manual not specifically concerned with transmissions, mainly rites executed before and after the acts of investiture, resolve themselves into a number of themes. The first of the motifs was the pilgrimage to the sacred marchmount. That undertaking commenced when the officiants, attired in liturgical vestments, and the ordinands, dressed in coarse yellow habits and black hats, made three circumambulations around the outside of the altar (Appendix Two, section III, part B, number 1). This peregrination represented the journey to the mountain. The pilgrimage continued with the ascension to the heights, which began when the preceptor mounted the lowest tier to recite the Invocation for Entering the Portal that opened communication with the unseen world (Appendix Two, section III, part B, number 3). Next the officiant stepped up to the Capital Altar (second tier) to conduct the Audience with the Nine Heavens, the first notification dispatched to the ethereal powers informing them that the transmission of the canon was about to take place (Appendix Two, section III, part B, number 5). He then commanded the ordinands to join him on that level for the Chanting of the Gold Perfected's Petition of the Great Space, which possessed the power to subjugate the myriad demons. At the conclusion of that recitation the congregation moved up to the Inner Altar (Appendix Two, section III, part B, number 7). The highest tier of the altar, the peak of the mountain, was the ultimate objective of the devotees. There they completed the final stage of their pilgrimage by circling the Inner Altar in a series of visitations *(hsieh)* to the sacred stations, that is the five gates and ten gates (Appendix Two, section III, part B, numbers 8, 10, 15, 23, and 33).

The sacred stations, the portals, were not sites that were hallowed because they were associated with heroic or miraculous events in the lives of the gods or the saints. As noted, they were the terminals of channels that stretched out from the altar to nodes in the distant directions which they represented. Through those channels flowed the energies which vitalized the ordination. Taoists had personified these ethers in the forms of divinities; thus the gates were also the mouths of ducts that extended upward to those spheres on the heavenly plane where the Celestial Venerables and other deities presided, and outward to those mysterious regions on the earthly plane where the Five Sovereigns or Elders resided. As the members of the congregation made their tour of the stations, they halted at each to pay homage to the deities. The forms of their adoration resembled the kinds of obeisances required of secular attendants when they appeared before the emperor at imperial levees. The gods were, after all, sovereigns of the cosmos, so officiants and ordinands appeared before them with their visitation boards upraised, bowed as if being received in audience, and offered incense as tribute. But their veneration also had a specifically religious character to it because they sang, chanted, or recited prayers and hymns. The objective of these acts was not only to express the devotees' profound reverence for the rulers of the universe, but also to establish bonds of allegiance between themselves and their superiors (Appendix Two, section III, part B, number 10). The priest was the servant of the gods, and homage was a demonstration of the vassal's fidelity to his liege lord. The gods were not the only masters of the clergy. The protocols also imposed an obligation on ordinands to pay ceremonial respects to their mortal preceptors, undoubtedly with the same intent of instilling a degree of subordination and allegiance in them (Appendix Two, section III, part B, numbers 30 and 32).

The third motif, after homage, was consecration, and this had two facets. The first entailed energizing the altar. A well-tempered altar welcomed the cosmic ethers and had the inherent potential for generating spiritual force. However, it rested inert without the intervention of the priest. It was his duty to activate its engine, and his instrument for accomplishing that task was visualization. Through use of his imagination, the officiant assimilated the primal ethers (Appendix Two, section III, part B, number 3) and the energies of the Ten Directions (Appendix Two, section III, part B, number 9). Then he envisioned a radiant light in the form of the sun at the nape of his neck and broadcast it in all directions (Appendix Two, section III, part B, number 8). Imbued with this aura, the altar was fully operational and ready to perform its task in the ordination.

The second facet involved erecting a spiritual bulwark for protecting the sacred precincts against attacks from malevolent powers. To no small degree Taoists saw themselves beset on all sides by demons (the gods of heterodox, that is non-Taoist, cults) and specters (troubled souls, primarily of those who had fallen in battle), which inundated the universe and posed a dire threat to the security of their rites. It was incumbent upon the clergy to prevent these evil beings from wreaking havoc. Again physical countermeasures were built into altars for this purpose, but they were not complete without the spiritual participation of the officiant. Wielding his ultimate weapon of visualization, he was able to summon forth a legion of warriors, a host of numinous officials, and a cluster of jade maids from his body (Appendix Two, section III, part B, numbers 2, 8, and 11). These spirits stood guard inside and outside his body ready to slay, control, or otherwise deter any specters or demons who might attempt to disrupt the proceedings. He also conjured up canopies of clouds, which acted like shields against any malevolent assaults from above (Appendix Two, section III, part B, numbers 2 and 11). So sheltered, the officiant could execute the rite in full confidence that nothing untoward would occur.

Ordination was, as the title *Su-ch'i* indicates, mainly a rite of annunciation, meaning that the whole proceeding was a form of notification. However, only part of it was strictly devoted to this fourth theme. Lu Hsiu-ching's protocols required that the officiant inform the Nine Heavens, the three Celestial Venerables, the Five Elders, local deities in whose territories the rite took place, and all other gods of the cosmos that he was going to transmit the canon (Appendix Two, section III, part B, numbers 5, 6, 9, 11, 13, and 14). Lu's manual also provided the devices by which such communication was conveyed. Usually the officiant alerted those whom he was to address by clacking his teeth or drumming his fingers on the sides of his head. Afterward he read statements whose formats resembled those for public documents, such as memorials *(piao)* or announcements *(ch'i),* issued by imperial officials. These texts reflected the typically bureaucratic concerns for proper identification of the subjects (people and topics) covered in the notices, exact specifications of the time when and place where the event occurred, verification by signature, and errorless transcription. Although they were recited, these messages were actually written communiqués that had to be delivered physically. Since the priest remained encumbered by his mortal flesh, he was incapable of presenting them himself. He was compelled to rely on the spirits of his body to carry out the task.

## The Transmission of Writs

Up to this point Lu Hsiu-ching's liturgy proceeds much as it might have for any of the great Ling-pao retreats. However, in the last major

annunciation of the prelude, the officiant proclaims the commencement
of the first of three acts in the rite devoted specifically to investiture. In
it he declares that he is going to transmit: (a) the True Writs and Treasure Talismans of the Five Elders from the Primordial Origin of the
Numinous Treasure in Red Script, (b) the Jade Graphs for the Esoteric
Intonations of the Eight Effulgent Spirits in the Three Divisions and the
Twenty-Four Divine and Perfected Officials, Clerks, and Warriors in
All Heavens, (c) the Slip Writs of the Eight Authorities, and (d) the
Divine Staffs. This statement marks the end of the preliminaries and
sets the agenda for the next phase of the *Su-ch'i*. After finishing his declaration, the preceptor and his students rise and make a tour of the
Inner Altar, kneeling at each of the five directions to offer incense in the
braziers on the tables positioned there. Then the officiant chants five
hymns to the Five Perfected while the students salute twice and sing
praises. At that moment in the ordination for Princesses Gold-Immortal
and Jade-Perfected, "just as the True Writs were about to be exposed, a
propitious cloud drifted over the altar covering it like a canopy."[21]

### The True Writs and Treasure Talismans

Following the annunciation and the hymn, the preceptor and the
ordinands return to their stations, he in the north and they in the south.
Facing his students, the officiant unrolls the True Writs on a table and
reads the preface. Afterward the ordinands salute twice, and the preceptor interprets the writs graph by graph *(tzu-tzu chieh-shuo)* according to
the proper intonations in the Jade Instructions *(Yü-chüeh cheng-yin)* and
transmits them by reading the texts out loud *(k'ou-shou tu-tu)*. The
ordinands acknowledge reception of the oral instructions.[22]

The True Writs *(Chen-wen)* were texts spontaneously generated in the
Empty Cavern *(K'ung-tung)* before the Primordial Commencement
*(Yüan-shih)*, before heaven and earth rooted, and before the sun and
moon radiated. They had no ancestors or progenitors. The Celestial
Venerable of the Primordial Commencement refined and smelted them
in the Courtyard of Flowing Fire *(Liu-huo chih t'ing)* at the Foundry of
Cavern-Yang *(Tung-yang chih kuan)*. Because the ether of the Cavern-
Yang (south) was red, the writs were called the Red Scripts *(Ch'ih-shu)*.
At an audience with the Ten Thousand Sovereigns, the Celestial Vener-
able ordered gold cast to make tablets *(chien)* for them and had the texts
engraved on Jade Slats *(Yü-p'ien)*. The Five Elders *(Wu-lao)* took charge
of recording them and secreted them in the Mysterious Terrace at the
Palace of Purple Tenuity in the Numinous Metropolis of the Nine
Heavens. The writs were the superior texts of the Nine Heavens (hence
the title Celestial Texts, *T'ien-shu)*, of which the specters and spirits had

not heard. The divine officials who served as the attendant guard of the Five Sovereigns issued them, according to the regulations of the Mysterious Code *(Hsüan-k'o)*, once every four eons when the ethers of the Six Heavens (the celestial regions associated with the excessive and heterodox, that is, non-Taoist, cults, which were the chief rivals of early Taoism) had dissipated and the True Tao prevailed. The first recipients of the sacred texts were the Most Exalted Lord of the Great Tao, the Eminent Superior Jade Sovereign, the Utmost Perfected of the Ten Directions, the Great Saints of all Heavens, and the Perfected of Marvelous Deportment, who requested the Celestial Venerable of the Primordial Commencement to transmit them. He ordered these deities first to withdraw and study the Celestial Intonations in the Golden Rules *(T'ien-yin yü chin-ko)*, also known as the Rules of Deportment *(Fu-yang chih ko)*. Three months later, having fulfilled this precondition, they returned to court. Satisfied that they were worthy of the gift, the Celestial Venerable commanded the Five Elders to open the wrappers of the nine beams in eight colors and the bags of cloud brocade, take out the Jade Slats of the Primordial Commencement, and convey them to the gods according to the procedures for transmission in the Mysterious Code.[23]

Lu Hsiu-ching does not reproduce in his manual the actual writs which were written in "secret seal script *(pi chuan wen)*," a form of celestial calligraphy undecipherable to the uninitiated. These sets of mysterious characters survive in the *Yüan-shih wu-lao ch'ih-shu yü-p'ien chen-wen t'ien-shu ching* (HY 22), the first of the revealed scriptures in the original Ling-pao canon (see Figure 4). It was in that form that the writs possessed talismanic powers. However, Lu only supplies versions rendered into standard Chinese script *(k'ai-shu)*. Each of the five writs is a passage consisting of four graph lines dedicated to the deity of the direction that it represents. They vary in length: 120 characters for the east, 152 for the south, 144 for the center, 136 for the west, and 120 for the north. All of the writs are divided into four paragraphs or stanzas whose ends are marked by lines giving the total number of graphs in the parts. Appended to each writ is a statement in conventional Chinese calligraphy which defines the magical properties of its sections. The description for the writ of the east (see Figure 4) reads:

> The upper text of twenty-four graphs [first paragraph] on the Jade Slats of the Numinous Treasure in Red Script for the Blue-Green Sovereign of the Eastern Region is that by which the Governor for the Primal Terrace of the Nine Heavens summons the Superior Sovereigns of the Nine Heavens to audit the charts and registers of the immortals [that is, enter or delete names in the celestial records].

Beneath it the text in thirty-two graphs [the second stanza] is that by which the Governor for the Hall of the Eastern Blossom in the Palace of Purple Tenuity summons the stellar mandarins to rectify the numbers for celestial lots [that is, alter human destinies].

Beneath it the text in thirty-two graphs [the third paragraph] is that by which the Governor for the Institute of the Eastern Mulberry that Presides over the Powers evokes the specters and demons to rectify the ethers of the Nine Heavens.

Beneath it the text in thirty-two graphs [the last stanza] is that by which the Governor for the Cinnabar Terrace and Jade Gate-Tower in the northeast sector of the Nine Heavens evokes the Water Sovereign of the Eastern Ocean according to the calculation for the enormous cataclysm [at the end] of the Great Kalpas to summon the scaly dragons and water gods for service.

Altogether there are 120 graphs, all of which were texts spontaneously generated at the Primordial Commencement. They are also called the Mysterious Petition of the Perfected Cavern which Produces the Divine Treasure and the Slip Writ of the Eastern Mount's Divine Invocation of the Eight Authorities.[24]

The format of the statements for the remaining four writs is roughly the same with different values, titles, and names substituted.

It is not clear from Lu Hsiu-ching's manual precisely what text the officiant used to interpret the writs. The present version of the Jade Instructions, the *T'ai-shang tung-hsüan ling-pao ch'ih-shu yü-chüeh miao-ching* (HY 352), which was the second of the revealed scriptures in the Ling-pao canon, does not supply a graph-by-graph exegesis of the texts. What it does provide is an elaboration on the statements translated above, defining their numinous power. Its description for the eastern writ reads:

These twenty-four graphs [the first paragraph] govern the summoning of the Superior Sovereigns of the Nine Heavens to audit the charts and registers of the immortals. On the first days of their original destinies [birthdays] and the first days of the spring season, priests who are studying to become immortals always write these twenty-four graphs out in blue-green script on white slips, recording their names and the dates at the bottom of the slips. Then they cast the slats off the peaks of numinous mountains. After [practicing this procedure for] nine years the immortal bureaucrats will arrive to commission the nine Jade Maids of blue-green waists, and [the priests] themselves will acquire [the status of] flying immortals.

These thirty-two graphs [the second stanza] govern the summoning of the stellar mandarins of the celestial asterisms to rectify the celestial lots and remedy all excesses and errors of the asterisms caused by celestial cataclysms [that is, astrological disasters]. Inscribe the thirty-two graphs in vermilion script on blue-green paper and expose the paper in a central courtyard. For nine days and nine nights [intone] nightly the separate invocation [not provided] according to liturgical procedure. At the end of this period burn the paper in a fire and scatter its ashes in blue-green smoke. Also carve the text in thirty-two graphs on a blue-green stone and bury it in the east. Celestial [astrological] calamities will then dissipate on their own accord, and the asterisms will return to their stations.

These thirty-two graphs [the third paragraph] evoke the specters and demons to rectify the ethers of the Nine Heavens. To accomplish this procedure inscribe the text in vermilion script on a slip of blue-green wood. Take the text, face east, and thrice intone the invocation according to the text of the separate invocation [not provided]. The specters will then fetter their forms on their own, and the demons will exterminate themselves. Practice this with a pure mind.

These thirty-two graphs [the last stanza] govern the evocation of the Water Sovereign in the Eastern Ocean according to the calculation for the celestial cataclysms [at the end] of the Great Kalpas, and summon the scaly dragons and water gods for service. When one encounters a flood or wishes to cross a great waterway, inscribe the thirty-two graphs in yellow script on blue-green paper and with the separate invocation [not provided] cast it into the water. Then one will be able to pass over because the scaly dragons will bear one on their backs over the father of waters. One cannot practice this rite when one is worshipping and welcoming beside a river.[25]

For the most part, the beginning lines of the second set of descriptions (HY 352) are identical to the corresponding passages from the first (HY 22) except that the names of the celestial governors who wielded the writs have been deleted. This alteration transforms the writs. The first version vests only the ethereal beings with the right to exercise the powers of the writs. The second entrusts that prerogative to mortals, the priests, who have received the writs through a legitimate, sanctified transmission. Hence, the remaining lines of the Jade Instructions (version two) also supply specific directions for liturgical procedures which enable the priests to activate the powers. With the writs in hand the cleric who executed these rites was able to acquire immortality, dispel astrological catastrophes, subjugate specters and demons, and overcome floods and waters.

Although the agenda of the annunciation declares that the Treasure

Talismans would be transmitted with the True Writs, Lu Hsiu-ching does not provide directions for their conferral, and they do not appear in his manual. However, it is inconceivable that ordinands would not have received these writs, better known as the Five Ling-pao Talismans *(Ling-pao wu-fu)*, during investitures because they were inextricably bound to the secret seal-script versions of the True Writs (HY 22). The original versions of the talismans appear in the *T'ai-shang ling-pao wu-fu hsü* (HY 388), the only work in the Ling-pao canon that predates A.D. 400, and may actually have been in the hands of Ko Hsüan (trad. 164– October 4, 244), the putative recipient of the canon's revelation. Yü (trad. 2205–2197 B.C.), the mythological founder of the Hsia dynasty (trad. 2205–1766 B.C.) and tamer of the floods, purportedly received these mysterious graphs along with oral instructions from one of the Perfected on Mt. Chung and, after using them to accomplish heroic deeds, hid the writs in a cavern on Mt. Pao. Yü himself allegedly wrote out the five talismans as Numinous Treasure Writs, relying on one talisman to produce the next. In the *Yüan-shih wu-lao ch'ih-shu yü-p'ien chen-wen t'ien-shu ching* (HY 22), the talismans are joined to the True Writs, but are given in forms different from the originals (compare the reproductions of the talisman for the west from both texts in Figure 5), being divided into two parts which possess different powers. The first half of the talisman for the east is called the Celestial Numinous Treasure Writ of the Nine Ethers for the Talisman of the Blue-Green Sovereign in the East which Transforms to Produce the Ethers of the Red Heaven (south), and is:

> the ether of the lesser yang that transforms to produce the three ethers of the greater yang of the Cinnabar Heaven [south]. In lesser kalpas it is the earthly branch *ssu* and in the Great Kalpas the earthly branch *wu*. It revolves around the Red Sovereign. If one activates it and wears it at the waist, one will pass through catastrophes [unharmed]. Inscribe [this half of the talisman] in vermilion ink on blue-green silk 22 centimeters (8.5 inches) in length for wearing at the waist on one's person.

The second half is called the Eastern Talismanic Mandate for Lord Lao of the Commencement to Pacify the Blue-Green Powers of the Jeweled Blossom Grove, and it is:

> the ether of the primal yang which gives birth to the blue-green treasure of the nine ethers [the eastern region]. When the Blue-Green Sovereign of the eastern region regulates the nine by nine, the eighty-one circuits, the nine ethers comingle so that the Great Kalpa [when the Tao prevails] begins anew. Wear this talisman at the waist to follow the revolution [of

the Kalpa] and pass over the great calamity [that occurs at the end of a kalpa]. Write [this half of] the writ with a blue-green brush [that is, in blue-green ink].[26]

Similar statements with different names, titles, and values appear after each of the remaining talismans. The first half of each talisman, known as the *ling* (celestial portion), is the generative power of the ethers associated with the region or direction and season it represents, a power which produces the ethers and talismans of its successors. This concept of creation, based on the Han (206 B.C.–A.D. 220) theory of the five elements or phases, predicates the existence of an endless cycle of change that starts with the east and proceeds to the south, west, north, and center only to begin again in the east. The second half, known as the *pao* (terrestrial portion), is that which the first cause, the primal yang, produced along with the ethers for the region that it represents. Although both parts of the talisman provided the possessor with certain protections against harm, they appear to have been primarily instruments for providing access to cosmogonic and cosmological forces which could be used in rituals. In particular, the True Writs, undoubtedly with the Five Ling-pao Talismans attached, played the central role in the Retreat of the Gold Register, one of the functions of which was to put an end to natural calamities and the excesses and errors of the asterisms (astrological disasters) as well as to restore the cosmic ethers to their normal, beneficent operation. At the end of this ritual the writs were burned.[27]

In Lu Hsiu-ching's manual, the True Writs are followed by five lines entitled the Jade Taboos of the Five Demons. These lines supply the titles, cognomens *(hsing),* and taboo names *(hui)* for the monarchs of the demons *(mo-wang).* Each of the sovereigns is associated with one of the writs. To possess knowledge of a deity's secret cognomen and taboo was to have power over it. Priests employed these names to summon the gods and command them to repel spectral forces and dispel other misfortunes. Lu Hsiu-ching's source for these names was the *Tu-jen ching* (HY 1, ch. 1), one of the most important scriptures in the Ling-pao canon. They also appear in the *Tung-hsüan ling-pao erh-shih-ssu sheng-t'u ching* (HY 1396), another Ling-pao scripture, where they are rendered into talismanic script (Figure 6). Lu offers no directions for the conferral of the Taboo Names.[28]

## The Jade Graphs for the Esoteric Intonations

The second item in the agenda of the annunciation calls for the transfer of the Jade Graphs of the Esoteric Intonations. However, before turning to the Jade Graphs, the officiant transmits *(tu)* the Jade Instructions in

Red Graphs for the Eight Effulgent Spirits and Rulers of the Upper
Section and the Ch'ing-wei Heaven; the Middle Section and the Ta-
ch'ih Heaven; and the Lower Section and the Yü-yü Heaven. These
instructions are in three stanzas of eight lines and thirty-two characters
each, and were to be written in jade graphs of blue-green, vermilion,
and yellow calligraphy, respectively. Lu's versions of them are again
renditions in standard Chinese script. The talismanic originals appear
in the *Tung-hsüan ling-pao erh-shih-ssu sheng-t'u ching* (HY 1396). In that
text each of the three passages follows a register that lists the numinous
subordinates of its eight deities (see Figure 6). Possession of the writs
was a kind of commission which permitted the priest to evoke the
twenty-four spirits and their minions through various rites. In the
Taoist pantheon there were three sets of eight effulgent spirits, which
resided and presided in the head, chest, and lower abdomen (the three
divisions) of the human body. These deities were personifications of the
twenty-four cosmic ethers that energized nature, rising successively to
dominant positions of influence over the cosmos during the half-months
of the year assigned to them. Furthermore, the internal gods of the body
had celestial analogues in the twenty-four astral deities of the zodiac.
The latter were the potentates of Ch'ing-wei, Ta-ch'ih and Yü-yü
Heavens.[29]

The actual Writs of the Spontaneously Generated Jade Graphs for
the Esoteric Intonations of the Eight Assemblies are four passages of
four graph lines, purportedly originating as coagulations of mysterious,
flying ethers. In order of their appearance in the scriptures they represent: (a) the Blue-Green Sovereign of the East, whose Nine Ethers Control Various Heavens, (b) the Red Sovereign of the South, whose Three
Ethers Control Various Heavens, (c) the White Sovereign of the West,
whose Seven Ethers Control Various Heavens, and (d) the Black Sovereign of the North, whose Five Ethers Control Various Heavens. In his
liturgy, Lu Hsiu-ching divides each of the passages into two parts. The
first part is the Esoteric Intonations proper. The officiant supplies
instructions *(chüeh)* for these sections of the writs. When he finishes, the
ordinands turn in their minds to face the direction appropriate to the
writ, prostrate themselves, and close their eyes. The preceptor then
clacks his teeth the proper number of times (nine, three, seven, and
five, respectively) and recites the second part of the text as an invocation. Afterward the students raise their heads and ingest their breaths
nine, three, seven, or five times. Next the officiant (?) reads the writ's
tiny graphs *(tu hsi tzu)*, transmits them by singing *(ch'ang tu chih)*, and
reads them horizontally *(heng tu chih)*. Since Chinese was written verti-
cally in traditional times, the second reading produced a radically different rendering from the first.[30]

The first half of each passage is an excerpt from the "Hidden Discourse of the Great Brahman *(Ta-fan yin-yü)*" that appears in the *Tu-jen ching.* For the most part the lines of the discourse are meaningless. The reason for this is that many of the phrases are transliterations of Sanskrit terms that were derived from early translations of Buddhist sutras and resemble the *dharani,* magic spells, in the sutras. Like mantras, which also contain nonsense syllables, the efficacy of the Esoteric Intonations does not depend on their intelligibility, but on their evocative powers when they are pronounced. Utterance of them empowered the cantor to summon the gods of the ten directions and direct them to do his bidding, particularly with regard to affecting the salvation of the dead. The Writs for the Esoteric Intonations appear again in the *T'ai-shang ling-pao chu-t'ien nei-yin tzu-jan yü-tzu* (HY 97), another scripture from the original Ling-pao canon, where they are cast into the Jade Graphs, a form of talismanic script (see Figure 7). As with the True Writs, the Jade Graphs possessed magic power when written in this type of script and were undoubtedly used in this form during the performances of liturgics. Following each of the four writs is another roster of spirits which presumably obey the commands of the text's owner. One section of HY 97 is devoted to prescriptions for procedures by which the lines of the Esoteric Intonations were applied during rituals that were conducted on specific days to activate their powers, and another section to explanations of their meanings. The latter was the source for the invocations which constituted the second half of the writs in Lu's liturgy, where they are transcribed into standard Chinese.[31]

### The Slip Writs of the Eight Authorities

The third conferral of talismanic texts in the agenda of the annunciation was the transmission of the Slip-Board Writs of the Eight Authorities. During this procedure the usual order of precedence is reversed, as the ordinands' names are read before the officiant's. The preceptor provides two instructions—very short declarations—for the talismans of the upper boards and two instructions for those of the lower. Then he performs a visualization in which he externalizes a group of Jade Lads and Jade Maids, twelve each, to act as the Five Sovereigns' attendant guard. The students receive the Slip-Boards and execute long kneelings before the officiant. He recites an invocation for the Talisman that Commands the Multitudes *(Ch'ih chung fu)* and one for sealing the ends of the last board. Afterward the preceptor clacks his teeth nine times, raises his face to heaven, whistles thrice, inhales three times ingesting the breaths, and uses the Signet of the Primordial Commencement and the Signet of the Five Elders *(Yüan-shih wu-lao yin)* to stamp the third board. This sealing officializes the transfer of the boards to the ordinands and activates the numinous powers of their talismans.[32]

Chang Wan-fu called these boards Belt Talismans *(P'ei-fu)*. Three in number, they were supposed to be made of ginkgo wood *(yin-mu)*, 39.3 centimeters (15.3 inches) long and 5.9 centimeters (2.3 inches) wide. On the first was written in vermilion script the Three Heavens' Most Exalted Writ of the Mountain Spirit for Summoning and Subduing Dragons, Tigers, and Leopards *(San-t'ien t'ai-shang chao-fu chiao-lung hu pao shan-ching wen)*. On the second was inscribed the date and the preceptor's surname and given name written in vermilion script, and on the third a second talisman (see Figure 8). The last slip was stamped at both ends with the signets just mentioned. The first two boards were joined and placed in a bag made from dark-red cloth 3.54 meters (11.5 feet) in length. The third was attached to the outside of the bag. Normally this package was stored in a box of cypress wood. When a priest had occasion to use the slips, he withdrew them, attached them to a belt on his waist, and employed the same visualization and invocation given in Lu's liturgy to activate them. These talismans were potent amulets which guaranteed that the possessor of them would never again suffer the three evil fates—rebirth as a denizen of hell, as a domestic animal, or as a hungry ghost. After the owner's demise they became safe-conducts which permitted him or her to bypass Mt. T'ai, where the souls of the dead were judged, and to ascend directly to the Nine Heavens. In short, they were instruments for accomplishing the salvation of the ordinands/priests. They were also powerful liturgical devices for soliciting the assistance of celestial and terrestrial deities in performing rites, for causing specters to exterminate themselves, and for establishing communication with the gods, among other things.[33]

## The Divine Staffs

The final act in this series of bestowals is the Sealing of the Staffs. It commences when the officiant clacks his teeth thirty-six times. With his eyes closed he visualizes the five Clerks of the Five Sovereigns' True Talismans *(Wu-ti chen-fu li)*, each of whom is clad in raiments of the color appropriate to the direction that he represents; beams of five-color lights which flow down and illuminate the tops of the staffs; and the five Jade Maids of the Five Sovereigns, who stand guard to the right and left of the staffs. When this is completed, the ordinands present the staffs horizontally to the preceptor with their tops pointed to the left. The officiant seizes the talismans of the Blue-Green Sovereign (east) and orders the students to read the talismans' instruction, which says: "The cogno-men of the Blue-Green Sovereign['s clerk] is Ch'ü, and his given name is Keng-sheng." Then the talismans are given to the ordinands who accept them, face east, and clack their teeth nine times. They visualize blue-green vapors entering their mouths and flowing into their livers, where they produce nine layers of glorious, precious light that radiates to the napes of their necks. When they finish, they return the talismans to the preceptor, who takes them, inserts them into the holes of the sec-ond segment from the top of the staffs, and recites an invocation. After that, the students inhale nine times, ingesting the breaths. The same procedure is followed for the remaining talismans, with different names and values filled into the formula as illustrated in Table 3. When all of the visualizations are finished, the officiant seals the openings at the ends of the staffs with vermilion wax. He then impresses the Signet of the Primordial Commencement in the wax of the top segment and the Signet of the Five Elders in that of the bottom. The ordinands clack their teeth thirty-six times and perform the same visualization of the Clerks of the Five Sovereigns' True Talismans, the beams of five-color lights, and the Jade Maids that the preceptor employed to open the rite. Then, while the students hold the staffs horizontally with the tops point-ing to the left, the officiant recites an invocation. Afterward he inhales and ingests the twenty-five vapors of the Five Sovereigns.[34]

Chang Wan-fu called these instruments Bamboo Staffs (Ts'e-chang). These batons were supposed to be straight, dry stalks of bamboo, 2.07

**Table 3.** Elements in the Visualizations for the Five Talismans

| Direction | East | South | Regal Gate? | West | North |
|---|---|---|---|---|---|
| Clerk's Cognomen | Ch'ü | Chu | Ssu | Ju | Hsüan |
| Clerk's Name | Keng-sheng | Ch'ang-chung | Ching | Ch'ü-cheng | Yin-feng |
| Talisman | Blue-Green | Red | Yellow | White | Black |
| Number | Nine | Three | Twelve | Seven | Five |
| Organ | Liver | Heart | Spleen | Lungs | Kidneys |
| Area of Radiation | Nape of neck | Chest | Entire body | Lower abdomen | Behind the back |
| Segment of Staff | Second | Third | Fourth | Fifth | Sixth |

meters (6 feet, 8.5 inches) long with seven segments, which had been obtained from the south face of a numinous mountain. The hollows of the middle five segments were the receptacles for the talismans. The upper, or first, and lower, or last, were left empty.[35]

The writs implanted in the staffs were the True Talismans of the Five Sovereigns (see Figure 8). Five in number, they are not to be confused with the Five Ling-pao Talismans. "The Five Elders of the Primordial Commencement issued the True Talismans of the Five Sovereigns to save the people of the Five Sovereigns." As with the revelation of the True Writs, this act took place in the palaces of the Mysterious Metropolis. The talismans, seal scripts, appear in the *Yüan-shih wu-lao ch'ih-shu yü-p'ien chen-wen t'ien-shu ching* (HY 22), with instructions for employing them attached beneath. The directions for the first or east, the True Talisman for the Blue-Green Sovereign of the Primordial Commencement, read:

> Summon Keng-sheng, [the Clerk of] the True Talisman, to guard the Celestial Writ of the Numinous Treasure. When a priest swallows it, the numinous ethers are impressed *(chen)* on his liver, producing the blue-green spirit of the jeweled blossom in nine petals, which becomes the servant that communicates with the powers and conveys to the immortals.

Following each of the talismans is a second passage, which gives a fuller account of the writs' powers and the ritual procedures for employing them. In part the statement for the east reads:

> Priests whose destinies fall under the purview of the Eastern Marchmount [T'ai-shan in Shantung Province] write out this talisman in blue-green calligraphy on a piece of dark-red silk to attach to a belt at the waist on their persons. Furthermore, on the days of their original destinies [that is, their birthdays, which occur in the spring], they write it out in red calligraphy, face east, and ingest it in nine pieces. The Clerk of the True Talisman Ch'ü Keng-sheng follows the talisman and enters the office within the viscera of the stomach and liver. If priests continuously practice this procedure for nine years, they all generate a treasure blossom of the blue-green essence in nine layers whose beams radiate outside their bodies.[36]

Similar statements with different names, titles, and values appear after the remaining talismans. When manipulated individually during rituals, these amulets produce an aura visible outside the priest's body. When implanted and sealed in the staffs, they transform the batons into magic scepters. A priest need only point them upward or downward and perform the prescribed liturgical acts to induce the celestial or terrestrial deities to do the priest's bidding, communicate with the gods, or annihilate the specters.

## Transmission of the Canon and the Registers

The Sealing of the Staff is the final conferral in the agenda for the first act of transmission. The second begins with another annunciation. During a rite called the Declaration of the Cinnabar Ink Writ, the officiant, who apparently reads the document, supplies his titles and name and the names of the ordinands. Then he describes the emergence of the canon before the creation of the cosmos and mentions the transmission of the scriptures to Ko Hsüan in the Ch'ih-wu era (238–251). Afterward he reminds the ordinands of their duties, warning them that they and their ancestors will fall into hell if they deviate from the standards. Finally, he declares that he has established this Yellow Altar to inform the Five Sovereigns that covenants will be sworn to and to transmit the Marvelous Canon of the Treasure Writs in Ten Sections *(Pao-wen shih-pu miao-ching)*. In all of this he says that he will act in accordance with the regulations of the Bright Code of the Four Poles *(Ssu-chi ming-k'o)*.[37]

Afterward the ordinands read their own covenants. In these documents they provide the names of their native prefectures, subprefectures, villages, and hamlets; their titles as Masters of such-and-such Marchmounts, Students of the Cavern-Mystery; and their own names. Following that, they swear never to violate their covenants, forsake their oaths, deceive their preceptors, or show disrespect for the Tao. They ask the gods to consider their ancestors to the seventh degree and their parents as guarantors of their word. All of this the ordinands declare to the Celestial Venerables above and vow to the Five Sovereigns below.[38]

The establishment of covenants as a prerequisite for receiving scripture was an old convention in Taoism. Ko Hung (283–343), the eminent proponent of alchemy, states that he had "received under covenant" *(meng-shou)* three texts of that arcane art from his master at an altar on Mt. Ma-chi. Such compacts were the legal basis for the transfer of the Ling-pao canon as well. The ultimate bestowers and guardians of the sacred texts were the gods, and they required assurances that the recipients were worthy of their gifts. So as a condition for dispensation of this grace they demanded that ordinands render such guarantees in the form of covenants. In these documents the ordinands promised not to violate their oaths, which imposed upon them the obligation to maintain the sanctity and secrecy of the scriptures and not to betray the preceptors who presented the canon to them.[39]

Given the importance of the canon to investiture, it is curious that Lu Hsiu-ching offers no instructions for the actual transmission of the Ling-pao scriptures in his liturgy. It is quite clear from the text of the Cinnabar Ink Writ that it took place at this time, but Lu remains mute on the question. It is difficult to believe that he deliberately omitted this climactic act or that there were no specific procedures for the transfer of the texts as there had been for the conferral of the writs. It may well be that the extant version of his manual is corrupt at this point. Some sections of the text, notably the directives for the transmissions of the last four of the True Writs, the Jade Taboos of the Five Demons, and the Jade Instructions for the Eight Effulgent Spirits, are conspicuously missing. Perhaps some later copyist inadvertently deleted them while transcribing the text. Whatever the case, the editors of the *Wu-shang pi-yao* did not overlook the presentation when they constructed their version of the Nocturnal Revelation for Ling-pao ordinations more than a century later. According to their protocols the bestowal of the scriptures occurred just after the Reading of the Covenant's Writ, a visualization, and a Hymn for the Transmission of the Canon. Their rendition of the rite is not entirely trustworthy either. The editors not only drastically abridged the liturgy for investiture, they also left out two decisive elements, namely, the transmissions of the True Writs and the True Writ Registers. It is totally inconceivable that an ordination could have been complete without these. Despite the weaknesses in the sources, it is probably safe to assume that Princesses Gold-Immortal and Jade-Perfected received the scriptures shortly after the Reading of the Covenant's Writ.[40]

As the Cinnabar Ink Writ announces, the scriptures to be transmitted were the Marvelous Canon of the Treasure Writs in Ten Sections. This was nothing more than an alternate title for the Ling-pao canon, or, more specifically, its first part. According to Ling-pao tradition, these texts were coagulations of primordial Brahman ether that spontaneously formed on gold tablets in the Empty Cavern before the creation of the cosmos. Thereafter these tablets were sealed up in the Mysterious Terrace of the Seven Treasures at the Palace of Purple Subtlety in the Heaven of the Mysterious Metropolis and in caverns on the Five Marchmounts. They remained there undisturbed for five eons. At the end of that period the Celestial Venerable of the Primordial Commencement, having determined that the time for their revelation to mortal man was at hand, released them from the archives and entrusted them to the Most-Exalted Lord of the Great Tao for propagation. The latter, in turn, delegated this task to certain Perfected who chose to confer these texts on Ko Hsüan. By virtue of his suffering through innumerable rebirths and his vowing to devote himself to the salvation of all mankind, Ko had qualified as a worthy recipient of these gifts and received the scriptures from the Perfected, one by one, on Mt. T'ien-t'ai or Mt. Yü (southeast of Hangchow) during the Ch'ih-wu era (238–251). While this myth of revelation was extremely important to the validation of the canon's sanctity, it was totally contrived. The true author of the corpus was Ko Ch'ao-fu, a distant relative of Ko Hsüan. During the late fourth century, Ko Ch'ao-fu extracted sections from older Taoist texts which were probably in the possession of his family, added elements from Buddhist sutras, and constructed a new body of texts. When he had finished, he transmitted the canon to his disciples, probably in the year A.D. 400, under the pretense that it had originally been revealed to Ko Hsüan and subsequently passed down through successive generations to him.[41]

What is now known of the original Ling-pao canon derives mainly from a catalog, the Ling-pao ching-mu, which Lu Hsiu-ching compiled in A.D. 437. Only Lu's preface to it survives in the Tao-tsang, but a corrupt and mutilated version of his inventory was incorporated into a text which is partially preserved among the Tun-huang manuscripts and has been identified as part of the T'ung-hsüan lun. Its author was probably Sung Wen-ming (flourished 549–551). As the Cinnabar Ink Writ indicates, the first part of this list is divided into ten sections, based roughly on the general themes of the scriptures in these groups. This system of organization was implicit in the structure of the Ling-pao canon from its inception because one of the scriptures mentions it. In Sung Wen-ming's version, part one enumerates the titles to thirty scriptures in thirty-six scrolls, of which eighteen titles in twenty-three scrolls had already been revealed, leaving twelve titles in fifteen scrolls (including two scrolls from revealed texts) that had not. The unrevealed portion of the corpus represented works or parts of works from the canon, as it existed in Heaven, which the Perfected were not authorized to bestow on Ko Hsüan.

The second part of the catalog contains the titles to nonscriptural works—the ancient text in which appears the original copies of the Five Ling-pao Talismans, dialogues between Ko Hsüan and the Perfected, hagiographies of Ko Hsüan, instructions, and liturgical protocols—ten titles in eleven scrolls. Although there is no provision for the transmission of these texts in the Cinnabar Ink Writ, they were probably bestowed on ordinands along with the scriptures, because they supplied directives, clarifications, explanations, and invocations necessary for executing the retreats and other rites. In sum, the total number of texts, revealed only, extant in the Ling-pao canon during Lu's time was twenty-eight in thirty-four scrolls.[42]

This was not, however, the corpus that was bestowed on Princesses Gold-Immortal and Jade-Perfected in A.D. 711. Chang Wan-fu states that they received the Canon of the Middle Covenant in Eight Satchels, forty-seven scrolls. Obviously, the corpus had undergone a substantial expansion between the middle of the fifth and the beginning of the eighth century. This growth was complete by the middle of the sixth century, when Chin-ming Ch'i-chen (flourished 543–554) compiled the *Tung-hsüan ling-pao san-tung feng-tao k'o-chieh ying-shih* (HY 1117). In this work, Chin-ming incorporated an "Inventory of Ling-pao Scriptures for the Middle Covenant *(Ling-pao chung-meng ching-mu)*, which listed forty-two titles in forty-seven scrolls. This list is an enumeration of the texts that were actually turned over to ordinands during investitures and therefore contains none of the titles for unrevealed scriptures from Lu Hsiu-ching's catalog. Otherwise, with the exception of variant readings, the titles and their number of scrolls is identical to those given in Lu's list. In Chin-ming's inventory, however, two titles from the second part of Lu's are missing, presumably lost sometime before A.D. 550, and sixteen new titles have been added. Nearly all of these accretions in HY 1117 were manuals for conducting various rites, especially the great retreats. In sum, the canon in the "Inventory of Ling-pao Scriptures for the Middle Covenant" of 550 was essentially the same as it had been in 437, but had been augmented to incorporate a cluster of works included for the purpose of supplying ordinands with sets of liturgical protocols that would enable them to execute their offices. It can be said with almost total certainty that the corpus of forty-two texts whose titles appear in Chin-ming Ch'i-chen's enumeration was that which Chang Wan-fu designated the Canon of the Middle Covenant in forty-seven scrolls and which the Princesses received at their ordination.[43]

Following the transmission of the canon the officiant proceeds to confer the two True Writ Registers. He stands facing north and holds the two True Writ Registers in his left hand. The ordinands execute long kneelings, supporting the pledges in their right hands. Clacking his teeth thirty-six times, the preceptor visualizes the colors of his five viscera, causes them to intermingle completely and forces them to form the cloud of a treasure canopy which covers the scriptures, himself, and his followers like a net. Then everyone, following the officiant, recites an invocation warning that those who improperly transmit the canon without obeying the regulations will fall into hell. The ordinands kneel and bow nine times, rising thrice and prostrating thrice. Afterward they receive the True Writ Registers with both hands, attach the Slip-Boards to their belts, and seize their staffs. So armed, they circle the altar, starting in the north and proceeding eastward, saluting each of the Ten

Directions with one bow. Lastly, they visualize the true forms of the Most Exalteds in the images of the Celestial Venerables.[44]

The Celestial Master order which founded Taoism as a religion in the late second century A.D. formulated a large corpus of registers from antecedents in Han dynasty apocrypha. What remains from this body of writs survives in the *T'ai-shang san-wu cheng-i meng-wei lu* (HY 1199), a text which was probably edited and published in the T'ang dynasty. The order also made the most extensive use of registers to designate various stages of initiation and ordination as well as to dispel various kinds of disasters (see Chapter Four, numbers 1, 2, 3, and 5). Subsequently, as other Taoist orders, six in number, emerged in the fourth and fifth centuries A.D., they adopted the practice and created their own registers for investitures. As a result, by the sixth century the minimal definition for a Taoist order was possession of a unique scripture or set of scriptures and a particular register or set of registers (Chapter Four, numbers 5 through 11). Concurrently, beginning with the Ling-pao canon and reaching its most mature or elaborate state in Chin-ming Ch'i-chen's *Tung-hsüan ling-pao san-tung feng-tao k'o-chieh ying-shih,* an organization of the priesthood evolved in the form of a hierarchy for the orders. One of the basic criteria for assigning status in this new system was the conferral of the register appropriate to the rank to which the ordinand was aspiring.

Although a register might contain a transmission formula, talismans, icons, or injunctions, it was basically a roster of the gods which supplied their titles and ranks. The conferral of the register gave the newly ordained priest access to those cosmic divinities on the celestial plane which protected the numinous versions of the scriptures that he had received. Thus the roster was an entitlement which bestowed on the cleric the privilege of communicating with deities of equal status in the heavenly hierarchy. The register also supplied the priest with the power to summon and command the internal spirits of his own body. Through evocation and visualization of these gods he was able to consummate the rituals that constituted his offices. Thus the roster was an instrument of commission which vested dominion over these gods in the cleric.[45]

The True Writ Registers do not appear in the Ling-pao canon, elsewhere in the *Tao-tsang,* or among the Tun-huang manuscripts under that title. However, as previously noted, two sets of rosters for titles of spirits can be found in the scriptures: those preceding each of the three Jade Instructions in Red Graphs and those following each of the four Spontaneously Generated Jade Graphs for the Esoteric Intonation. In his description of matter transmitted to Ling-pao ordinands, Chin-ming Ch'i-chen lists two registers whose titles correspond to those of the two writs in the canon (Chapter Four, number 10, part *a*). On the face of this information, it would appear that these rosters were extracted from their milieus to form the two registers specified in the protocols and conferred separately from the texts. However, Chin-ming also mentions a register whose name clearly indicates that it was somehow associated with the True Writs. Consequently, there remains some confusion as to precisely what were the two True Writ Registers that Princesses Gold-Immortal and Jade-Perfected received.

After the bestowal of the registers, the officiant rises and chants the Lyrics for Pacing the Void in ten stanzas while touring the Inner Altar. At the conclusion of each stanza, during his recitation, the ordinands sing praises, scatter flowers, and bow once. One whole scripture, the *Tung-hsüan ling-pao Yü-ching shan pu-hsü ching* (HY 1427), of the original Ling-pao canon, is devoted to this hymn, which Lu Hsiu-ching reproduced verbatim in his manual. According to this text, three times a month the Immortal Lads sing the Lyrics for Pacing the Void, while the Jade Maids perform a dance on the Mountain of the Jade Capital in the Heaven of the Mysterious Metropolis. According to another text from the canon, the *T'ai-chi chen-jen fu Ling-pao chai-chieh wei-i chu-ching yao-chüeh* (HY 532), mortal participants in retreats execute the chanting of the lyrics as an imitation of the celestial performance. The second stanza in the hymn begins with the lines, "Twirling as we walk we tread upon the cloudy hawsers/Mounting the void we pace the mysterious marlines." These two pieces of evidence indicate that as the preceptor made his peregrination on the upper tier of the altar during Ling-pao investitures, he performed a kind of dance while singing or chanting the verses. Pacing the Void was not peculiar to ordinations. In fact it played a role in many of the public retreats and private devotions which Taoist priests conducted. The protocols assigned particular functions for it in such rites, but unfortunately, Lu does not specify what purpose they served at investitures.[46]

Immediately after chanting the hymn for Pacing the Void, the officiant faces north and sings the Hymn for the Salute to the Canon, three stanzas of eight five-character lines. This hymn marks the end of the section in the liturgy devoted to the transmission of the canon and its registers.[47]

## The Transmission of the Vows and Injunctions

Lu Hsiu-ching supplies no annunciation for this last section in the acts of investiture. In his manual it begins simply with the Singing of the

Three Salutes. The congregation sings three lines as a pledge of allegiance to the Three Treasures—the Tao, the Venerable Canon in Thirty-Six Sections (Taoist scriptures in general), and the Grand Canon Preceptors. The notion of the Three Treasures was a borrowing of the concept *triratna*—the Buddha, the Teaching, and the Sangha (Clergy, Community)—from Buddhism, but Taoists recast it to fit their own peculiar tenets. The ultimate focus of Taoism was not a deity, but an impersonal entity, the Tao, which caused the creation of the cosmos and which all devotees strove to acquire through religious endeavor. The scriptures were objects of reverence less because they were repositories of beliefs, wisdom, and procedures than because they were crystallizations of vital cosmic energies. And it was the status of preceptor and officiant that was prized, rather than the mere commitment to the pursuit of religious life under vows. The Three Treasures constituted the most fundamental articles of faith in Taoism to which ordinands swore fidelity by singing these lines.[48]

Next, the officiant conducts the Discourse on the Interdictory Injunctions of the Primordial Commencement. The congregation sits flat on the ground. The ordinands face the preceptor and prostrate themselves. The officiant then imparts the precepts while the students chant responses phrase by phrase, saying "Student . . ." after each. It is not clear to which set of ethical dictates in the canon that the title Interdictory Injunctions of the Primordial Commencement refers. Most likely this was another name for the Great Injunctions, Superior Grade, of Wisdom, which Chang Wan-fu says were transmitted during the Middle Covenant, that is, during the Nocturnal Annunciation for the transmission of the canon. This set of precepts, which the Celestial Venerable of the Primordial Commencement issued, appears in a scripture in the original canon, the *T'ai-shang tung-hsüan ling-pao chih-hui tsui-ken shang-p'in ta-chieh ching* (HY 457). It encompasses ten commandments in all.

1. Do not let envy overcome you. Suppress and check your virtue and brilliance;
2. Do not drink wine or indulge in dissipation which defiles and agitates the Three Palaces [located at the highest point in the human brain];
3. Do not licentiously violate another man's wife or lust after the soft and supple [avoid adultery and sex];
4. Do not abandon or despise the aged, infirm, impoverished, or humble;
5. Do not defame the virtuous man or slanderously attack a fellow student;

6.  Do not covet or amass rarities and treasures or be unwilling to donate and disperse them;
7.  Do not slay living beings or offer sacrifices to the specters and spirits of the Six Heavens;
8.  Do not opine in discourse on the scripture and canon as this is empty boasting;
9.  Do not turn your back on your preceptor's gracious intent or defraud and deceive a novice; and
10. Be humane and filial to everyone with equality and single-mindedness.[49]

Unlike the Injunctions for Arresting the Six Emotions received by the ordinands during the Rending of the Spontaneously Generated Tally, this body of precepts focused more on molding the behavior of the soon-to-be priests by advocating the elimination of vices and undesirable attitudes, rather than on shaping their mental state by urging the development of quiescence. Restated in positive terms, these charges to the ordinands committed them to the virtues of temperance, chastity, compassion, benevolence, altruism, respect for life, humility, gratefulness, magnanimity, tolerance, humaneness, and filiality. The intent of the injunctions, which the students swore to uphold, was to eradicate or diminish the ordinands' self-interest and self-centeredness so as to instill values in them which would contribute to a tranquil, well-run religious order and a peaceful, harmonious relationship between it and the secular community at large.

The officiant brings the discourse on the injunctions to a close by making a long declaration. It begins with a description of the cosmogonic, cosmological, spiritual, material, and political power of the canon, and ends with a list of conditions that are violations of the regulations governing the proper transmission of the scriptures and a warning to the ordinands that seven generations of their ancestors will fall into hell if they disobey the rules.

As that declaration intimates, the next step in this section of the rite is the transmission of the Writ for the Six Oaths. At this point the ordinands rise, bow thrice, and return to their prostrations. The officiant then administers the oaths.

1.  I vow never to divulge the canon frivolously,
2.  I vow never to disparage the scriptures vulgarly,
3.  I vow never to transmit the canon indiscriminately,
4.  I vow never to converse about the scripture's contents openly,
5.  I vow never to violate the canon's interdictions, and
6.  I vow never to transmit the scriptures for a fee.

Before the preceptor's pronouncement of each oath, incense is offered three times, and the ordinands raise one hand toward heaven, men raising the left hand and women the right. When the recitation of the oaths has been completed, the ordinands salute six times, and the officiant stands to chant a hymn to the oaths.[50]

The purpose of these vows was, first and foremost, to elicit the solemn word of the students that they would maintain the secrecy of the canon. Only the elect anointed by the testimony of their preceptors, qualified by their presentation of pledges and establishment of covenants, and bound by their vows to uphold the injunctions were entitled to receive the divine gift. In effect, the ordinands swore in these oaths to deny anyone who was not initiated into the order through the esoteric rites access to the texts or their contents.

The section on vows and injunctions in Lu Hsiu-ching's manual ends with the Transmission of Liturgical Positions to the Ordinands by Means of Slips. The students execute long kneelings and receive the slips from the officiant. These slips assign the ordinands the titles Students of the Most Exalted Numinous Treasure and Peerless Cavern-Mystery and Masters of such-and-such Marchmounts. The final act of investiture at ordinations was the conferral of the titles, to which the transmission of the canon entitled the ordinands.[51]

The remainder of the proceedings in Lu Hsiu-ching's manual was devoted to salutes, readings, a confession, the deconsecration of the altar, some hymns, and the activation of talismans. The ritual concluded in the early hours of the morning. Chang Wan-fu relates an unusual incident that probably occurred shortly after the end of the investiture for Gold-Immortal and Jade-Perfected in February of 711. "In the fourth watch (around 2:00 to 4:00 A.M.), Lord Lao (Lao Tzu Deified) descended to the altar and spoke to the Princesses."[52]

The completion of the Nocturnal Annunciation was by no means the final act in the ordination of the ladies. There was a third segment to the Middle Covenant which Chang calls the "Transmission of the Procedures (Ch'uan-fa)." He says that this took place on another day, perhaps the day after the Nocturnal Revelation (February 12). Unfortunately, Chang does not specify what took place on that occasion, but the Wu-shang pi-yao offers an explanation. It says that if the number of ordinands is small, then the emplacement of the talismans in the staffs and the conferral of the Slip-Boards should be performed according to the regulation for later conferrals of writs and incantations. If the number is large, then these instruments should be bestowed at the same time as the canon during the retreat. This rule seems to have been applied in 711, when only two ordinands took vows, and accounts for the addition of the extra stage in Chang's description. Chang goes on to say that after the Transmission of the Procedures, the Princesses abandoned their couches and reclined on armrests and layered cushions.[53]

Chang Wan-fu calls the third covenant the Great Covenant of the Numinous Treasure *(Ling-pao ta-meng)* and says that the One Hundred and Eighty Injunctions of the Three Primes *(San-yüan pai-pa-shih chieh)* were conferred in conjunction with its establishment. He does not, however, indicate when this occurred. Lu Hsiu-ching associates the Great Covenant with the Nocturnal Revelation in his title for the latter. This suggests that the compact was part of that rite. The liturgy does call for two readings of covenants (Appendix Two, section III, part B, numbers 18 and 22). However, it is also possible that the same covenant was read twice, and that there was an additional rite for establishing the third covenant, at least in the early eighth century.[54]

According to Lu Hsiu-ching, upon completion of the investiture the ordinands were required to conduct a retreat of thanksgiving for mercy *(she-chai hsieh-en)* that occupied three days, followed by the rite of Casting the Dragon Tablets *(T'ou lung-chien)*. Chang Wan-fu mentions neither of these, but the Princesses undoubtedly performed the latter because the instruments for accomplishing it were included in the altar's furnishings. The Casting of the Dragon Tablets took place on the same altar that was used for the investiture and was executed at the gates that corresponded to the ordinands' birthdates. It was a simple tripartite rite which began with a *Fa-lu* (Lighting of the Censer) and concluded with a *Fu-lu* (Return to the Censer). In between, the ordinands performed the *Tu-chien* or Reading of the Slips. Facing the direction of the Regal Gate, they recited the texts of the inscriptions written on their slips.[55]

These slips or tablets, three in number for each ordinand, are to be made of ginkgo wood, 34.4 centimeters (13.4 inches) long, 5.9 centimeters (2.3 inches) wide, and 7.4 millimeters (.29 inches) thick. Each of the inscriptions on them, which are to be written in vermilion ink, begins with an ordinand's title as Master of such-and-such a Numinous Treasure Sovereign (the name of the particular deity among the Five Elders who is associated with the student by virtue of her or his, the student's, birthdate). Next the ordinands fill in their names, their ages, and the months of their births. The text of the first tablet, which contains a prayer for immortality, requests that the Water Sovereign of the Nine Administrations and the Grand Sovereigns of the Sources of the Twelve Rivers and the Yangtze, Yellow, Huai, and Chi Rivers erase the students' sins from their ledgers. The text of the second, which contains a prayer for immortality and salvation, notes the ordinands' places in the lineages of their particular Sovereigns on Mt. T'ai and requests that the Perfected of the Highest Spirit and Greatest Power on the Five Marchmounts of Superior Purity eradicate their sins from their ledgers. The text on the third, which also has a prayer for immortality and salvation, mentions the entries of the students' names in the registers at the Eastern Dipper *(Tung-tou)* of the Nine Heavens and requests that the Five Sovereigns of the Soil Administration *(T'u-fu)* remove their sins from their ledgers. The ordinands date each of the tablets giving the hours, days, months, and years when they are performing the rite and noting the place (countries, marchmounts, and districts) in which it is taking place. After reading each text the students recite an invocation for it. The tablets are then wrapped in blue-green paper and tied with blue-green thread. One gold dragon plaque and nine gold knobs are attached to each of them. After the rite is completed, the first tablet is to be cast into the sources of a clear river, the second buried on the marchmounts associated with the ordinands' birthdates or tossed into a mountain cavern, and the third buried in their places of residence *(kung, abbeys?)*.[56]

The Casting of the Dragon Tablets was a rite of metamorphosis whose purpose was to transform the ordinands, to affect their salvation through the remission of sins. However, the rite did not require them to enumerate any specific sins that they had committed. Furthermore, although they had been required to express their sincere remorse for having erred in the form of head knocking and brow beating during the Nocturnal Annunciation (Appendix Two, section III, part B, number 34), this liturgy did not demand that they do penance to demonstrate their contrition. Instead, exculpation was essentially a bureaucratic action involving the alteration of accounts. The ordinands sought absolution for any and all, conscious or unconscious, remembered or forgotten errors of the past that were recorded in the ledgers of the gods, whose vigilant surveillance was ever-present. The mechanism of forgiveness resembled the normal routine of the imperial state. The supplicants tendered documents of a prescribed format, and this ensured that they would reach the proper address, that is, the offices of the numinous mandarins concerned. They filled the blanks in these forms with information—their names and affiliations—which enabled the numinous officials to identify the petitioners readily. And they noted the exact time that they dispatched their papers in order to guarantee prompt processing of them. The dragon plaques carried their messages forth to the governments of the waters, earth, and heaven, where the bureaucratic machinery, well oiled by the pledges (bribes) presented by the ordinands, acted upon them. In short, absolution was the function of a political apparatus that processed written appeals and passed judgment through paperwork. Once these formalities were completed, the numinous functionaries entered the ordinands' names in the register of the immortals, and they were saved from the torments of rebirth as denizens of hell, domestic animals or hungry ghosts. After death, armed with the Slip-Board Writs, they were exempted from judgment and punishment and guaranteed free passage in their ascent to heaven.

The Casting of the Dragon Tablets was the final act in the drama of the Princesses' ordination. Thereafter, they were fully ordained priests entitled to conduct the Ling-pao liturgical offices that devolved upon them by virtue of their investiture.

CHAPTER FOUR

# Denouements

THE DENOUEMENT in Lu Hsiu-ching's liturgy for ordination occurred toward the end of the proceedings when the officiant bestowed titles on the ordinands, an act which formally recognized them as fully empowered members of the Ling-pao order. This was not the first, last, or only occasion when an aspirant seeking a religious vocation might experience such a climactic event. By the end of the Nan-pei ch'ao seven clerical orders had emerged in Taoism. Four of them—those based on the *Tao-te ching, San-huang wen,* Ling-pao canon, and Shang-ch'ing scriptures, and probably the other three as well—admitted candidates to their ranks by means of dramatic investitures that had denouements during which new titles were conferred on ordinands. These orders, based on corpora of scriptures sanctified by traditions of revelation, differed from their counterparts in other religions. With some exceptions, notably the Shang-ch'ing center at Mt. Mao, south of present-day Nanking, they did not establish separate cloisters devoted to propagating and perpetuating their own dogmas or disciplines, nor did they dominate specific regions. Furthermore, excluding the conflict between the older, familial Celestial Master and the newer, celibate priesthoods, they did not contend with each other. Instead, they occupied rungs in a ladder of learning, the lower in rank accepting subordination to the upper.

The first effort made to define this canonical and ecclesiastical hierarchy appeared in the Ling-pao scriptures around A.D. 400. Subsequently, some of the texts in that early list lost favor, and others emerged to take their place. Around A.D. 550, Chin-ming Ch'i-chen codified these changes by composing a new hierarchy in his *Tung-hsüan ling-pao san-*

*tung feng-tao k'o-chieh ying-shih* (HY 1117). In this work he defines Taoist orders by the titles which they bestowed during their investitures, and enumerates the matter—scriptures, commentaries, writs, registers, tallies, talismans, injunctions, and the like—which they transmitted to ordinands. More often than not, the orders conferred several titles, each of which was associated with a different segment of its corpus and apparently represented a phase in its ordination. Most of the orders conducted retreats of their own and had distinctive liturgical vestments which readily identified their members at such rites. A century and a half later, at the time of the investiture for Princesses Gold-Immortal and Jade-Perfected, Chin-ming's scheme was in general as valid as it had been in his own day. In the *Ch'uan-shou san-tung ching-chieh fa-lu lüeh-shuo* (HY 1231), to which he appended his account of the Princesses' Ling-pao ordination, Chang Wan-fu undertook the same task of outlining the clerical hierarchy for the Taoist priesthood. In doing so, however, Chang was less systematic than his predecessor. He provides three different groups of criteria for assigning status in the religion: a short list of six steps, a catalog for sixteen sets of injunctions, and five inventories of matter transmitted. In keeping with the term *lüeh-shuo* (synopsis) in the title of his work, he does not supply a complete roster of orders or ordinations. It is clear from other works written by him that he was familiar with the remainder (see Appendix Three, numbers 3, 5, and 7). Furthermore, in only one instance, the description of the canon transmitted with the *Tao-te ching,* does he supply all of the titles for a corpus. Nevertheless, although changes occurred again in the intervening period, the state of the priesthood was basically the same in A.D. 711 as it had been in 550. Since Chin-ming Ch'i-chen's delineation is more comprehensive and lucid, the following account of the Taoist hierarchy of initiation and investiture, orders and ordination, is based upon it. Chang Wan-fu's comments have been appended to various sections, and notes from other works have been added to flesh out what is otherwise a bare skeleton in Chin-ming's text.[1]

## Initiation

As used here the term "initiation" refers to a number of formal acts which validated the confirmation of youth, acknowledged the conversion of nonbelievers, certified a layman's membership in the faith, or recognized a novice's admission to a cloister. It should be noted, however, that some stages of ordination included phases which were clearly initiations of a sort.

1. *NAN-SHENG NÜ-SHENG* (MALE OR FEMALE PUPILS): titles conferred on children seven or eight *sui* (six or seven years old) who had received:

   *a)*  the *Keng-ling lu* or *Keng-ling chiu-kuan lu* (Register of the Nine Officials' Reform Commands) and

   *b)*  the *I chiang-chün lu* (Register of One General).[2]

2. *LU-SHENG* (REGISTER PUPIL): a title reserved for children ten *sui* (nine years old) or older to whom the following were presented:

   *a)*  the *San chiang-chün fu-lu* (Talismanic Register of Three Generals),

   *b)*  the *Shih chiang-chün fu-lu* (Talismanic Register of Ten Generals), and

   *c)*  the *San-kuei wu-chieh* (The Three Refuges and Five Injunctions) or *Lu-sheng san-chieh wen* (Writ of the Three Precepts for Register Pupils) and *Cheng-i chieh wen* (Writ of the True-Unity's Precepts).[3]

3. *MOU CHIH-CH'I NAN-KUAN NÜ-KUAN* (MALE OR FEMALE MANDARINS OF SUCH-AND-SUCH PARISH): titles conferred on young men and women twenty *sui* (nineteen years of age) who had received:

   *a)*  the *Ch'i-shih-wu chiang-chün lu* (The Register of Seventy-Five Generals),

   *b)*  the *Pai-wu-shih chiang-chün lu* (The Register of One Hundred and Fifty Generals),

   *c)*  the *Cheng-i chen-chüan* (The Perfect Chapter of True-Unity),

   *d)*  the *Erh-shih-ssu chih cheng-i ch'ao i* (The Protocols for the True-Unity Audience of the Twenty-Four Parishes), and

   *e)*  the *Cheng-i pa-chieh wen* (The Writ of the True-Unity's Eight Injunctions).[4]

Actually there was only one register for the final level of initiation, the Register of One Hundred and Fifty Generals. However, it had two parts. The first, called the *Hsien-kuan ch'i-shih-wu chiang-chün lu* (The Immortal Mandarins' Register of Seventy-Five Generals), was given to men, and the second, entitled *Ling-kuan ch'i-shih-wu chiang-chün lu* (The Numinous Mandarins' Register of Seventy-Five Generals), was presented to women. The conferral of the title *kuan* (mandarin) on young men and young women marked the end of childhood and the attainment of full status as a lay adherent in the Taoist community. At this age, nineteen or shortly after, the initiate was enrolled as a member of a parish by means of a ritual which was separate from that for the transmission of the registers. The Celestial Master or Cheng-i sect originally established most of the parishes in western China at the end of the second or the beginning of the third century A.D. By the T'ang period (618–907), however, the parishes had ceased to have spatial reference, at least as far as registration was concerned. Cyclical dates from the Chinese calendar were assigned to them. A young man or woman was enrolled in that parish whose date corresponded to the month of his or her birth.[5]

*Chang Wan-fu:* in Chang's scheme of things, distinctions in initiation based on age and the conferral of registers carried less weight than the bestowal of injunctions.

a) Injunctions *(chieh):* "receiving various injunctions will protect the recipient from calamities and arrest sin." Of the sixteen sets that Chang names at the beginning of his work only seven are relevant to initiations. The remainder apply to various levels of ordination.[6]

   (1) *San-kuei chieh* (Injunctions for Taking Refuge in the Three): an aspirant received these when the thought of becoming a Taoist first entered his mind. They were intended to establish allegiance to the Three Treasures *(San-pao:* the Tao, the Venerable Scriptures in Thirty-Six Sections [the Taoist canon in general], and the Grand Preceptors). The swearing of an oath to observe these precepts admitted the professor to membership in the faith. The Three Formulas of Refuge or Surrender *(San-kuei)* and Three Treasures were concepts that Taoists borrowed from Buddhism and adapted to their own needs.[7]

   (2) *Wu-chieh* (The Five Injunctions): these eliminate the five desires (senses) so that the recipient can cultivate the five virtues and expel the five turbities *(wu-cho).* Chang lists these precepts in another of his works. They are not related to the five *sila* or commandments that were given to pious laymen in Buddhism. Instead they deal with the five roots or senses (eyes, ears, nose, mouth, and body), a Buddhist notion which was again modified to suit Taoist doctrines. The Five Injunctions of True-Unity preserved in the *Wu-shang pi-yao* are somewhat similar to Chang's, but his are more Buddhistic in character.[8]

   (3) *Pa-chieh* (The Eight Injunctions): these were conferred on Register Pupils together with the preceding. The eight precepts permitted students to bond with the gods and energies *(ch'i)* of the Eight Directions. The eight which Chang lists in the *San-tung chung-chieh wen* are strictly Taoist in character, but they may have been inspired by the Buddhist notion of the eight directions and gods. In the Celestial Master tradition, initiates received sets of three,

five, and eight injunctions in the same order given here. Chang
Wan-fu, however, does not recognize the Injunctions for Taking
Refuge in the Three (number [1] above) as an element in Cheng-
i confirmations. They are only the initial conferrals to anyone,
child or adult, who converts. Furthermore, he derived his sets
from the *Tung-shen ching* (Scripture of the Cavern-Divine), which
was the scripture for the *San-huang wen* (Writ of the Three Sovereigns), not a text from the Celestial Master canon.[9]

(4) *Wu-shang shih chieh* (The Ten Peerless Injunctions): these were
presented to laymen. They allowed them to avoid committing the
ten abominations *(shih-e)* and enabled them to cultivate the ten
virtues *(shih-shan)*. Since conferral of these precepts does not
appear to have played any role in conversion, this bestowal was
simply a formal recognition of lay status.[10]

(5) *Ch'u-chen chieh* (The Injunctions for Beginning Perfection): these
precepts were reserved for novices who had left their families (cast
off their secular clothes) and joined Taoism (entered an abbey).
The novices were required to swear an oath for each of the
injunctions, promising not to violate the precept. The seventh
commandment constituted a vow of celibacy. "After leaving the
family I swear not to have intercourse with men or women, since
this will produce licentious desires or thoughts."[11]

(6) *Ch'i-shih-erh chieh* (The Seventy-Two Injunctions): a set of precepts which Students of True-Unity, *Cheng-i ti-tzu*, received along
with the *Hsien-kuan* and *Ling-kuan* Registers (see *Mou chih-ch'i nan-
kuan nü-kuan* above). Obviously, this set of injunctions was not the
same as that which Chin-ming Ch'i-chen gave for this level of initiation.[12]

*b)* Registers *(lu):* "wearing talismanic registers enables the recipient to
control and impede the demonic influences and protect the gods and
energies of the center [that is, the inner gods of the human body]."
Chang stipulates that the Register of One General and Register of
Ten Generals were transmitted to children *(t'ung-tzu)*. He gives no
age for the conferral of the Register of One Hundred and Fifty Generals, which he notes had two parts, the *Hsien-kuan* and *Ling-kuan,* as
explained above. According to his note on the Seventy-Two Injunctions, Students of True-Unity received these registers.[13]

There is a subtle shift of emphasis on the question of initiation and
ordination between these two authorities. In Chin-ming Ch'i-
chen's view, the registers are the determinants of status for young
believers within the Taoist community. Injunctions play a role in
his order, but they do not appear to have been decisive elements.
He assigns injunctions to only eight of the nineteen phases of initiation and investiture. More significantly, although he was well

aware of the distinction between the laity and the priesthood, he fails to designate when the novice was required to take a vow of celibacy and does not mention the *Ch'u-chen chieh* at all. Finally, precepts do not function as measures of progress at various levels of ordination. His only criteria for distinguishing ranks at various stages and phases of initiation and investiture are the titles conferred at each. A priest was supposed to write these honorifics on declarations and memorials, which were submitted to the gods during the rites that the priest conducted. In contrast, Chang Wan-fu sees registers as secondary to injunctions. He not only places the inventory of precepts before that of registers, but also uses the injunctions to mark ranks of initiation and ordination. In his scheme of things, these sets function in a manner similar to credentials. They certify that the recipient has been admitted to the faith, has acquired registers, has been recognized as a lay adherent, or has been inducted into a cloister as a celibate novice. At various stages of investiture they also serve to mark the rungs of the novice's advancement up the ladder of learning. Chang lists the titles to four sets of injunctions that were given to students aspiring to be ordained at one level or another and six more that were bestowed with scriptures. The conferral of the former seems to have constituted a kind of formal acknowledgment that a preceptor had accepted the recipient as a pupil under his tutelage. The latter were elements of the scriptural corpus, the transmission of which verified that the student had earned his master's trust and had satisfactorily completed his training.[14]

4. *CH'ING-HSIN TI-TZU* (STUDENT OF PURE FAITH): a title reserved for those who had received the *T'ien-tsun shih-chieh shih-ssu ch'ih-shen chieh* (The Celestial Venerable's Ten Injunctions and Fourteen Precepts for Sustaining Self), and *Shih-erh k'o-ts'ung liu-ch'ing chieh* (The Observable Twelve Injunctions for the Six Emotions). The exact role of this conferral in the Taoist order is not clear. The title Ch'ing-hsin ti-tzu appears in one of the scriptures from the original Ling-pao canon which dates back to A.D. 400. Chin-ming Ch'i-chen notes that it was bestowed on initiates, who received the two sets of injunctions. However, although he mentions the titles and the injunctions at the beginning of his account on the hierarchy of Taoist initiation and investiture, he provides no slot for this conferral in his order. In the same period, the "New Protocols Imperially Compiled" that were issued during the Northern Chou dynasty (557–581) under the auspices of Wu-ti (r.

561–578) muddled the issue considerably. These regulations stipulated that ordinands could assume the title Students of Pure Faith
when they were about to receive any of three different sets of scripture: the Ten Injunctions, *Tao-te ching,* and *San-huang wen;* the *Chen-
wen* (True Writs) and Shang-ch'ing scriptures; or all five canons
transmitted at the same time on the same altar. Clearly, Ch'ing-
hsin ti-tzu was a title for ordination, not initiation, at that time.[15]

> *Chang Wan-fu:* the titles for these sets of precepts appear in Chang's
> inventory of injunctions, where he concurs with Chin-ming Ch'i-chen
> in stating that they were presented to the Students of Pure Faith. How-
> ever, Chang also contends that commitment and natural ability were
> prerequisites for the conferral of the title. In his list, Ch'ing-hsin ti-tzu
> appears immediately after a set of precepts given at ordinations for
> Cheng-i priests, and just before one that was bestowed on novices who
> were admitted to the study of the *Tao-te ching,* indicating that the presen-
> tation was apparently some kind of preliminary step to the transmission
> of the latter corpus.[16]

## Ordination

The Taoist hierarchy of ordination emerged in a primitive form at least
as early as the last decade of the fourth century A.D., when Ko Ch'ao-fu
compiled the Ling-pao canon. One of the texts in that corpus is devoted
to providing instructions on the functions and treatment of sacred texts.
It opens with an account of the order for bestowal of scriptures and the
rites employed for their conferral.

(a) *Tao-te ching,*
(b) *Ta-tung chen-ching* (Perfect Scripture of the Great Cavern),
(c) *T'ai-shang ling-pao tung-hsüan ching* (Most Exalted Scripture of
    the Numinous Treasure and Cavern-Mystery), the Ling-pao
    or Tung-hsüan canon,
(d) *T'ai-shang san-huang t'ien-wen* (Most Exalted Celestial Writs of
    the Three Sovereigns), the *San-huang wen* or Tung-shen canon,
(e) *Shang-ch'ing p'in ching fu* (Talismans and Scriptures of the Supe-
    rior Purity Category), the Shang-ch'ing or Tung-chen canon.

By the sixth century the *Ta-tung chen-ching* had been dropped from the
hierarchy, the *San-huang wen* had been moved to second place in it, and
several newer texts had been added. Furthermore, some of the canon,
namely, those for the *Tao-te ching* and *San-huang wen,* had been greatly
expanded, and the rituals of investiture had become far more elaborate.

In the fourth century, the rites for transmission *(ch'uan, shou, ch'uan-shou)* were basically the same for all scriptures: a prostration, a submission of pledges, a visualization, an invocation, and several obeisances. Soon after that time, grand ordination liturgies developed that were specifically tailored to the canon bestowed. The oldest surviving example is Lu Hsiu-ching's *T'ai-shang tung-hsüan ling-pao shou-tu i* (HY 528), which he finished about A.D. 454. By the end of the Nan-pei ch'ao each of the major canons had its own individual rite of transmission taking three to nine days to complete. It was at this time that Chin-ming Ch'i-chen set about the task of codifying the hierarchy of ordination.[17]

5. THE TRANSMISSION OF THE *CHENG-I* (TRUE-UNITY) CANON: in Chin-ming Ch'i-chen's hierarchy, this level of ordination is divided into four phases.

a) *San-i ti-tzu, Ch'ih-yang chen-jen* (Perfected of Red Yang, Student of the Three and One), a title given to those who received:

(1) one tally-contract *(ch'üan-ch'i),*
(2) three tallies *(ch'üan),* and
(3) three contracts *(ch'i).*

b) *Mou chih-ch'i cheng-i meng-wei ti-tzu* (Student of True-Unity and Covenantal-Authority from Such-and-Such Parish); this title was bestowed with the conferral of:

(1) one contract, and
(2) ten registers.

c) *Cheng-i meng-wei ti-tzu yüan-ming chen-jen* (Perfected of Primal Clarity, Student of True-Unity and Covenantal-Authority), a title presented after the transmission of:

(1) one tablet *(pan),* and
(2) seven registers.

d) *Cheng-i meng-wei yüan-ming chen-jen* (Perfected of Primal Clarity in True-Unity and Covenantal-Authority), a title for ordinands who completed the final stage of investiture, during which they received:

(1) fourteen registers,
(2) the *Ch'ien-erh-pai ta-chang* (The Twelve Hundred Grand Petitions),
(3) the *San-pai-liu-shih chang* (The Three Hundred and Sixty Petitions),
(4) the *Cheng-i ching* (The Scripture of True-Unity) in twenty-seven chapters,

(5) the *Lao-chün i-pai-pa-shih chieh* (The One Hundred and
Eighty Injunctions of Lord Lao),

(6) the *Cheng-i chai i* (Protocols for Conducting the Retreat of
True-Unity), and

(7) the *Lao Tzu san-pu shen-fu* (Divine Talisman of Lao Tzu in
Three Sections).[18]

According to the Cheng-i tradition, T'ai-shang Lao-chün (Lao
Tzu Deified) revealed the corpus of Celestial Master scriptures to
Chang Tao-ling on June 11, 142, at Mt. Ho-ming (in modern Sze-
chuan Province). Purportedly, the texts transmitted were:

(a) the *Cheng-i meng-wei fu-lu* (Talismanic Registers of True-
Unity and Covenantal-Authority) in 120 *chieh* (steps?),

(b) the *Ch'ien-erh-pai kuan i* (Protocols of the Twelve Hundred
Mandarins),

(c) the *San-pai ta-chang* (Three Hundred Grand Petitions), and

(d) the *Fa-wen* (Canonical Writs).

Since these scriptures have been lost it is impossible to ascertain
how these primitive works related to those conferred at Cheng-i
ordinations in the sixth century. However, the titles convey some
sense of continuity between the older and newer traditions.
According to Tu Kuang-t'ing (850–933) the *Cheng-i chai i* was a
retreat for the transmission of registers and scriptures.[19]

*Chang Wan-fu:* in his inventory of this canon, all that remains of the substantial Celestial Master corpus that was transmitted to ordinands during Chin-ming Ch'i-chen's time is the set of precepts which Chang calls
*Pai-pa-shih chieh chung-lü* (The Hundred and Eighty Injunctions of the
Weighty Code) and a set of twenty-four registers. As far as he was concerned, the function of Cheng-i investitures was to transmit the precepts
and registers only. Of the twenty-four, seventeen titles (one is split in
two) can be identified with relative certainty as the same as sixteen
given in Chin-ming Ch'i-chen's list of thirty, and three more with less
confidence. The role which Chang assigns the registers in his comments
is apotropaic in nature. Those who receive them will be protected
against injury, especially illness, inflicted by the specters and demons of
the Six Heavens. In its earliest stage of development the Celestial Master Sect established itself as the standard-bearer of the "Three Heavens" and waged war against the followers of the "Six Heavens," who
were the priests, sorcerers, that promoted and conducted the worship of
a plethora of local cults. Registers provided the arms and armor which
adherents of the "true" faith, Cheng-i, employed in their struggles
against the heterodox cultists. This proclivity to see its competitive relationship with popular religions as basically combative explains the

heavy military symbolism inherent in the registers. The Celestial Master sect's fulminations against its rivals were nothing more than elements in a propaganda campaign whose purpose was to convince believers and potential converts that its way was superior to that of the cultists, even though the two religions shared much in common.

Confronted only with Chang's inventory, one would have to assume that Cheng-i priests performed no offices and engaged only in drafting talismans, an enterprise which has supplied a modest income for certain Taoist priests from ancient times to the present. However, this was probably not the case. Lu Hsiu-ching and later Taoists strove to bring some order to their liturgical tradition by creating a hierarchy for their rituals. At least two of the retreats in their systems were Celestial Master rites of repentance that were of ancient origin:

(a) the *T'u-t'an chai* (Mud and Soot Retreat), during which drums were employed to induce a frenzy among participants in order to uproot sin and thus ensure the salvation of the living and the dead, and

(b) the *Chih-chiao chai* (Retreat for Instruction in the Teachings), which sought divine blessings for healing the sick and averting calamities.

Although the compilers of this hierarchy do not specifically state that performances of these rites were reserved for the Cheng-i priesthood, they occupied precisely the same position in the order of things as the clergy. It is reasonable to assume that these retreats remained the special preserve of the Celestial Master clergy in the early eighth century. Unfortunately, in his inventory Chang lists no liturgies for them that would confirm this assumption.[20]

6. THE TRANSMISSION OF THE *SHEN-CHOU CHING* (SCRIPTURE OF THE DIVINE INCANTATIONS): the title bestowed on the occasion of this transmission was *Tung-yüan shen-chou ta-tsung san-mei fa-shih hsiao-chao chen-jen* (Perfected of the Lesser Omen, Canon Preceptor of *Samadhi,* Grand Master of the Cavern-Deep's Divine Incantations). The scripture that was the core of this corpus is still extant in the *Tao-tsang, T'ai-shang tung-yüan shen-chou ching* (HY 335), ch. 1–10 only. The contents of this investiture were:

a) *Tung-yüan shen-chou ching* (The Cavern-Deep Scripture of Divine Incantations), in ten chapters,

b) *Shen-chou ch'üan* (Tally of Divine Incantations),

c) *Shen-chou lu* (Register of Divine Incantations),

d) *Ssu-shen t'u* (Illustrations for Visualizations of the Gods),

e) *Shen-hsien chin-chou ching* (Scripture for the Interdictory Incantations of the Divine Immortals) in two chapters, *f)*   *Heng-hang yü-nü chou yin-fa* (The Method for Imprinting the Jade Maid's Incantations in Horizontal Lines), and

*g)*   *Huang-shen ch'ih-chang* (The Red Petition of the Yellow Spirit).[21]

T'ai-shang Tao-chün (the Most Exalted Lord of the Tao) purportedly revealed the *Shen-chou ching* and *San-wu ta-chai chih chüeh* (The Oral Instructions for the Great Retreat of the Three and Five) to a certain Wang Tsuan during the troubled times at the fall of the Western Chin (ca. A.D. 316). In ancient times this scripture had been issued from the Tu-yang Palace in heaven, and transmitted to the Perfected T'ang P'ing for publication in the world of mortals. Contrary to the myth, internal evidence shows that the first chapter of the text dates from the end of the Eastern Chin dynasty (ca. A.D. 420). Chapters 2 through 10 were written between 420 and 550. During the T'ang dynasty (618–907), the text was enlarged by the addition of ten more chapters. The scripture is a work on demonology which promises that those who receive, recite, maintain, and venerate it will be graced with divine assistance in the form of spirit warriors, stalwarts, and officials who will protect them against evil specters, especially those that cause disease. Three sets of protocols for conducting retreats based on this scripture edited by Tu Kuang-t'ing have survived in the *Tao-tsang:*

(a)   *T'ai-shang tung-yüan san-mei shen-chou chai ch'an-hsieh i* (HY 525),

(b)   *T'ai-shang tung-yüan san-mei shen-chou ch'ing-tan hsing-tao i* (HY 526), and

(c)   *T'ai-shang tung-yüan san-mei shen-chou shih-fang ch'an i* (HY 527).

Tu's collection of accounts on Taoist miracles, the *Tao-chiao ling-yen chi* (HY 590), contains several examples of the application of the text and its retreats to heal those who were ill and repel barbarian incursions during the T'ang.[22]

> *Chang Wan-fu:* Chang omits this phase in his work on ordination, but includes it in other texts that he wrote.[23]

7.   THE TRANSMISSION OF THE *TAO-TE CHING:* Chin-ming Ch'i-chen divides this stage into four phases:

*a)*   *Lao Tzu ch'ing-ssu chin-niu ti-tzu* (Student of Lao Tzu's Gold Knob and Blue-Green Thread); this title was bestowed on those who had received:

(1) the *Lao Tzu chin-niu ch'ing-ssu,* and
(2) the *Shih-chieh shih-ssu ch'ih-shen chieh* (The Ten Injunctions and Fourteen Precepts for Sustaining Self).[24]

At first glance the latter appears to be the same precepts that were transmitted to the Students of Pure Faith. However, such is not the case. These injunctions, unrelated to those given the Ch'ing-hsin ti-tzu, were extracted from two scriptures in the original Ling-pao canon to form a new scripture, which now bears the title *Tung-hsüan ling-pao T'ien-tsun shuo shih-chieh ching* (HY 459). Four copies of HY 459 with covenantal writs *(meng-wen)* have survived among the Tun-huang manuscripts:

> *(a) Shih-chieh ching* (P. 2347). This text is attached to a copy of the *Tao-te ching* and has a writ of covenant written by the Student of Pure Faith, T'ang Chen-chieh, a nun sixteen years of age, who received the text from the Canon Preceptor of the Three Caverns, Yen Lü-ming. It is dated June 29 or 30, 709.
>
> *(b) Shih-chieh ching* (P. 2350). This text is attached to a copy of the *Tao-te ching.* The writ of covenant for the *Shih-chieh ching* was written by the Student of Pure Faith, Li Wu-shang, age twenty-six, who received the text from the Canon Preceptor of the Three Caverns, Chang Jen-sui. It is dated February 11, 714.
>
> *(c) Shih-chieh ching* (S. 6454). The writ of covenant was written by the Student of Pure Faith, Chang Hsüan-pien, age twenty-six, of the K'ai-yüan Abbey in Tun-huang Subprefecture, who received the text from the Canon Preceptor of the Three Caverns, Ma Yu-?. It is dated February 26, 751.
>
> *(d) Shih-chieh ching* (P. 3770). The writ of covenant was written by the Student of Pure Faith, Wang Yü-chen, age fifteen, who received the text from the Canon Preceptor of the Three Caverns, So Ch'ung-shu. It is dated June 5, 757.

Since in the first two cases the texts of the injunctions (only twenty-five lines long in the *Tao-tsang* version) are joined to the students' copy of the *Tao-te ching* along with a covenant, the conferral of these precepts appears to have been part of the transmission rite for the canon that formed around the *Tao-te ching.*[25]

*b*)  *Kao-hsüan ti-tzu* (Student of the Eminent Mystery), this title
was bestowed with:

(1)  the *Lao Tzu Tao-te ching,* two chapters. See *Tao-te chen-ching*
(HY 664) and *Tao-te chen-ching ku-pen p'ien* (HY 682), collated and certified by Fu I (555–639).

> *Chang Wan-fu:* (1) *Tao-te,* two chapters.

(2)  the *Ho-shang Kung chen-jen chu* (Annotation of the Perfected
Duke on the River), two chapters. See *Tao-te chen-ching chu*
(HY 682).

> *Chang Wan-fu:* (2) *Ho-shang kung chu,* two chapters.

(3)  the *Hsiang-erh chu* (The Hsiang-erh Commentary to the
*Tao-te ching*), two chapters. See *Lao Tzu Hsiang-erh chu
chiao-chien,* collated and annotated by Jao Tsung-i (Hong
Kong, 1956).

> *Chang Wan-fu:* (3) *Hsiang-erh chu,* two chapters.

(4)  the *Wu-ch'ien-wen ch'ao-i* (The Protocols for the Audience
of the *Tao-te ching*), one chapter.

> *Chang Wan-fu:* (6) *Ch'ao-i,* one chapter?

(5)  the *Tsa-shuo* (Miscellaneous Discourses), one chapter.
(6)  the *Kuan-ling nei-chuan* (Hagiography of the Guardian of
the Pass), one chapter, a biography of Yin Hsi.

> *Chang Wan-fu:* (13) *Wu-shang chen-jen chuan* (Hagiography of
> the Peerless Perfected), one chapter.

(7)  the *Chieh-wen* (Writ of the Injunctions), one chapter.

> *Chang Wan-fu:* *T'ai-ch'ing yin-yang chieh* (Injunctions for the
> Yin and Yang of Supreme Purity); these precepts were given
> to Students of the Register for the Five Thousand Words *(Tao-
> te ching).*

*c*)  *T'ai-shang kao-hsüan fa-shih* (Canon Preceptor of the Most
Exalted and Eminent Mystery); this title was reserved for those
who had received the preceding and the following:

(1) the *Lao Tzu miao-chen ching* (Lao Tzu's Scripture of Marvelous Perfection), two chapters.

> *Chang Wan-fu:* (9) *Miao-chen,* two chapters.

(2) the *Hsi-sheng ching* (The Scripture of Lao Tzu's Ascension in the West), two chapters. See HY 666.

> *Chang Wan-fu:* (8) *Lao Tzu hsi-sheng,* one chapter.

(3) the *Yü-li ching* (The Scripture of the Jade Almanac), one chapter.
(4) the *Li-tsang ching* (The Scripture of Successive Repositories), one chapter.
(5) the *Lao Tzu chung-ching* (Lao Tzu's Scripture of the Center), one chapter. Preserved in the HY 1026, chapters 18 and 19.
(6) the *Lao Tzu nei-chieh* (The Esoteric Interpretation of Lao Tzu), two chapters.

> *Chang Wan-fu:* (10) *Nei-chieh,* two chapters.

(7) the *Lao Tzu chieh-chieh* (The Interpretation of the Lao Tzu by Sections), two chapters.

> *Chang Wan-fu:* (11) *Chieh-chieh,* two chapters.

(8) the *Kao-shang Lao Tzu nei-chuan* (The Esoteric Hagiography of His Eminence Lao Tzu), one chapter.

> *Chang Wan-fu:* (12) *Kao-shang chuan,* one chapter.

(9) the *Huang-jen san-i piao-wen* (The Writ of the Yellow Man's Three and One Memorial).

> *Chang Wan-fu: Hsiang-erh erh-shih-ch'i chieh* (The Twenty-Seven Injunctions for the Hsiang-erh Commentary). These were the precepts that were given to the T'ai-shang kao-hsüan fa-shih.

d) *T'ai-shang ti-tzu* (Student of the Most Exalted); this title was conferred with:
(1) the *T'ai-i pa-t'ieh t'un-chia hsien-lu* (T'ai-i's Immortal Register for Divining the Chia in Eight Tablets).

(2) the *Tzu-kung i-tu ta-lu* (The Great Register of the Purple Palace's Motions).

(3) the *Lao-chün liu-chia pi-fu* (Lord Lao's Secret Talisman of the Six Chia Spirits).

(4) the *Huang-shen yüeh-chang* (The Surpassing? Petition of the Yellow Spirit).

> *Chang Wan-fu:*
> (4) *Ta-ts'un t'u* (Illustration for the Grand Visualization), one chapter.
> (5) *Ch'uan-i* (Protocols for the Transmission of the Canon), one chapter.
> (7) *Chai-i* (Protocols for the Retreat), one chapter.
> (14) *Tzu-hsü lu* (Register of the Purple Vacuity), one chapter.[26]

The tradition of the *Tao-te ching*'s revelation, recorded in the *Shih chi* by Ssu-ma Ch'ien (ca. 145–ca. 85 B.C.), is older than the religion itself. Lao Tzu, who was serving as an Archivist (*Chu-hsia shih,* Scribe Stationed beneath the Pillar) in the Chou dynasty (trad. 1122–256 B.C.), became disheartened by the degeneration at the court. So he decided to resign his post and leave the kingdom. When he arrived at the Han-ku Pass on his journey westward, he met its keeper Yin Hsi, who asked him to compose a book on his philosophy. Lao Tzu agreed and wrote a work in two chapters of more than five thousand words, the *Wu-ch'ien wen,* which subsequently acquired the title *Tao-te ching.* He then departed, and no one knew where he met his end. By the late second century A.D., Lao Tzu had been deified as Lord Lao, Lao-chün. This transfiguration transformed the historic Lao Tzu into one of Lord Lao's avatars and the tale of the text's transmission, merely a transfer of a text from master to disciple in the original version, into a myth of divine revelation. The *Tao-te ching* was elevated to the status of scripture, and new annotations for it were written that reinterpreted it in terms that conformed to the expectations and notions of the religion. Furthermore, new scriptures—as well as registers, injunctions, talismans, and the like—were composed which, with the annotations, formed a canon that was transmitted to ordinands during investitures. By the beginning of the T'ang dynasty, the myth of the revelation had been greatly elaborated. When Lord Lao meets Yin Hsi at the Han-ku Pass, he subjects the keeper to a threefold test, which Yin passes successfully. Lord Lao then transmits to him the *Yü-li chung-ching* (a text on the ingestion of breath, in three chapters and fifty-five sections), the *Tao-te ching,* the *Lao Tzu chieh-chieh,* and the *Lao Tzu hsi-sheng ching.* In this manner three more texts were sanctified by the legend of divine revelation. One item in Chang Wan-fu's inventory, number (7) above, is a liturgy for conducting a retreat. It is not at all clear to what Chang was referring. There is no reference to a retreat associated with the *Tao-te ching* in any of the lists for such rites dating from the early T'ang nor do the *Wu-shang pi-yao* and other compendia completed in the sixth, seventh, and eighth centuries contain any protocols for executing it. Consequently, despite Chang's notation, it is doubtful that priests invested with this canon performed any office specifically related to the corpus of texts that they received at ordination. Judging by the character of the commentaries transmitted with the *Tao-te ching,* it seems more likely that this order was devoted more to personal, inner, spiritual, and physiological cultivation than to public, external service to the community of the faithful.[27]

> *Chang Wan-fu:* Chang's inventory is juxtaposed with Chin-ming Ch'i-chen's above. This is the only instance when Chang supplies a more-or-less complete catalog of the items conferred on ordinands at their investitures, and he appears to have had some trouble constructing it. He says that it is clear from the *T'ai-hsüan ching* (now lost), a scripture that was part of that section of the *Tao-tsang* devoted to the philosophical texts of Taoism, that items 1 to 7 in his list ought to be transmitted and observed for the cultivation of behavior. The remaining items, 8 to 14, he adopted from the Duke of the Great Bourne (Ko Hsüan) and Chin-ming [Ch'i-chen]. Judging from this evidence, Chang was well aware of the latter's work (HY 1117), but did not have complete confidence in it. It seems that no concensus was reached among authorities in the Nan-pei ch'ao or T'ang as to the precise contents of this canon.[28]

8.  THE TRANSMISSION OF THE *SAN-HUANG WEN* (WRIT OF THE THREE SOVEREIGNS): Chin-ming Ch'i-chen divides this stage into two phases. However, the protocols for the investiture given in the *T'ai-shang tung-shen san-huang i* (HY 802), which may date from the T'ang period, call for the transmission of items from both phases at a single rite.

    *a)*    *Tung-shen ti-tzu* (Student of the Cavern-Divine); this title was conferred with:
        (1)    the *Chin-kang t'ung-tzu lu* (Register of the Diamond Lad) (HY 802, p. 11b [conferral of the *T'ung-tzu lu*]).

*Chang Wan-fu:* (1) *Chin-kang t'ung-tzu lu.*

(2)   the *Chu-shih fu* (The Talisman of the Bamboo Emissary) (HY 802, p. 11b [conferral of the . . .]).

(3)   the *P'u-hsia pan* (The Tablet of the Pusya Asterism?).

*Chang Wan-fu:* (2) *P'u-hsia pan.*

(4)   the *San-huang nei-ching fu* (The Talisman of the Three Sovereigns' Esoteric Essence) (HY 802, p. 7b [the intoning of the *Nei-ching fu*]).

(5)   the *San-huang nei-chen hui* (The Three Sovereigns' Taboos for Esoteric Perfection) (HY 802, p. 7b [transmission of the *hui*]).

(6)   the *Chiu-t'ien fa-ping fu* (The Talisman for Issuing the Warriors of the Nine Heavens). In this text the talisman is split into two parts (see the following) (HY 802, p. 7b [transmission of the *Chiu-t'ien fa-ping fei-teng fu*]).

(7)   the *T'ien-shui fei-teng fu* (The Talisman of the Celestial Waters for Flying and Ascending) (HY 802, p. 7b).

(8)   the *Pa-ti ling-shu nei-wen* (The Esoteric Writ and Numinous Text of the Eight Sovereigns) (HY 802, p. 10a [transmission of the *Ling-shu nei-wen*]).

(9)   the *Huang-ti tan-shu nei-wen* (Huang-ti's Esoteric Writ of the Cinnabar Text) (HY 802, p. 10b [transmission of the *Tan-shu nei-wen*]).

(10)  the *Pa-ch'eng wu-sheng shih-san fu* (The Thirteen Talismans of the Eight Accomplishments and Five Victories) (HY 802, p. 10b [transmission of the *Pa-wei wu-sheng shih-san fu*, The Thirteen Talismans of the Eight Authorities and Five Victories]).

(11)  the *Pa-shih lu* (The Register of the Eight Scriveners).

(12)  the *Tung-hsi liang-chin* (The Two Interdictions of the East and the West).

*Chang Wan-fu:* Chang Wan-fu does not list this text in his inventory, but does describe it in another section of his work (HY 1231, ch. 1, p. 14a).

(13)  *San-huang san-chieh wu-chieh pa-chieh wen* (The Writs of the Three, Five and Eight Injunctions for the Three Sovereigns) (HY 802, p. 11b [transmission, *tu,* of the injunc-

tions by recitation, *sung*] and p. 13b [transmission, *shou,* of the essential injunctions, *yao-chieh,* after the close of the ordination rite]).

> *Chang Wan-fu:* Chang lists a *Tung-shen san-tung yao-yen wu chieh shih-san chieh ch'i-pai erh-shih chieh men* (The Gates of the Five, Thirteen, and Seven Hundred and Twenty Injunctions for the Essential Words in the Cavern-Divine and Three Caverns) in his inventory of precepts.

*b)*   *Wu-shang tung-shen fa-shih* (Canon Preceptor of the Peerless Cavern-Divine), a title bestowed with:

(1)   the *T'ien-huang nei-hsüeh wen* (The Celestial Sovereign's Writ of Esoteric Study) (HY 802, p. 5a [chapter one of the *Tung-shen ching,* see 17 below], p. 8b [transmission of the writ], and pp. 12b–13a [a discussion of its title]).

> *Chang Wan-fu:* (6) *San-huang nei-wen* (The Esoteric Writs of the Three Sovereigns). Chang also describes these writs separately (HY 1231, ch. 1, pp. 18b–19a).

(2)   the *Ti-huang chi-shu wen* (The Terrestrial Sovereign's Writ for Recording Texts) (HY 802, p. 5a [chapter two of the *Tung-shen ching;* see 17 below], p. 8b [transmission of the writ], and pp. 13a [a discussion of its title]).

> *Chang Wan-fu:* (6); see the preceding.

(3)   the *Jen-huang nei-wen* (The Human Sovereign's Esoteric Writ) (HY 802, p. 5a [chapter three of the *Tung-shen ching;* see 17 below], p. 8b [transmission of the writ], and pp. 12b–13a (a discussion of its title).

> *Chang Wan-fu:* (6); see (1) above.

(4)   the *San-huang t'ien-wen ta-tzu* (The Celestial Writ of the Three Sovereigns in Giant Graphs) (HY 802, p. 7b [the opening of the Giant Graphs]).

> *Chang Wan-fu:* (7) *San-huang ta-tzu.*

(5)   the *Huang-nü shen-fu* (The Divine Talisman of the Yellow Maid) (HY 802, p. 7b [transmission, *tu,* and reading, *tu* of the . . .]).

(6)    the *San chiang-chün t'u* (The Illustration of the Three Gen-
       erals) (HY 802, p. 7b [transmission *tu,* of the *San-huang
       chiang chün*]).

       *Chang Wan-fu:* (4) *San chiang-chün t'u.*

(7)    the *Chiu-huang t'u* (The Illustration of the Nine Sover-
       eigns) (HY 802, p. 7b [transmission of the . . .]).

       *Chang Wan-fu:* (5) *Chiu-huang t'u.*

(8)    the *Sheng-t'ien ch'üan* (The Tally for Ascension to Heaven)
       (HY 802, p. 11b [transmission of the . . .]).
(9)    the *San-huang ch'uan-pan* (The Three Sovereigns' Trans-
       mission Tablet).
(10)   the *San-huang chen-hsing nei-hui pan* (Tablet of the Esoteric
       Taboos of the Three Sovereigns' True Forms) (HY 802,
       p. 11b [transmission of the *San-huang nei-hui pan*]).
(11)   the *San-huang san-i chen-hsing nei-hui pan* (Tablet for the
       Esoteric Taboos of the Three Sovereigns' Three and One
       True Forms) (HY 802, p. 11b [transmission of the *San-i
       nei-hui pan*]).

       *Chang Wan-fu:* (3) *San-i chen-hui.*

(12)   the *San-huang chiu-t'ien chen-fu ch'i-ling* (The Three Sover-
       eigns' and Nine Heavens' Contract of the True Talis-
       man) (HY 802, p. 11b [transmission of the *Chiu-t'ien
       fu-ch'i*]).
(13)   the *San-huang yin* (The Three Sovereigns' Seal) (HY 802,
       p. 11b [transmission of the *Chiu-t'ien yin,* Seal of the Nine
       Heavens] and p. 12a–b [the impressing of the seal on tab-
       lets]?).
(14)   the *San-huang yü-ch'üan* (The Jade Tally of the Three Sov-
       ereigns) (HY 802, p. 4a [the reading of the tally-contract
       which is also called *yü-ch'üan* or *chin-ch'üan,* jade or gold
       tally]).
(15)   the *San-huang piao* (The Three Sovereigns' Memorial).
(16)   the *P'an-tai* (The Large Girdle).
(17)   the *Tung-shen ching* (The Cavern-Divine Scripture), 14
       chapters (HY 802, p. 5a–b [transmission of the . . .]).
       The contents of the scripture are also given here.[29]

The core of this canon was the *San-huang wen,* issued by his divine majesty Shen-pao chün (Lord of the Divine Treasure) and inscribed by Hsi-ling chen-jen (Perfected of the Western Powers). The text was stored in the celestial Jade Treasury, and immortals transmitted it by hiding copies in grottoes on holy mountains. However, only that version in a cave on Mt. E-mei in modern Szechuan Province was complete. When Po Ho went there to study with Lord Wang (Wang Fang-p'ing or Wang Pao), Wang told him in secret that he should stare at the north wall of the grotto. After a time Po would see the graphs of the writ and would attain the Tao. On February 10, 100 B.C., after staring at the wall for three years, Po was able to discern the writing, writs which the ancients had carved there. The texts of those etchings were the *San-huang wen, Wu-yüeh chen-hsing t'u* (Illustrations of the Five Marchmounts) and the *T'ai-ch'ing chung-ching shen-tan fang* (The Formulas for the Divine Elixirs from the Middle Canon of the Supreme-Purity). Although he memorized (*sung,* recited) ten thousand words, Po was unable to understand what he had acquired. So he returned to Lord Wang, who transmitted the texts through oral instructions. Ko Hung (283–343) says that his master Cheng Yin told him that no texts were more important than the *San-huang wen* and *Wu-yüeh chen-hsing t'u.* Po Ho's version of the *Writ of the Three Sovereigns* was not the set which served as the basis for the *Tung-shen ching,* however. On March 7, A.D. 292 (or A.D. 301) the *San-huang wen* abruptly carved itself into the wall of Lord Liu's Grotto on Mt. Sung (south of Loyang in modern Honan Province), where Pao Ching was fasting and meditating. In accordance with stipulations in the writs, Pao deposited a pledge of pongee measuring four hundred feet in length and then copied the texts. Subsequently, Pao passed the scriptures on to Ko Hung or Ko's sons and grandsons. Later Lu Hsiu-ching (406–March 31, 477) obtained them. He, in turn, transmitted them first to his disciple Sun Yu-yüeh (399–June 28, 489) and later to T'ao Hung-ching (456–April 18, 536). The original scripture grew through gradual accretions during the Nan-pei ch'ao. The text in Ko's possession had three chapters; the text acquired by Lu Hsiu-ching had four, and that transmitted to T'ao Hung-ching eleven or thirteen. The *Tung-shen ching* extant in the T'ang consisted of fourteen chapters with the following contents:

Chapter 1: *Ta-yu lu-t'u T'ien-huang nei-wen* (Esoteric Writ of Heaven's Sovereign, Registers, and Illustrations of the Ta-yu Heaven).

Chapter 2: *Ta-yu lu-t'u Ti-huang nei-wen* (Esoteric Writ of Earth's Sovereign, Registers, and Illustrations of the Ta-yu Heaven).

Chapter 3: *Ta-yu lu-t'u Jen-huang nei-wen* (Esoteric Writ of Man's Sovereign, Registers, and Illustrations of the Ta-yu Heaven).

Chapters 4–6: *Pa-ti miao-ching ching* (Scripture of the Eight Sovereigns' Marvelous Essence).

Chapters 7–9: *Pa-ti hsüan-pien ching* (Scripture of the Eight Sovereigns' Mysterious Transformations).

Chapters 10–11: *Pa-ti shen-hua ching* (Scripture of the Eight Sovereigns' Divine Transformations).

Chapter 12: *San-huang chai-i* (Protocols for the Three Sovereigns' Retreat).

Chapter 13: *San-huang ch'ao-i* (Protocols for the Three Sovereigns' Audience).

Chapter 14: *San-huang ch'uan-shou i* (Protocols for the Transmission of the Three Sovereigns' Writs).

The first three chapters of this text, now lost, were the Writs of the Three Sovereigns. The *Tung-shen pa-ti miao-ching ching* (HY 640) and *Tung-shen pa-ti yüan (hsüan)-ching ching* (HY 1193) may be surviving chapters from the fourth and fifth sections of the *Tung-shen ching*. The liturgies for its investiture and retreat were included in the text itself (chapters 13 and 14). A hierarchy of retreats that probably dates from the Sui dynasty (589–618) ranks the *Tung-shen chai* just beneath the Ling-pao rites, and states that performances of it could assist the emperor and protect the nation.[30]

> *Chang Wan-fu:* The titles from Chang's inventory of this corpus, listing only seven texts, are noted above. Chang says that the *Tung-shen ching* as transmitted by T'ao Hung-ching had only thirteen chapters.[31]

9. THE TRANSMISSION OF THE *SHENG-HSÜAN NEI-CHIAO CHING* (THE SCRIPTURE OF THE ESOTERIC TEACHINGS FOR THE ASCENSION TO THE MYSTERY).

   a) *Sheng-hsüan fa-shih* (Canon Preceptor of the Ascension to the Mystery); this title is reserved for those who have received:

      (1) the *T'ai-shang tung-hsüan ling-pao sheng-hsüan nei-chiao ching,* one title in ten chapters, and the

      (2) the *Sheng-hsüan ch'i-shih-erh tzu ta-lu (ch'üan)* (The Great Register or Tally of Ascension to the Mystery in Seventy-Two Graphs).[32]

This text, which originally had ten chapters, is now lost except for the seventh chapter, *T'ai-shang ling-pao sheng-hsüan nei-chiao ching chung-ho p'in shu-i shu* (HY 1114), which survives in the *Tao-tsang* and a number of manuscript copies, in varying states of disorder, for chapters five through ten in the Tun-huang archives. It was one of several Ling-pao scriptures composed in the late fifth or early sixth century as extensions or elaborations of the original canon. What role it played in the Taoist hierarchy of investiture is not at all clear, though its transmission appears to have been some sort of preliminary stage to the conferral of the Ling-pao canon itself.[33]

*Chang Wan-fu:* Chang omits the investiture for this scripture in his text on ordination, but recognizes its existence in his work on the taboo names for an officiant's preceptors.[34]

10. THE TRANSMISSION OF THE LING-PAO (NUMINOUS TREASURE) CANON.

  a)  *T'ai-shang ling-pao tung-hsüan ti-tzu* (Student of the Most Exalted Numinous Treasure Cavern-Mystery); this title was bestowed on ordinands who received:

  (1)  the *Yüan-shih tung-hsüan ling-pao ch'ih-shu chen-wen lu* (The Register for the True Writs in Red Script, a Cavern-Mystery and Numinous Treasure Text of the Primordial Commencement),

  (2)  the *T'ai-shang tung-hsüan ling-pao erh-shih-ssu sheng t'u* (The Illustrations of the Twenty-Four Life Energies),

  (3)  the *San-pu pa-ching tzu-jan chih-chen yü-lu* (The Spontaneously Generated Jade Register of the Utmost Perfection and Eight Effulgent Spirits in Three Sections),

  (4)  the *T'ai-shang tung-hsüan ling-pao chu-t'ien nei-yin lu* (The Most Exalted Numinous Treasure and Cavern-Mystery's Register for the Esoteric Intonations of All Heavens),

  (5)  the *Ling-pao tzu-jan ching-ch'üan* (The Spontaneously Generated Scriptural Tally of the Numinous Treasure), and

  (6)  the *Yüan-shih ling-ts'e* (The Numinous Slips of the Primordial Commencement).

  b)  *Wu-shang tung-hsüan fa-shih* (Canon Preceptor of the Peerless Cavern-Mystery): a title reserved for priests who had received:

  (1)  the *Ling-pao chung-meng ching* (The Numinous Treasure Canon of the Middle Covenant) in forty-two titles and forty-seven chapters.[35]

The Ling-pao canon emerged spontaneously from the Brahman-ether and, like the *San-huang wen,* was tucked away in the holy mountains, in this case the Five Marchmounts, for five eons. Finally, the Celestial Venerable of the Primordial Commencement decided that the time was ripe and ordered the Most Exalted Lord of the Tao to propagate it among mortal men. The latter commissioned a number of the Perfected to reveal the holy texts, one by one, to Ko Hsüan, who, after suffering countless reincarnations and having compassionately vowed to strive for the salvation of mankind, had qualified as worthy to receive them. The conferrals purportedly took place on Mt. T'ien-t'ai or Mt. Yü (southeast of Hangchow in Chekiang Province) during the Ch'ih-wu era (238–251). In reality, Ko Ch'ao-fu, a descendant of Ko Hsüan, wrote the corpus and transmitted it to his disciples between 397 and 402. Only one text in the canon, the *T'ai-shang ling-pao wu-fu hsü* (HY 388), dates from Ko Hsüan's time. Ko Ch'ao-fu extracted the essence from older Taoist texts in his possession and infused it with elements from Buddhist sutras to form his new scriptures. For his efforts he was rewarded with something less than an enviable reputation. T'ao Hung-ching charged that he had "fabricated" the Ling-pao scriptures. T'ao's intent was to distinguish between Ko's inferior scriptural legacy and the higher, truly revealed canonical heritage of the Shang-ch'ing order. However, the denigration of his work as the issue of human hands and not the gift of the gods should not be permitted to minimize Ko's original contributions, which were largely responsible for the enormous institutional changes in Taoism that occurred during the fifth century. Ko established a scriptural hierarchy that elevated the Ling-pao, San-huang, and Shang-ch'ing texts to the highest ranks of prestige and banished the works of the Cheng-i tradition to obscurity. His injection of Buddhist notions into Taoism led to the growth of a new priesthood based on celibacy, in contrast to the older, familial clergy of the Celestial Master sect. His texts also inaugurated a new system of retreats, six in number, whose function was to serve the spiritual needs of the community and the priesthood (see the Finale). By the sixth century, the institutions which emerged from his canon had supplanted the older Cheng-i traditions. Although Ling-pao doctrines enjoyed less prestige than Shang-ch'ing tenets, they were the dominant force that shaped the clergy and its offices until at least the eleventh century.[36]

*Chang Wan-fu:* Chang lists the *Tzu-jan ch'üan* (Spontaneously Generated Tally), the *Chung-meng ching* (Canon of the Central Covenant) in forty-seven chapters, the *Ta-meng chen-wen* (The True Writs of the Great Covenant), and the *Pa-ching nei-yin* (Esoteric Intonations of the Eight Effulgent Spirits) in his inventory. He does not enumerate the titles of the scriptures, but does discuss the *Ling-pao wu-fu* (The Five Talismans of the Numinous Treasure) and names the registers, talismans, and staffs that were presented at ordinations. Since the number of chapters that he supplies for the corpus is identical to that given by Chin-ming Ch'i-chen, the canon circulating in the early eighth century was probably the same as that extant around 550.[37]

## 11. THE TRANSMISSION OF THE SHANG-CH'ING (SUPERIOR PURITY) CANON.

a) *Tung-chen fa-shih* (Canon Preceptor of the Cavern-Perfected); this title is for those who have received:

(1) the *Wu-yüeh chen-hsing t'u* (Illustrations of the Five Marchmounts' True Forms),

(2) the *Wu-yüeh kung-yang t'u* (Illustrations for Worshiping the Five Marchmounts),

(3) the *Wu-yüeh chen-hsing t'u hsü* (Preface to the Illustrations of the Five Marchmounts' True Forms),

(4) the *Ling-pao wu-fu* (The Five Talismans of the Numinous Treasure),

(5) the *Wu-fu hsü* (Preface for the Five Talismans),

(6) the *Wu-fu ch'uan-pan* (Transmission Tablet for the Five Talismans),

(7) the *Shang-ch'ing pei-ti shen-chou wen* (The Shang-ch'ing Writ of the Northern Sovereigns' Divine Incantations),

(8) the *T'ai-hsüan ho-t'u* (The River Chart of the Great Mystery),

(9) the *Chiu-huang pao-lu* (The Treasure Register of the Nine Sovereigns).

The conferral of these items appears to have been a prelude to the transmission of the Shang-ch'ing canon. Only number (7) claims to be related specifically to that corpus. In pre-T'ang times number (1) was linked to the *San-huang wen*, and number (4) was, of course, a part of the Ling-pao canon. The bestowal of the nine may have been a variation of the *Wu-fa* transmission, mentioned by Chang Wan-fu as part of the Shang-ch'ing investiture for Princesses Gold-Immortal and Jade-Perfected. The *Wu-fa*, as described in another text by Chang (HY 1230), included numbers (1) and (4). That text is devoted to providing schedules for conducting ordinations and kindred rites. In it the conferrals of the *Wu-fa*, the River Chart, and Treasure

Register (8 and 9 above) appear just after the transmission of the Ling-pao canon and immediately before the bestowal of the Shang-ch'ing corpus in precisely the same place that the nine items occupy in Chin-ming Ch'i-chen's order.[38]

(10)  twenty-three registers,
(11)  one writ,
(12)  one illustration,
(13)  seven contracts,
(14)  four tallies,
(15)  two incantations,
(16)  one scripture,
(17)  one document,
(18)  one tablet.

b)  *Shang-ch'ing hsüan-tu ta-tung san-ching ti-tzu, Wu-shang san-tung fa-shih* (Student of the Three Luminaries in the Great Cavern of the Mysterious Capital, Canon Preceptor of the Peerless Three Caverns), these titles were reserved for recipients of:

(1)  the *Shang-ch'ing ta-tung chen-ching* (The Superior Purity Canon of the Great Cavern), forty-three titles in ninty-two chapters.[39]

Of all the Taoist revelations, this is the only one that is well documented and appears to have been the product of true ecstatic experiences—experiences reminiscent of Allah's revelations to Muhammad. Between 364 and 370 a cluster of the Perfected descended to transmit scriptures, hagiographies, and instructions to Yang Hsi (330–?) near Mt. Mao south of Nanking. Yang, and his associates Hsü Mi (303–373) and Hsü Hui (341–ca. 370), made a transcript of these nocturnal visions, carefully noting the matter that Yang received from his benefactors. After the deaths of Yang, Hsü Mi, and Hsü Hui, their record was partially lost as it passed down through the hands of a very small number of heirs. T'ao Hung-ching reassembled parts of the original transcript and fragments from the scriptures penned by Yang and the Hsü's, authenticated the manuscripts on the basis of handwriting, and published his critical edition as the *Chen-kao,* around A.D. 500. This text soon found a place in the corpus of Shang-ch'ing scripture. Meanwhile, the order which formed to perpetuate the canon established itself as the most prestigious in Taoism. It was the elite, and its retreats reflected that status.

(1)  Title unknown: this rite was performed "to transcend the

multitude [common men] and abide in quiet solitude, to
calm the *ch'i* [energies] and lose the form [*hsing*, body].

(2)  Title unknown: this rite was conducted according to the
Statutes of the Protocols for Grand Perfection *(T'ai-chen i-
ko)*. It may be the same retreat which this source says was
executed to "seek the immortals and recall the Perfected in
order to sublimate the body and hide the shadow." If so, it
was part of the Shang-ch'ing regime for acquiring immortality and invisibility by means of visualizations.

(3)  *Hsin-chai* (Mind-Fasting): this rite was practiced to
"cleanse the mind and purify the essence and spirit." The
phrase *hsin-chai* derives from the *Chuang Tzu* and denotes a
form of Taoist meditative practice, mind-fasting or sitting
in forgetfulness *(tso-wang)*, whose purpose was to purge the
mind of discursive thought.

These liturgies made no demands on priests to perform services for
the community or the state. They were actually forms of discipline
intended only for the personal physical, mental, and spiritual perfection of their officiants. However, by the sixth century, ordination in lower orders before or simultaneously with Shang-ch'ing
investitures appears to have become a common practice. Consequently, although primarily devoted to the pursuit of higher individual goals, members of this order were active in performing public rituals as well.[40]

*Chang Wan-fu:* Chang mentions this level of ordination in his text on
Taoist investitures and other works, but he supplies no inventory for the
matter presented to ordinands.

Taoist ordinations, the liturgies of investiture practiced in the late Nan-
pei ch'ao and the early T'ang periods, originated in the rites for conferring registers of the Celestial Master movement and the rites for transmitting texts among the alchemical, occult, and contemplative schools
during the second, third, and fourth centuries A.D. Most of the instruments—oaths, covenants, tallies, pledges, injunctions, and the like—
employed to consummate ordinations existed long before the creation of
the liturgies. However, with the exception of the Cheng-i tradition, the
objective of the earlier rites that used these writs was to ensure the secret
transmission of texts, not to produce clerical institutions for service to
the community. The latter development began at the very end of the
fourth century, when Ko Ch'ao-fu published the Ling-pao canon, and

reached its first stage of maturity around the middle of the fifth century. In the south, Lu Hsiu-ching organized the scriptures revealed in the fourth century (the *San-huang wen,* Ling-pao, and Shang-ch'ing texts) as the Three Caverns, imposed order on Taoist liturgy by creating a hierarchy of retreats, and composed the Ling-pao ordination rite. In the north, K'ou Ch'ien-chih (ca. 415–died 448) launched a reform movement which strove to eliminate the abuses of the Celestial Master clergy of Libationers *(Chi-chiu)* and to replace the older hereditary priesthood with a celibate clergy of *tao-shih.* In the following century, additional orders based on the transmission of a scripture or scriptures emerged which found niches in Chin-ming Ch'i-chen's hierarchy. Foreign influence was responsible for some of these changes. The new priesthood adopted celibacy from Buddhism and increasingly came to see investiture as "receiving precepts" *(shou-chieh),* a Buddhist notion. The latter trend is most evident in Chang Wan-fu's work on ordination, which relies on various sets of injunctions to define the stages and phases of initiation and investiture.

The evolution of the new sacerdotal orders entailed a decline in the prestige and power of the Cheng-i sect. Although they were loathe to abandon completely their affiliation with the older tradition to whose legacy they were heirs, they wished to establish their preeminence over it. They resolved this contradiction by formulating an ecclesiastical hierarchy which preserved the libationers, but relegated them to the lowest rung in the clerical ladder. The *chi-chiu* occupied a position just beneath the clergy who remained with their families *(tsai-chia),* who in turn were ranked just beneath those who left their families *(ch'u-chia).* Celibacy was a virtue superior to familial loyalty. The new priesthood "departed from the dust of the secular world to guard the Tao *(shou-tao)* and complete Perfection *(ch'üan-chen),*" which required residence in an abbey. Their admission to the cloisters and their attainments of various levels of ordination were not contingent upon familial custom, predilection, or favor. The celibate orders secured victory over the Celestial Master sect long before the T'ang. By 713 the Libationers survived in what is now Szechuan Province and the region south of the Yangtze River, where they practiced healing arts. Leadership of Taoism had passed into the hands of the new orders, where membership was open to talent; learning became the criterion for initiation and advancement, and the character of the priesthood was more impersonal than it had been in its earliest days.[41]

# Finale

LIKE THE TRADITIONAL secular theater in China that developed many centuries later, Taoist investiture was a form of opera, combining dialogue with music and singing. The altar functioned like an elevated stage. It had an architectural structure that defined the arena in which the drama unfolded, lighting that permitted evening performances, furniture that designated the positions where the actors executed the actions assigned to them, and props that were manipulated to produce desired effects. The script, the liturgy, supplied detailed stage directions choreographing the movements, postures, and gestures of the players. It also provided the speeches and lyrics that were uttered or sung. The cast, composed of visible mortals and invisible immortals, wore costumes whose colors, designs, and fabrics were prescribed in the regulations of the divine codes. In short, the protocols for ordination created an ambience that was theatrical in nature even though the rite was never intended to entertain.[1]

Unlike secular theater, the drama of Ling-pao investitures had no plot. Lu Hsiu-ching made no effort to construct a liturgy patterned on the divine transmission of the scriptures or the legend of the Perfecteds' revelations to Ko Hsüan. In fact, these momentous events are only mentioned in his manual. Admittedly, the traditions of the Ling-pao conferrals lacked the intimate details and constant excitement that characterized the transcript of the Perfecteds' bestowal of the Shang-ch'ing scriptures on Yang Hsi (330–?) during nocturnal visitations that occurred between 364 and 370. But, just as important, there was no

99

compelling reason for Lu to develop a sustained plot because he had no
audience, no congregation of devotees, to please. If spectators were not
discouraged or forbidden to attend, they were at the very least excluded
from the actual proceedings. The true drama at ordinations did not
unfold on stage through the songs, speeches, movements, and gestures
of the cast. It took place in the minds of the officiants and ordinands as
an exercise of their imaginations. These actors performed the real rite
within their skulls, animating the investiture by conjuring up legions of
armored warriors, regalia-clad bureaucrats, jade maids, radiant stars,
variegated vapors, and purple clouds. It was within their inner sanc-
tums that the cosmic ethers consecrated the writs, registers, and talismans that thereafter became the instruments of liturgical power for the
newly ordained priest.[2]

The liturgy of the Nocturnal Annunciation as adapted for Ling-pao
ordinations was a tripartite transmission to ordinands. The first set of
acts entailed the conferral of writs—the True Writs, Five Talismans,
Jade Taboos, Jade Instructions, Esoteric Intonations, Slip-Board
Writs, and Divine Staffs—all instruments of power which enabled the
priest to perform his offices. These were the most treasured passages
from the scriptures and required special ritual procedures—horizontal
recitation, implantings, sealings, visualizations, ingestions of breath,
secret instructions, esoteric interpretations, and the like—for their
transfer. The second set involved the presentation of the canon—the
source of the writs, injunctions, liturgies, and other matter—and the
registers, the documents of entitlement which certified the cleric's right
to possess the scriptures and exercise dominion over the spirits. The last
set was the administration of vows and injunctions—the restraints
whose purpose was to prevent the recipients of the writs, canon, and
registers from abusing them and to establish standards of decorum for
the priesthood.

The scriptures possessed immense spiritual powers, powers capable
of influencing the fate of nature, the spirits, the empire, the people, and
individuals. For this reason the liturgy of ordination devoted considera-
ble attention to ensuring that men who might improperly or maliciously
use them for the wrong ends would not acquire them. A substantial portion of the rite focused on various forms of oath-taking. The ordinands
had to establish covenants and swear oaths, which were validated with
all due legal formalities: sealed with signets; certified by signatures;
secured with bonds (pledges) and guarantors (preceptors, parents, and
ancestors); and enforced by threatened sanctions that would be imposed
on them and their ancestors in the afterlife should the students violate
their vows. These oaths were binding agreements committing the

ordinands to preserve the esoteric tradition of transmission, to keep the secrecy of the canon inviolate except from those worthy of initiation. But the oaths had other implications. The vows imposed on the students the obligation of observing the divinely legislated injunctions which circumscribed their behavior and thought. Strict adherence to the precepts guaranteed that the newly ordained priests were worthy of the trust that their master and the gods had placed in them.

Above all, covenants and vows were legal instruments for bonding the ordinands to their superiors, their preceptors, and the gods. They created enduring ties of allegiance which could be undone only at the risk of suffering cruel punishment in the hereafter. The students were not merely becoming priests in an order. They were also entering the canonical lineage. Oath-taking and the transmission of the scriptures established them as heirs to a legacy which originated with the emergence of the scriptures before the creation of the cosmos and was passed down from god to god and bequeathed to Ko Hsüan, and conveyed generation after generation from master to disciple until it reached them. Ordination was a rite of succession in which the officiant endowed his ordinands with that heritage. In return, his students pledged their undying fealty to him and the gods, swearing never to betray their trust. The ritual awarded the ordinands a place in the line of textual transmission that stretched backward and upward from their preceptors to the immortals, Perfected, and gods.[3]

Investiture was also a rite of political appointment, during which established officeholders delegated the authority and powers to perform certain tasks to new appointees. During the rite, the officiant conferred upon the ordinands the titles of their posts in the hierarchy of the numinous bureaucracy that ruled the cosmos. Thereby the appointees acquired the rights to command a group of subordinates and to communicate with their superiors in order to petition them for action. The bestowal also imposed the obligation of obeying the dictates of their overlords as set forth in the divine codes as recorded in the scriptures. The canon—specifically its protocols, injunctions, registers, talismans, and other documents—set the limits of their authority, defined their prerogatives, and prescribed their duties. Foremost among their responsibilities was the charge to perform the great Ling-pao retreats.

1. *Chin-lu chai* (The Gold Register Retreat): conducted for the salvation or protection of the emperor. The *Ta T'ang liu-tien* interprets this to mean that the rite harmonizes yin and yang, eradicates natural calamities and dispels damage, and prolongs the reign of and causes blessings to descend upon the emperor.

2. *Huang-lu chai* (The Yellow Register Retreat): executed to save the ancestors of the age.

3. *Ming-chen chai* (The Retreat for Clarifying Perfection): performed as penance to secure absolution for the souls in the nine dark sectors of hell.

4. *San-yüan chai* (The Retreat of the Three Primes): conducted on the fifteenth day of the first month (Upper Prime) as an act of veneration for the celestial mandarins, on the fifteenth day of the seventh month (Middle Prime) as an act of worship for the numinous terrestrial governors, and on the fifteenth day of the tenth month (Lower Prime) as an act of reverence for the spirit officials of the waters. At each of these the priest confesses for his violations of the regulations in the religious codes.

5. *Pa-chieh chai* (The Retreat of Eight Segments): executed on the solstices, equinoxes, and first days of each season as an act of contrition for newly committed transgressions and for sins remaining from past incarnations (karma).

6. *Tzu-jan chai* (The Retreat of Spontaneity): performed to petition the gods for bestowing blessings on mankind.

The priest was a true public servant in the government of the cosmos, obliged to minister to the needs of the state, society, and family.[4]

Such were the major duties that devolved upon Princesses Gold-Immortal and Jade-Perfected by virtue of their ordination. Although there is a paucity of information about the pastoral careers of these women, the record shows that at least Jade-Perfected twice conducted Taoist rites, and on one of those occasions she performed the Gold Register Retreat. However, in both instances she executed these tasks at the behest and for the benefit of the throne. It is by no means certain that these aristocratic women deigned to provide such services for the people at large. Nevertheless, the evidence demonstrates that they were full-fledged priests (unlike Princess T'ai-p'ing) who took their offices seriously, if perhaps in a limited sense.

The investiture of Gold-Immortal and Jade-Perfected established a precedent for the ordinations of later daughters of royal blood. Their example inspired emulation on the part of T'ang princesses in the eighth and ninth centuries.

Emperor Hsüan-tsung    Princess Yung-mu (first daughter). She was
   (r. 713–756)        ordained in 748, had been married previously,
                       and donated her mansion in Ch'ang-an for
                       conversion into an abbey.

Princess Wan-an (seventh daughter). Her investiture took place sometime between 742 and 756, and an abbey may have been renamed in her honor.

Princess Hsin-ch'ang (eleventh daughter). She took vows after the death of her husband in 747, and an abbey named after her was established at the time of her ordination.

Princess Ch'u-kuo (sixteenth daughter). She was ordained and took her vows in 747; she had been married previously.

Princess Hsien-i (twenty-second daughter). She was married twice before her ordination and died about 784.

Emperor Tai-tsung
(r. 763–780)

Princess Hua-yang (fifth daughter). She requested permission to take vows because of illness in 722.

Emperor Te-tsung
(r. 780–805)

Princess Wen-an (seventh daughter). She requested permission to be ordained between 827 and 836.

Emperor Shun-tsung
(r. 805–806)

Princess Hsin-yang (seventh daughter). All three of Shun-tsung's daughters who asked for permission to take vows did so at the same time and received yearly stipends of seven hundred lengths of stuffs.

Princess P'ing-en (tenth daughter). She died in her youth.

Princess Shao-yang (eleventh daughter). She died in her youth.

Emperor Hsien-tsung
(r. 806–821)

Princess Yung-chia (second daughter).

Princess Yung-an (fifteenth daughter). She was betrothed about 821 to the Uighur Khan, but the Khan died before the marriage ceremony took place. The Princess requested permission to be ordained between 827 and 836.

| Emperor Mu-tsung | Princess I-ch'ang (seventh daughter). She died |
| (r. 821–825) | between 860 and 874. |
| | Princess An-k'ang (eighth daughter). She was recalled from her abbey to the Southern Palace in 877.[5] |

Between 618 and 906 seventeen T'ang princesses (including Princesses T'ai-p'ing, Gold-Immortal, and Jade-Perfected) out of two hundred and twelve were inducted into Taoist orders. Although the number of these ordinations, which constitutes eight percent of the total number of women, may appear to be small, it is a remarkable statistic because not a single daughter of any emperor took vows as a Buddhist nun. Since Buddhism reached the apex of its popularity in this period it would be unreasonable to assume that none of the princesses had a desire to enter a Buddhist convent. It is more likely that there was a rule, written or understood, governing the affairs of the royal clan which prohibited them from being ordained as anything but Taoist nuns.

The reason for this tilt toward Taoism in investitures is not difficult to uncover. At the beginning of the dynasty the royal house established a claim that its members were descendants of Lao Tzu. This assertion was based on the notion that the imperial surname Li was the same as that of the ancient Taoist sage. Guided by this initial premise the T'ang developed a dynastic ideology based on philosophical and religious Taoism, Lao Tzu being esteemed as the founder of both at the time. The ideology, in turn, influenced the throne's religious patronage and shaped its policies on a number of questions. Consequently, when a princess decided to commit herself to religious life, she apparently had only one recourse. In a real sense, questions about family affairs were governed by applying the familial, that is genealogical, pretensions of the court. This does not mean that the emperor prescribed personal beliefs or affiliations for his kin. In fact, Princess Tai-kuo, another of Jui-tsung's daughters, was an ardent adherent of Buddhism. Apparently, princesses were free to choose whatever faith they desired, but not if they elected to pursue a religious vocation. While the options of the latter were restricted, there was compensation. These princesses received approbation from the throne as well as substantial endowments for their own maintenance and occasionally for the establishment of abbeys for them.[6]

T'ang ideology also helps to explain the epiphany which occurred at the investiture of Princesses Gold-Immortal and Jade-Perfected early in the morning on February 20, 711. On at least three occasions before

711, Lao Tzu appeared, to bless the royal house. The first of these, actually a series of five apparitions, occurred in 620 and 622, shortly after the dynasty was founded. At the time, the Li's were hard pressed by rivals for the throne who were attempting to unseat them. The second and third appearances took place during the reign of Kao-tsung, at the dedication of a new temple for Lao Tzu on Mt. Pei-mang just north of Lo-yang in 662, and again at the same abbey in 679 when the Emperor and his court visited it to observe the performance of a retreat. These early epiphanies were concrete manifestations of the divine ancestor's approbation for the descendant's conquest and reign, the god's sanction for the god-king's exercise of power. Given this history it is not surprising that the particular deity who appeared in the Princesses' visions was none other than the divine protector of their clan. The ladies' knowledge of the divine interventions may well have influenced their ecstatic experiences. The traditions seem to have left a strong impression on the imagination of their elder brother, Emperor Hsüan-tsung, who thrice experienced visions in which Lao Tzu appeared to him.[7]

Politics and familial beliefs, however, only partially account for the Princesses' visions. Taoist protocols note that epiphanies and kindred phenomena were not only to be expected, but were at times also required at investitures and other rites. One Shang-ch'ing scripture instructs the preceptor to enter a place that is totally isolated from contact with people, to fast, and to make a declaration to the gods requesting a secret response from them before he transmits the sacred texts to his students. This regulation applies, of course, to the officiant, not the ordinands. However, a scripture from the original Ling-pao canon makes it clear that such divine responses were by-products of the pieties practiced by all participants as preliminaries to ordinations and other retreats. It promises that if you fast, meditate, recite scripture, repent, burn incense, and worship,

> you will see the flying celestial men. The immortal lads and jade maids will descend to you. Some will hear the singing of praises in space. Others will see beams of light shining upon their bodies or hear the tinkling of jade and gold or the sound of the eight tones.

There is a recognition here that deprivation of sustenance, studied exercise of the imagination (visualization), and rhythmic, monotonous chanting of texts generate psychological states of ecstasy in which practitioners experience illusions. In Taoism, such states were deliberately cultivated. Adepts consciously sought to create such phantasms by pursuing a calculated discipline for which the scriptures provided exact instructions.[8]

On the First of December, 712, Princesses Gold-Immortal and Jade-Perfected received the Five Procedures *(Wu-fa)*—the Talismans of the Six Chia Spirits *(Liu-chia fu)*, the Mountain Interdictions *(Chin-shan)*, the Illustrations of the Five Marchmounts' True Forms *(Wu-yüeh chen-hsing t'u)*, the Talismans of the Three Sovereigns *(San-huang fu)*, and the Five Talismans *(Wu-fu)*—and the Shang-ch'ing canon on an altar erected in a separate cloister of the Kuei-chen Abbey. This altar, constructed according to liturgical regulations, had a square lower tier or outer enclosure and a round upper level or inner altar, symbolizing earth and heaven, respectively. The panoply of pledges, colored silks for defending the sacred arena, destiny silks, and other furnishings vastly exceeded those supplied for the Princesses' Ling-pao ordination. The ascent of Gold-Immortal and Jade-Perfected up the ladder of investiture was complete with this final conferral.[9]

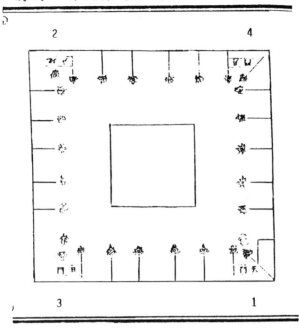

**Figure 1. The Structure of the Middle Enclosure, Capital Altar *(Tu-t'an)*, of the Altar for the Yellow Register Retreat**

1. The Celestial Gate: north-northwest corner, blue-green script on a black placard.
2. The Terrestrial Portal: south-southeast corner, yellow script on a red placard.
3. The Solar Gate: north-northeast corner, yellow script on a blue-green placard.
4. The Lunar Gate: south-southwest corner, yellow script on a white placard.

According to HY 508, this enclosure was constructed by erecting eight long blossom-poles (for the gates) and twenty short ones (for the intervening spaces). It goes on to say that all entrances and exits proceed through the Terrestrial Portal and that it is impermissible to come and go through the other three gates. This does not square with Lu Hsiu-ching's manual for conducting Ling-pao ordinations, which instructs the officiant(s) to enter through the Celestial Gate and the ordinands through the Terrestrial Portal *(Wu-shang huang-lu ta-chai li-ch'eng i* [HY 508], ch. 2, pp. 2b–3a and 6b).

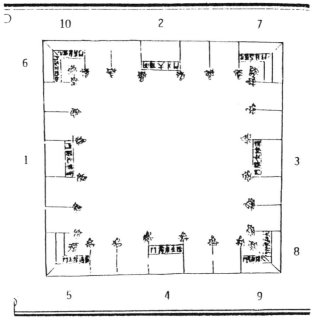

無上黃籙大齋立成儀

**Figure 2. The Structure of the Inner or Ten-Gate Enclosure on the Altar for the Yellow Register Retreat**

1. Ch'ing-hua yüan-yang men: east, vermilion script on a blue-green placard.
2. Tung-yang t'ai-kuang men: south, yellow script on a red placard.
3. T'ung-yin chin-ch'üeh men: west, black script on a white placard.
4. Yin-sheng kuang-ling men: north, blue-green script on a black placard.
5. Ling-t'ung chin-shang men: northeast (north-northeast), white script on a yellow placard.
6. Shih-yang sheng-ch'i men: southeast (east-southeast), white script on a yellow placard.
7. Yüan-huang kao-ch'en men: southwest (south-southwest), white script on a yellow placard.
8. Chiu-hsien fan-hsing men: northwest (west-northwest), white script on a yellow placard.
9. Ta-lo fei-fan men: upper regions (north-northwest), blue-green script on a white placard.
10. Chiu-ling huang-chen men: lower regions (south-southeast), yellow script on a blue-green placard.

This enclosure was constructed with eighteen long and ten short blossom-poles joined by three courses of dark-red or blue-green cordons. Additional ropes were strung between the tall poles of the gates from which were suspended small pennons and branches of flowers. Thirty-two Banners of the Thirty-Two Heavens were hung outside the gates. Blossom-poles to which lanterns were attached were planted inside the inner altar's enclosure between each pair of its poles (*Wu-shang huang-lu ta-chai li-ch'eng i* [HY 508], ch. 2, p. 1a–b).

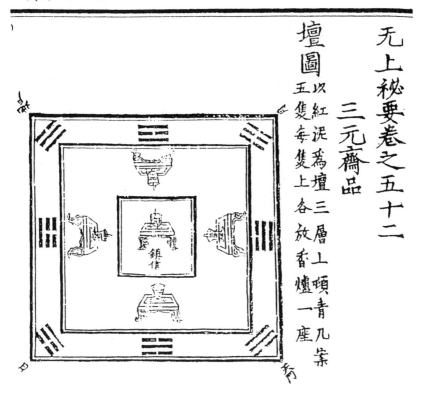

要祕上无

壇圖

无上祕要卷之五十二

三元齋品

以紅泥為壇三層上頂青几案玉隻每隻上各放香爐一座

**Figure 3. The Arrangement of the Altar Tables for the
Performance of the Retreat for the Three Primes**

This configuration does not represent the plan employed for altars at Ling-pao
investitures. The four gates of the outer enclosure depicted here were those for
the Capital Altar or second enclosure at Ling-pao retreats, the eight trigrams
from the *I-ching* represented placards that were suspended from the frame of the
outermost enclosure in the ten-gate altar for the Yellow Register Retreat, and
the tables were all deployed inside the Inner Altar at the five gates during Ling-
pao ordinations. Nevertheless, the illustration provides a general impression of
how the tables were arrayed, their heights, and their functions as supports for
incense burners during such ordinations (*Wu-shang pi-yao* [HY 1130], ch. 52,
p. 1a).

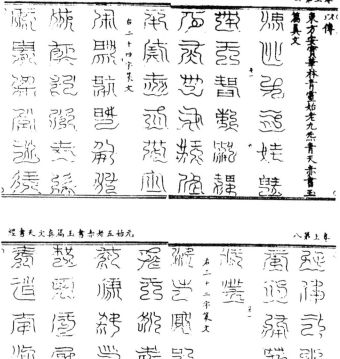

**Figure 4. The True Writ for the East**

The reproduction of the True Writ on the Jade Slats in Red Script for the Blue-Green Heaven of the Nine Ethers provided here encompasses the first, second, and most of the third paragraphs. The ends of the first and second stanzas are marked by lines in standard Chinese calligraphy giving the number of graphs in these sections. The word for secret *(pi)* has been erroneously deleted from the lines *(Yüan-shih wu-lao ch'ih-shu yü-p'ien chen-wen t'ien-shu ching* [HY 22], ch. 1, pp. 7a–8b. For a version of the writ in regular characters see the *T'ai-shang tung-hsüan ling-pao shou-tu i* [HY 528], pp. 25b6–26a1).

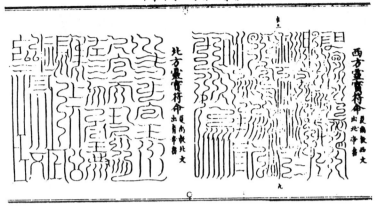

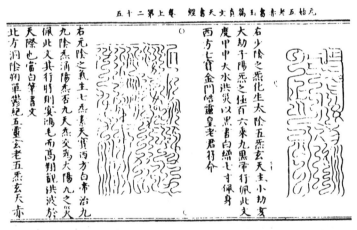

**Figure 5. The Ling-pao Talisman of the West**

The right half of the upper reproduction is the talisman for the Sovereign of the West, the fourth of the Five Ling-pao Talismans, as it appears in the *T'ai-shang ling-pao wu-fu hsü* (HY 388, ch. 3, p. 11a), a text that dates, in part, to the late third century A.D. According to its gloss it issues (generates) the talisman for the Emperor of the North, which appears to its left. The reproduction below is the version of the same writ as it appears in the *Yüan-shih wu-lao ch'ih-shu yü-p'ien chen-wen t'ien-shu ching* (HY 22, ch. 1, p. 25) of A.D. 400. This later rendition is split in two. The right half represents the lesser yin ether that transforms and gives birth to the five ethers of the black heaven (north) and the left the primordial yin ether that produces the treasure of the seven ethers for the plain white heaven (the west).

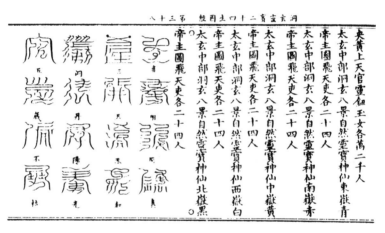

**Figure 6. The Jade Taboos of the Five Demons (Upper)
and The Jade Instructions in Red Graphs for the Middle Section
and the Governor of the Great Red Heaven (Lower)**

(Upper) Each of the cognomens and taboos for the five Demon Monarchs is given in talismanic graphs with their equivalents in standard calligraphy beneath in this passage. (Lower) This is the first half of the writ, four of eight lines, dedicated to the Eight Effulgent Spirits of the chest in the human body and the celestial monarch of the Ta-ch'ih Heaven. Preceding it is the concluding portion of the roster for the numinous functionaries presiding in that section of the body (*Tung-hsüan ling-pao erh-shih-ssu sheng-t'u ching* [HY 1396], pp. 20b–21a and 38a–b).

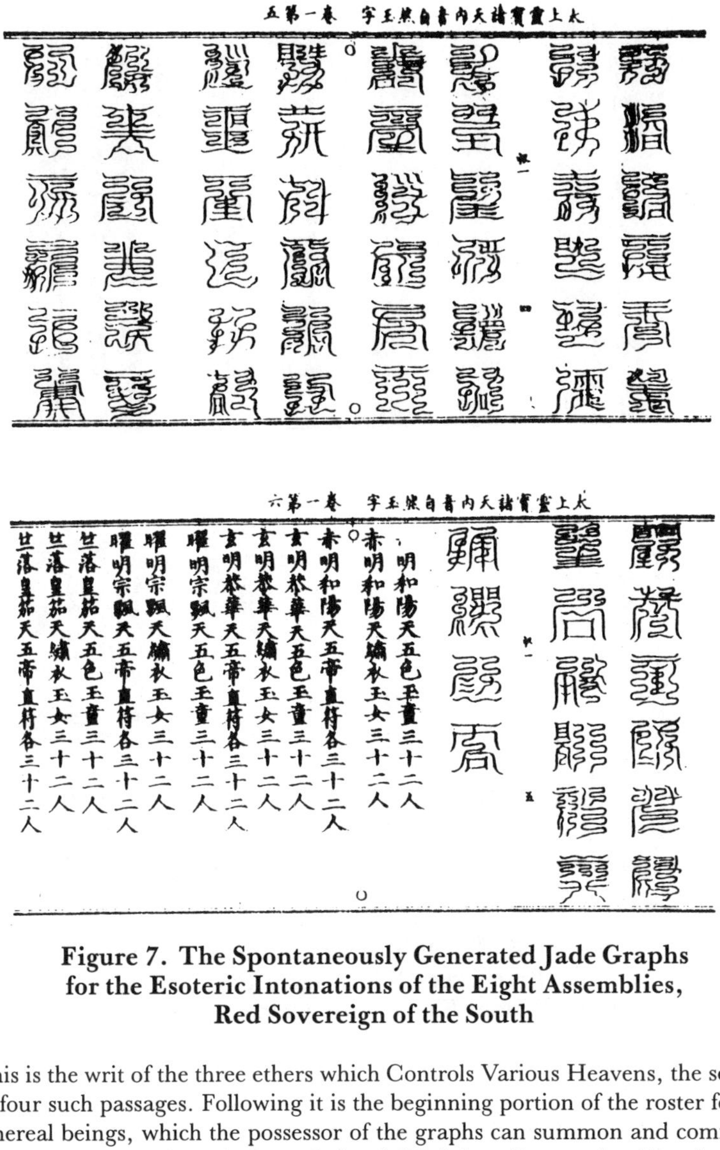
太上靈寶諸天內音自然玉字　卷一第五
太上靈寶諸天內音自然玉字　卷一第六
明和陽天五色玉童三十二人
赤明和陽天繡衣玉女三十二人
赤明和陽天五帝直符各三十二人
玄明恭華天五色玉童三十二人
玄明恭華天繡衣玉女三十二人
玄明恭華天五帝直符各三十二人
曜明宗飄天五色玉童三十二人
曜明宗飄天繡衣玉女三十二人
曜明宗飄天五帝直符各三十二人
竺落皇笳天五色玉童三十二人
竺落皇笳天繡衣玉女三十二人
竺落皇笳天五帝直符各三十二人

**Figure 7. The Spontaneously Generated Jade Graphs for the Esoteric Intonations of the Eight Assemblies, Red Sovereign of the South**

This is the writ of the three ethers which Controls Various Heavens, the second of four such passages. Following it is the beginning portion of the roster for the ethereal beings, which the possessor of the graphs can summon and command when he activates the writ through ritual *(T'ai-shang ling-pao chu-t'ien nei-yin tzu-jan yü-tzu* [HY 97], ch. 1, pp. 5–6. For the version of the Jade Graphs in standard Chinese calligraphy from "The Hidden Discourse of the Great Brahman" see the *Ling-pao wu-liang tu-jen shang-p'in miao-ching* [HY 1], ch. 1, pp. 16b9–17a4).

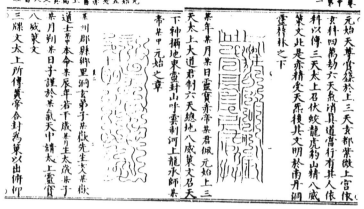

**Figure 8. The Slip-Board Writs (Upper)
and The Blue-Green Sovereign's True Talisman
of the Primordial Commencement (Lower)**

(Upper) The talisman on the right was inscribed on the first board, the statement which follows it on the second, and the talisman on the left on the third. The final passage on the left is a request for transmission of the writs which ordinands completed by supplying particulars about themselves. (Lower) This talisman was placed in the second segment from the top of the Divine Staffs (*Yüan-shih wu-lao ch'ih-shu yü-p'ien chen-wen t'ien-shu ching* [HY 22], ch. 2, pp. 1a–2b, and ch. 1, p. 35a–b).

# APPENDIX ONE
## Chang Wan-fu's Account of the
## Princesses' Ling-pao Investiture

This is a translation of a passage on pages 18a9–20b5 of chapter 2 in the *Ch'uan-shou san-tung ching-chieh fa-lu lüeh-shuo* (HY 1231), compiled by Chang Wan-fu (fl. 710–713), whose postscript is dated January 13, 713. Subtitles, which are not part of the original text, have been added to facilitate reference.

### Introduction

On the Tenth of February, 711, I witnessed Princess Gold-Immortal and Princess Jade-Perfected visit Reverend Preceptor Shih—

> Grand Canon Preceptor of the Three Caverns *(San-tung ta fa-shih);*
> Abbot of the Supreme Purity Abbey *(T'ai-ch'ing kuan chu);*
> Grandee of Illustrious Noble Rank, Gold Signet and Purple Ribbon *(Chin-tzu kuang-lu tai-fu);*
> Chief of the Service for Stentorian Annunciation *(Hung-lu ch'ing);*
> Principality-Founding Duke, Ho-nei Commandery *(Ho-nei chün k'ai-kuo kung);*
> Pillar of State, First Class *(Shang chu-kuo)*

—to receive investiture as Taoist priests [*shou-tao;* literally, receive the Tao], rend

> the Self-Generated Tally of the Numinous Treasure *(Ling-pao tzu-jan ch'üan),*

and secure

the Canon of the Central Covenant in Eight Satchels *(Chung-meng pa-chih ching)*, forty-seven scrolls,
two True Writ Registers *(Chen-wen erh lu)*,
Belt Talismans *(P'ei-fu)*, and
Staffs *(Ts'e-chang)*

in the Abbey of Refuge in Perfection (Kuei-chen kuan) at the Great Inner Palace (Ta-nei).

### *Altar:*

So earth was excavated to form an altar, in three tiers, which was one *chang*, two *ch'ih* (about 3.54 meters or 11.6 feet) high. Gold lotus blossom poles *(chin-lien hua-tsuan)*, purple and gold title-tablets *(tzu-chin t'i-pang)*, and a blue-green silk cordon *(ch'ing-ssu)* encircled the altar.

### *Floor Coverings:*

Cushions of layered cloth were made from

eastern blue-green brocade *(tung-fang ch'ing-chin)*,
southern cinnabar (red) brocade,
western white brocade,
northern purple brocade, and
central yellow brocade

and there were also dragon whisker *(lung-hsü)*, phoenix pinion *(feng-ko)*, and other types of mats for covering the earth.

### *Table Settings:*

Brocades were fabricated according to the colors of the directions for each of the five tables. Curly gold dragons *(ch'iu chin-lung)* and jade disks *(yü-pi)* [were placed on the tables] to defend them.

### *Articles of Appeasement:*

In addition,

eighteen lengths of blue-green silk net *(ch'ing-lo)*,
six lengths of scarlet silk net,
fourteen lengths of white silk net,
ten lengths of black silk net, and
twenty-four lengths of yellow silk net

were used to appease *(an)* [the gods of] the five directions.

*Pledges:*

To bind [the ordinands] to the numinous bureaucrats *(Ling-kuan)*

240 lengths of purple silk net,
480 lengths of pongee,
240 strings of cash,
200 ounces of gold,
25 lengths of five-color cloud brocade,
120 catties of incense,
500 ounces of continuous blue-green Seven Treasure thread *(Ch'i-pao chou-tsu ch'ing-ssu),*
24,000 sheets of memorial paper,
240 writing brushes and 240 inksticks,
12 knives for straightening documents *(t'ing-shu tao),*
38 knives and 38 kerchiefs for preserving injunctions *(hu-chieh tao-chin),*
6 gold dragons, and
54 gold knobs

were employed to defend at the altar's center.

*Braziers:*

There were also

coiled-dragon incense braziers *(p'an-lung hsiang-lu),*
dancing-phoenix incense braziers,
auspicious-leaf incense braziers,
propitious-blossom incense braziers,
lotus-blossom incense braziers, and
magic-mushroom incense braziers

together with incense caskets and incense chests, all of which were fabricated from pure gold and solid silver.

*Table Cloths:*

There were also brocade cloths with matched cranes and paired simurghs, flying dragons, and bowing phoenixes.

*Canon Wrappers:*

There were also wrappers for covering the scriptures embroidered with Divine Diamond Kings; Immortal Lads and Jade Maids; smoke-clouded landscapes; grasses, trees, insects, and fish; sacred beasts and numinous birds; and ornamented marvels and precious objects.

*Tables:*

There were also tables of carved jade, chased gold, purple sandalwood, white sandalwood, and aloeswood, all of which were made with carved or engraved ornamentations of soaring simurghs and dancing phoenixes, gold blossoms, and jade leaves.

*Canon Cases:*

There were also

    Seven Treasure cases *(Ch'i-pao han),*
    Nine Immortal cases,
    yellow-gold cases, and
    white-jade cases,

for holding the scriptures.

*Satchels:*

There were also

    bags of blue-green brocade, *ch'ing-chin chih nang,*
    bags of scarlet brocade,
    bags of plain white brocade,
    bags of purple brocade,
    bags of yellow brocade,
    bags of cloud brocade, and
    bags of polychrome brocade,

for holding the liturgical registers *(fa-lu).*

*Food Containers:*

There were also kitchen baskets and hampers, all embellished with pearl and jade ornaments of such marvelous craftsmanship and beauty as the world has never possessed nor the eye ever seen.

*Pennons:*

There were also

banners of the Perfected *(chen-jen fan)*,
banners of the Jade Lads and Jade Maids,
banners of the Divine Diamond Kings,
brocaded lotus-blossom banners *(lien-hua lou-fan)*,
brocaded magic-mushroom banners,
brocaded coiled-dragon banners,
brocaded dancing-phoenix banners,
brocaded soaring-simurgh banners, and
brocaded flying-crane banners.

Some [had motifs of] brilliant suns in flying clouds, dark shadows embracing smoke, revolving graphs and unfurling flowers, linked gold, and strung jade. Others [had designs of] painted landscape images, birds and animals of strange shapes, propitious grasses and auspicious blossoms, and the sun piercing the unfolding clouds. These banners were suspended from the altar's four sides.

*Lighting Accoutrements:*

There were also

gold-lotus lamp trees *(chin-lien hua-shu)*,
silver-lotus lamp trees,
Seven Treasure lamp trees, and
polychrome lamp trees.

Chiliads and myriads of them were arrayed on and below the altar as well as within the cloister of the abbey. The illumination of their beams pierced and penetrated [the dark]. There were also

polychrome blossom candles *(wu-se hua chu)*,
gold coiled-dragon candles,
silver soaring-simurgh candles,
thousand-petaled lotus candles,
nine-color cloud candles,
lanterns of like minds *(t'ung-hsin chih teng)*,
lanterns of split blossoms,
candles of strung pearls,
lanterns of threaded blossoms,
divine revolving lanterns,
numinous flying-terrace lanterns,
purple flaming-orchid lanterns *(tzu-t'ao lan teng)*,
blue-green beamed magic-mushroom lanterns *(ch'ing-kuang chih teng)*,
thousand boughs of rosy-blossom lanterns,

moonlit thousand-leaf lanterns *(yüeh chao ch'ien-yeh teng)*,
five-star lanterns *(wu-hsing teng)*,
seven planetoid lanterns *(wu-yao teng)*,
twenty-eight asterism lanterns *(erh-shih-pa hsiu teng)*,
thirty-six heaven lanterns,
sheathed-light lanterns, and
extinguishing-smoke lanterns

which radiated their brilliance within and without.

### The Su-ch'i:

On the eve of the twenty-seventh day (February 19, 711), the officiants performed the rites of the Tao *(hsing Tao li)*. Just as they began to chant the retreat of annunciation an auspicious snow drifted down like flowers. As they were about to reveal the True Writs, a propitious cloud floated [over the altar] like a canopy. During the fourth watch (2:00 to 4:00 A.M.) of that night, Lord Lao (Lao Tzu Deified) descended to the altar and spoke to the Princesses.

### The Transmission of the Procedures:

On the day for the transmission of the procedures an auspicious cloud of five colors and incense smoke of the eight inhalations [appeared]. When the transmission of the procedures had concluded, both Princesses abandoned their couches to recline on armrests and cushions.

### Conclusion:

The value of the musical instruments and clothing [for wearing] in secular life, 500 sets of pongee for each woman; 10,000 lengths of brocade and net; cash, colored silks, and the liturgical paraphernalia *(fa-chü)* exceeded 10,000 strings of cash (that is, 10,000,000 cash). And this figure does not include the liturgical objects which defended the altar.

# APPENDIX TWO
## A Synopsis of the Ordination Rite
### for the Ling-pao Canon

This outline is based largely on the *Tung-hsüan ling-pao tzu-jan ch'üan i* (HY 522) of unknown date (Section II, Part A) and the *T'ai-shang tung-hsüan ling-pao shou-tu i* (HY 528) by Lu Hsiu-ching (Sections III, V, and VI). Its purpose is to provide an overview of the investiture process as it may have existed in the early eighth century and to describe in some detail those facets of the liturgy omitted or cursorily treated in Chapter Three. Those ritual acts in the investiture already analyzed in that section of this study are generally listed by title only and marked by asterisks here.

*I.   Visiting the Preceptor and Submitting the Statement *(I-shih t'ou-tz'u* or *I-shih)*, February 11, 711 (HY 1130, ch. 35, p. 1a–b).

II.  The Initial Covenant *(Ch'u-meng)*.

    A. The Rending of the Spontaneously Generated Tally *(P'o Tzu-jan ch'üan)* (HY 522).

        1. Lighting the Censer *(Fa-lu)*. After the incense has been ignited the officiant faces east, thrice offers incense, clacks his teeth three times, and recites this invocation (HY 522, p. 1a–b). The format of this text is virtually identical to that given in the Nocturnal Annunciation (Section III, Part B, number 9 below).

        2. Externalizing the Bureaucrats *(Ch'u-kuan)*. The officiant executes a long kneeling, clacks his teeth twenty-four times, and recites this text, in which he states that

he is going to rend the tally for transmitting the canon and venerate the Red Petition on Yellow Silk (HY 522, pp. 1b–4a). The format of this document is roughly the same as that given in the Reading of the Yellow Silk Petition (Section III, Part A, number 3 below).

3. [Dispatching the Memorial *(Sung piao)*]. The officiant clacks his teeth three times and utters an invocation, in which he calls upon the spirit emissaries to split up, seize his Petition on Plain Red Silk for Rending the Tally of the Great Scriptures Containing the Peerless, Most Perfect Five Slats, and convey it to the upper regions (HY 522, p. 1a–b). This document is somewhat similar to that in the Nocturnal Annunciation (Section III, Part B, number 13 below).

4. The Annunciation of the Rite *(Ch'i-shih)*. The officiant executes a long kneeling and recites this text, in which he announces that he is going to rend the tally and transmit the canon (HY 522, pp. 4b–5b). Although the beginning resembles the text given in the Nocturnal Annunciation (Section III, Part B, number 14 below), it is, for the most part, entirely different.

5. Rending the Tally *(Fen-ch'üan)*. There is no description of this act in this text (HY 522, p.5b).

6. The Declaration of the Cinnabar Ink Writ *(Kao tan-shui wen)*. Before he transmits the tally, the officiant returns to the north and faces the ordinands, who turn to the left, face south, and execute long kneelings. The officiant raises the Cinnabar Ink Writ, faces north in his mind, and recites the writ (HY 522, pp. 5b–6b). Although this text contains many elements common to writs in the Nocturnal Annunciation, it is quite different from the version in Lu Hsiu-ching's liturgy (Section III, Part B, number 21 below).

7. The Transmission of the Tally *(Shou-ch'üan)*. There is no description of this act in this text (HY 522, p. 6b).

8. Chanting the Hymns for the Five Perfected *(Sung wu chen-jen sung)*. The officiant rises, burns incense, scatters flowers, and tours the altar, chanting this hymn in one stanza (HY 522, p. 6b). No text is supplied. This hymn has five stanzas in the Nocturnal Annunciation (Section III, Part B, number 15 below).

9. Bowing to the Capital *(Pai-tu)* (HY 522, p. 6b). There

is no section comparable to this rite in the Nocturnal Annunciation.

10. The Invocation *(Chu)*. The ordinands execute long kneelings and grasp their pledges. The officiant clacks his teeth thirty-six times and visualizes in his mind the colors of his five viscera. He causes them to intermingle completely and form a cloud that covers the scripture, himself, and his followers. Then the preceptor recites the invocation in which he states that he is conferring the canon and warns that those who transmit the scriptures in violation of the regulations will fall into hell (HY 522, p. 7a). This visualization is part of the transmission of the True Writ Registers in the Nocturnal Annunciation (Section III, Part B, number 23 below).

11. Receiving the Canon *(Shou ching)*. There is no description of this act in this text (HY 522, p. 7a).

12. The Salute and Bows to the Ten Directions in Circuit *(Li-pai chou shih-fang)*. Starting from the north and turning toward the east (the participants proceed to each point of the compass and stop there) to bow and salute. They visualize the true forms of the Most Exalted Ten Directions as images of the Directions (HY 522, p. 7a). This visualization and form of worship were parts of the transmission of the True Writ Registers in the Nocturnal Annunciation (Section III, Part B, number 23 below).

13. Chanting the Lyrics on the Three Paths and Five Sufferings *(Sung san-t'u wu-k'u tz'u)*. The officiant chants this, but no text is supplied (HY 522, p. 7a). See the Nocturnal Annunciation (Section III, Part B, number 35 below).

14. Chanting the Stanzas for Wisdom *(Sung chih-hui)*. The officiant chants these three stanzas. No text is supplied (HY 522, p. 7a).

*15. The Discourse on the Doctrine and the Transmission of the Ten Injunctions *(Shuo-fa shou shih-chieh)*. The officiant performs these tasks, but no text is provided (HY 522, p. 7a).

16. The Enunciation of Merit and the Restoration of the Bureaucrats *(Yen-kung fu-kuan)*. The officiant recites this passage. No text is supplied (HY 522, p. 7a). See

the Nocturnal Annunciation (Section III, Part B, number 36 below).

*B.  The Conferral of the Injunctions for Arresting the Six Emotions *(Pi-sai liu-ch'ing chieh)* (HY 177, p. 6a–b).

III.  The Central Covenant *(Chung-meng)*.

A.  The Reading of the Petition on Yellow Silk *(Tu huang-tseng chang)*, February 18, 711 (HY 528, pp. 4a–7b).

1.  The Entrance. The officiant and the ordinands enter through the Terrestrial Portal (the southeast gate of the second enclosure) and turn to the left. The preceptor enters the regal gate of the inner altar, faces north, and thrice offers incense. The two True Writ Registers were placed on a table earlier. The ordinands move to the southern side of the outer altar, face north, and make three bows *(pai)*, prostrating themselves and knocking their foreheads on the ground opposite the petition. The officiant sounds Heaven's Drum *(ming T'ien-ku,* taps his fingers on the sides of his head) thirty-six times (to alert the Thirty-Six Heavens) (HY 528, p. 4a–b).

Note: For the relative positions of the actors on the stage at various points during the rite, see Figures 2, 3, and 4. According to the *T'ai-chen k'o,* an ancient Taoist code, striking the drum and sounding the bell summon the immortals and cause the sages to assemble. It goes on to say that there were two types of liturgical drums: clacking of the teeth and metal drums or stone chimes (cited in HY 463, ch. 8, p. 10b).

2.  Lighting the Censer. Lu Hsiu-ching does not provide the text of this invocation at this point, but it probably included some statement to the effect that the officiant was burning incense for submitting the memorial at the altar erected for conducting the Nocturnal Annunciation (HY 528, p. 4b).

3.  Externalizing the Bureaucrats. The officiant recites a long text in which he summons forth clusters of deities from his own body designating them by their titles, describing their raiments, assigning them positions inside and outside of his body, and commissioning

spirit emissaries to announce his submission of this memorial to various regions of the macrocosm (the Twenty-Four Celestial Master Parishes, the Seventy-Two Elysian Fields, 360 numinous mountains, the sun, the moon, the stars, the Three Realms, and the like) as well as to the highest deities (the gods of the Five Marchmounts, Lao Tzu Deified, the Celestial Venerables, and the like). He concludes with a declaration that he, the preceptor, is about to transmit the True Writs, the Esoteric Pronunciations of the Eight Effulgent Spirits *(Pa-ching nei-yin),* and the two registers. All the while, the petition on plain yellow silk reposes on the table before him (HY 528, pp. 4a–6b).

*4. The Reading of the Yellow Silk Petition.

*5. The Rescript for Revering the Compact *(Chung-yüeh ch'ih).*

*6. The Invocation.

7. The Restoration of the Bureaucrats *(Fu-kuan).* The officiant orders the inner spirits to return to his body and assume their customary stations therein so that they can stabilize its microcosm and protect it. He cautions them to put themselves in order and wait for his summons for them to emerge again later. The preceptor then beats the Drum of the Law *(Fa-ku)* three strokes and thrice ingests his breath (HY 528, p. 7a–b).

8. Returning the Censer *(Fu-lu).* The officiant rises, bows twice, and orders the gods attending the incense to cause the spontaneous production of liquid gold, cinnabar's red and jade's green, and the magic mushroom's blossom in the oratory. A request that all the Perfected and Powers assemble in front of the censer follows. The officiant prays that this multitude of spirits will protect so-and-so (the participants in the ordination) so that they will attain immortality early, that the August Sovereign will greatly bless them, and that all under heaven will enjoy divine mercy. Finally, the officiant charges the Jade Lads and Jade Maids of the Ten Directions with the task of attending to and protecting the incense smoke so that it can convey his message to the Supreme Limitless Tao [the Jade Emperor] (HY 528, p. 7b; and HY 1130, ch. 39, p. 4b).

*Note:* Lu Hsiu-ching provides no instructions or text for this rite. The version of it given in the *Wu-shang pi-yao*'s protocols for the investiture conferring all groups of canon and that for the ordination transmitting the Ling-pao scriptures alone are identical to the form provided in the rules for the primitive Nocturnal Annunciation except that the texts of the prayers are different (HY 1130, ch. 35, p. 12a; ch. 39, pp. 4b and 11a; and HY 1400, p.39a).

9. Exit. When this has been completed, the officiant and the ordinands leave the altar by way of the Terrestrial Portal in the second enclosure (HY 528, p. 7b).

B. The Nocturnal Annunciation for Investiture, the night of February 19, 711 (HY 528, pp. 8a–50b).

1. The Procession. When all is ready, a Cantor strikes the bell. The Canon Preceptors and the ordinands approach the altar. The Three Preceptors and the Five Cantors *(Wu-pao)* are majestically attired in their liturgical vestments, and the ordinands are clothed in black caps and coarse yellow habits. First they lead the ordinands around the altar, making three revolutions, until they reach the southeast corner, where they stand facing west and sing praises without end. Next they lead the preceptors around the altar, making three revolutions, until they reach the northwest corner (HY 528, p. 8a).

*Note: Wu-pao* (the Five Guarantors) was an alternate, perhaps archaic, term for cantor (HY 445, p. 2b).

2. A Visualization. From a distance of seven or thirty paces the officiant clacks his teeth thirty-two times (to alert the Thirty-Two Heavens). Then he visualizes a purple cloud that covers the entire altar like a crown and a host of warriors—ten thousand for each of the Five Sovereigns. Then he utters an invocation (HY 528, p. 8a).

3. The Invocation for Entering the Portal *(Ju-hu chu)*. Walking gravely, the officiant ascends the altar from the Celestial Portal in the northwest and recites this invocation, in which he requests that the Jade Lads, Jade Maids, and other emissaries open communica-

tion with the Chamber of the Tao *(Tao-shih)* and asks that the Vital Energy of the Orthodox Spirit and Superior Prime enter his body (HY 528, p. 8b; and HY 1130, ch. 39, p. 5b).

> *Note:* There is a directive for executing this rite in Lu's manual, but no text.

4.  The Quiet Visualization of the Three Preceptors *(Ju ching-ssu san-shih)*. The officiant first visualizes his Scripture Preceptor in the place (direction) where he resides, bows thrice in his mind, and prays that the master will attain the Tao of immortality so that he, the officiant, can ascend and be saved. Second, he envisions his Register Preceptor in the place where he resides, bows thrice in his mind, and prays that the master will become a flying immortal so that he, the officiant, can save his ancestors to the seventh degree and his parents, who will then ascend to the Celestial Hall (T'ien-t'ang) before their alloted time; and to enable him, the officiant, to attain the True Tao and ascend to the realm of the formless. Lastly, he visualizes his Initiation Preceptor in the place where he resides, bows thrice in his mind, and prays that the master will rise to the highest ranks of the eminent immortals so that he can save him, the officiant, from the Five Destinies—as a spirit, man, domestic animal, hungry ghost, or denizen in hell—and the Eight Difficulties—forms of disease—have his name entered on an immortal register, and become a Perfected for eternity (HY 1130, ch. 35, p. 2b).

> *Note:* This rite has no place in Lu's liturgy, but by the early eighth century it was a standard fixture in all Taoist rites (HY 445, p. 1a). The text paraphrased here is part of the ordination ritual for conferring up to five canons.

5.  The Audience with the Nine Heavens *(Chiu-t'ien ch'ao)*. Ascending to the Capital Altar, the officiant turns to the left, faces the northwest, and bows nine times as if at an audience with the monarchs of the Nine Heavens. Clacking his teeth nine times, he recites an invo-

cation declaring that he is going to transmit the canon, the Treasure Scriptures of the Nine Heavens *(Chiu-t'ien pao-ching),* to so-and-so and requests that certain ethereal beings descend and inspect the Writ of the Covenant, what is to be announced, and what is to be transferred (HY 528, p. 8b).

6. The Announcement *(Ch'i).* The officiant must inform the altar. Walking to the left he returns (to the northwest), faces the southeast, and bows twice. Then he submits a prayer to the Eminent Exalted Celestial Monarchs of the Primordial Commencement, informing them that he is transmitting under covenant the mysterious canon on this mysterious altar during this auspicious hour of this day, and implores the gods to report the matter to the Five Sovereigns and numinous mountains so that the latter can inspect the rite (HY 528, pp. 8b–9a).

7. Chanting the Gold Perfected's Petition of the Great Space *(Sung Chin-chen t'ai-k'ung chang).* The officiant stands and orders the ordinands to enter the Capital Altar from the Terrestrial Portal in the southeast (corner of the second enclosure), where they perform nine bows facing the northwest. Afterward the preceptor turns to the left and stands above the Terrestrial Portal while the ordinands turn to the left and stand above the Celestial Portal. Turning toward the southeast, the students bow twice and then return to the north side, face south, and prostrate themselves. The officiant turns to stand facing north, clacks his teeth thirty-six times, and chants this petition, which has the power to control the myriad demons. When he has finished this, he walks to the left and, with the ordinands following him, enters the inner altar through the Main Portal (HY 528, pp. 9a–10a).

> *Note:* In this passage Lu Hsiu-ching says that the officiant and ordinands enter the inner altar through the Celestial Gate, but this is impossible since that gate was a portal to the middle or Capital Altar. However, in a note he states that someone said that they enter through the main gate, which means the Regal Gate.

8. Chanting the Invocation of the Guardian Powers and Gods *(Sung wei-ling-shen chu)*. Turning to the left, the officiant thrice offers the incense of the Five Directions at each station, starting in the east, circling the altar, and returning to the west side. Facing the east, the preceptor closes his eyes and visualizes his five viscera, the Five Marchmounts, five stars, and Five Sovereigns, which thereafter act as a defensive guard inside his body. Light, emanating from the rear of his lungs, covers his entire body, which takes on a golden hue. He then envisions a round beam in the image of the sun at the nape of his neck, and causes it to radiate to and illuminate the Ten Directions. After this the officiant chants the invocation (in five parts) to the Five Directions, evoking various ethereal beings associated with the radiant energies of these regions to restrain, obstruct, slay, and otherwise deter demons and specters (HY 528, p. 10a–11a).

9. Lighting of the Censer. After the incense has been ignited, the officiant clacks his teeth twenty-four times (to alert the twenty-four energies), calls on Lao Tzu Deified to summon forth several clusters of spirits, thirty-six in each group, from his, the priest's body. These spirits then announce to the Orthodox Deities and Perfected Bureaucrats of the soil and the hamlet's territory in the district where the rite is taking place that the officiant is burning incense to transmit the canon. The declaration concludes with a prayer requesting that the true and perfect vital energies of the Most Exalted Ten Directions descend and permeate his, the preceptor's, body and that what he is announcing will be conveyed promptly to the Limitless Tao [the Jade Emperor] (HY 528, pp. 11b–12a).

10. Singing the Formulas for the Celestial Venerables of the Ten Directions *(Ch'ang shih-fang t'ien-tsun fang)*. The officiant leads the ordinands, who walk to the left holding visitation tablets *(hsieh-pan)* in their hands, to the west side. Facing east they sing the formula for the Celestial Venerable of the east with their tablets upright, and everyone bows thrice (once is sufficient, but it is not necessary to bow at all). This act is

repeated for the Celestial Venerables of the south, west, north, northeast, southeast, northwest, the upper regions, and the lower regions. The ten formulas are oaths of allegiance to these deities in which the participants most earnestly place their fates in the hands of the gods. At the end, the officiant reminds the gods that he submitted the Yellow Silk Petition the day before at such-and-such an hour in accordance with the protocols of the Instructions for the Covenant of the Grand Perfection *(T'ai-chen meng chüeh)* and the Instructions for the Retreat *(Chai-chüeh)*. He asks that nothing, especially wind and rain, be allowed to hinder the proceedings. Everyone knocks his head and beats his brow (HY 528, pp. 12a–13b).

11. Externalizing the Bureaucrats. The officiant proceeds to his station and faces east. The ordinands return to the east side, face west, and prostrate themselves on the ground. The preceptor executes a long kneeling, clacks his teeth twenty-four times, and externalizes twenty clusters of emissaries, Jade Lads, and the like— twenty-four in each group; twenty-two armies of 910,000 mounted warriors each; and ten sets of Jade Maids and celestial clerks, twenty-four in each group, from his body. He arrays these bureaucrats and cavalrymen around himself and visualizes a five-colored cloud covering his body. Then he commands the spirit emissaries to split up in order to report the words, which he is about to utter, to the gods of various regions in the cosmos. In his statement, which follows, he addresses the Five Elders and other deities, informing them that so-and-so, whose destinies have assigned them the titles Perfecteds of such-and-such Marchmounts and who have already received the Numinous Writs of the Nine Heavens for the Superior Procedure *(Shang-fa chiu-t'ien ling-wen)* and presented pledges, seek the True Writs and Jade Slats in Red Script of the Five Elders of the Primordial Commencement *(Yüan-shih wu-lao ch'ih-shu yü-p'ien chen-wen)* and other writs as well as the Bamboo Staffs. The participants have fasted three days in preparation for performing the Nocturnal Revelation in accordance with the Code of the Powers and the Immortals *(Ling-hsien k'o-p'in)* in the Slip Writs

of the Yellow Register *(Huang-lu chien-wen).* The weather is clear, there is no wind, and the gold and silk are present to appease the powers (HY 528, pp. 13b–21a).

12. Reading the Memorial's Writ *(Tu piao-wen).* This is an oral recitation of the Yellow Silk Petition, which lies exposed on a table (HY 528, p. 21a).

13. Dispatching the Memorial. The officiant clacks his teeth three times and utters an invocation which calls upon the spirit messengers to seize and convey the petition to the Supreme Sovereigns, the Five Elders of the Primordial Commencement. He further requests that errors in the text which are not written according to the old procedures be corrected and warns the emissaries not to allow the superior officials and demons to interfer with their execution of the task which he has assigned them or to damage the document that he has entrusted to them (HY 528, p. 21a–b).

14. Annunciation and Veneration *(Ch'i-feng).* The ordinands turn to the left and face south. The officiant turns to the left, faces north, executes a long kneeling, clacks his teeth *(ming-ku,* sounds the drum) thirty-six times, and reads the announcement. He repeats his titles, evokes certain spirits to inspect the covenantal writ, and addresses the Five Elders and other deities. The preceptor assures the gods that the ordinands have the proper character and have submitted the appropriate pledges for ordination. He then declares that he is going to confer:

   a) the True Writs and Treasure Talismans of the Five Elders from the Primordial Origin of the Numinous Treasure in Red Calligraphy *(Ling-pao yüan-shih wu-lao ch'ih-shu chen-wen pao-fu),*
   b) the Jade Graphs for the Esoteric Intonations of the Eight Effulgent Spirits in the Three Divisions and the Twenty-Four Divine and Perfected Officials, Clerks, and Warriors in All Heavens,
   c) the Slip Writs of the Eight Authorities *(Pa-wei ts'e-wen),* and
   d) the Divine Staffs *(Shen-chang)*

on the prescribed altar under the covenants and oaths sworn to the Nine Heavens without violating the regulations governing improper transmissions (HY 528, pp. 21b–23b).

15. Chanting the Hymns of the Five Perfected *(Sung-yung wu chen-jen sung)*. They rise, and the officiant thrice offers the incense of the Five Directions with the ordinands following along behind him. Starting in the east, the procession circles the altar, stopping at each direction and quickly performing long kneelings to offer the incense. Then it tours the altar, making three revolutions and scattering flowers to the Ten Directions. When this has been completed, the preceptor chants the five hymns with the ordinands saluting twice and singing praises after each salute (HY 528, pp. 23b–25a).

*16. Chanting the Preface to the True Writs *(Sung chen-wen hsü)* (HY 528, p. 25a–b).

*17. The Transmission of the True Writs *(Shou chen-wen)* (HY 528, p. 25a).

*a)* The Jade Slats *(Yü-p'ien)* (HY 528, pp. 25b–28a).

*b)* The Jade Taboos of the Five Demons *(Wu-mo yü-hui)* (HY 528, p. 28a).

*c)* The Jade Instructions in Red Graphs for the Eight Effulgent Spirits who Rule the Upper Division and Ch'ing-wei Heaven, the Middle Division and Great Red Heaven, and the Lower Division and Yü-yü Heaven (HY 528, pp. 28a–29a).

*d)* The Writs for Managing All Heavens in the Spontaneously Generated Jade Graphs of Esoteric Intonations for the Eight Assemblies (HY 528, pp. 29a–31b).

*18. Reading the Covenant's Writ *(Tu meng-wen)*. The writ was read from the year *(t'ai-sui,* date) onward. Lu Hsiu-ching supplies no text at this point, and it is not clear to what he is referring (HY 528, p. 31b).

*19. The Transmission of the Slip-Board Writs *(Tu ts'e-wen)* (HY 528, pp. 31b–33a).

*20. Sealing the Staffs *(Feng chang)* (HY 528, pp. 32b–36a).

*21. The Declaration of the Cinnabar Ink Writ (HY 528, pp. 36b–37a).

*22. The Ordinands Read Their Own Covenants *(Ti-tzu tzu meng-wen)* (HY 528, pp. 37a–38a).

*23. The Transmission of the True Writ Registers *(Shou chen-wen lu)* (HY 528, p. 38a-b).

*24. Chanting the Lyrics for Pacing the Void *(Yung Pu-hsü tz'u)* (HY 528, pp. 38b-41a).

*25. Chanting the Hymn for the Salute to the Canon *(Li-ching sung)* (HY 528, p. 41a).

*26. Singing the Three Salutes *(Ch'ang san-li)* (HY 528, p. 41b).

*27. The Discourse on the Interdictory Injunctions of the Primordial Commencement *(Shuo yüan-shih chin-chieh)* (HY 528, pp. 41b-42b).

*28. The Transmission of the Writs for the Six Oaths *(Shou liu-shih wen)* (HY 528, p. 43a-b).

*29. The Transmission of Liturgical Positions to the Ordinands by Means of Slips *(Chien-shou ti-tzu fa-wei)* (HY 528, p. 43b).

30. The Salute to the Original Preceptor *(Li pen-shih)*. They [officiant and ordinands] withdraw and join the ends of their tablets. "I [Lu Hsiu-ching] call this Saluting the Original Preceptor [that is, the ordinand's true master]." The ordinands bow nine times, thrice rising and thrice prostrating. Then they crawl on their hands and knees (HY 526, p. 43b).

> *Note:* Apparently these tablets, like the tallies, were broken or divided, the preceptor retaining his halves and the ordinands theirs. During this ceremony the halves were joined in a symbolic gesture reaffirming the master-student bond.

31. The Audience with the Four Poles *(Ch'ao Ssu-chi)*. The ordinands move to the left, stop at the east side, face west, and bow twice. This ritual is then repeated for the north, east, and south, and is called the Audience of the Four Poles (HY 528, p. 43b).

32. The Salute to the Three Preceptors *(Li san-shih)*. The ordinands return to their stations and bow thrice as a salute to the three officiants who are conducting their investiture rite (HY 528, p. 43b).

33. Reading the Boards *(Tu-pan)*. They return [to their stations] to read the Visitation Boards for the Ten Directions *(Hsieh shih-fang pan)* and the Boards for the Five

Preceptors *(Wu-shih pan),* facing each of the ten directions as before, except in the case of the reading of the Tablets for the Five Preceptors, when they face west (HY 528, p. 43b).

34. The Great Confession *(Ta-hsieh).* The ordinands execute long kneelings, knock their heads and beat their brows countlessly. Then the officiant reads the confession in which he seeks forgiveness for his and the ordinands' sins and violations of the codes. He prays that the emperor, the people, the spirits, and the gods will attain their objectives and be successful in their endeavors, and that those in evil states will be saved (HY 528, pp. 43b–46a).

35. Chanting the Lyrics on the Five Paths and Five Sufferings, eight stanzas. These concern the three evil states —rebirth as a denizen of hell, rebirth as a domestic animal, and rebirth as a hungry ghost—and the five forms of suffering—life, aging, illness, death, and separation. Both of these notions were Buddhist in origin (HY 528, pp. 46a–47a).

36. The Announcement of the Petition for the Enunciation of Merit and the Restoration of the Bureaucrats. The officiant, designating himself by a Celestial Master title, notes his fortune at being a Taoist. He acknowledges the role of the spirit officials in assisting him with the performance of the investiture and recommends them for promotion in the immortal bureaucracy. Then he requests that the emissaries seize this Oral Petition for the Enunciation of Merit and convey it to the Bureaus of the Three Heavens *(San-t'ien ts'ao).* The preceptor signs the document, giving the name of his abbey in such-and-such subprefecture of such-and-such prefecture. This is followed by another Restoration of the Bureaucrats. Afterward the officiant ingests twenty-four breaths (HY 528, pp. 47a–49a).

37. Returning to the Censer. The format of this rite is basically the same as previously described (Section III, Part A, number 8 above), except for the prayer in which the officiant solicites the assistance of the gods to enable him to acquire the Tao and immortality, and to bestow blessings, internal and external, on the ordinands and mercy on their households (HY 528, p. 49b).

38. Chanting the Hymn for Worship of the Injunctions *(Sung feng-chieh sung)*, eighteen verses. Lu Hsiu-ching offers no instructions for this act (HY 528, pp. 49b–50a).

> *Note:* This hymn appears in a scripture from the original Ling-pao canon, *T'ai-shang tung-hsüan ling-pao pen-hsing su-yüan ching* (HY 1106, p. 4b).

39. The Hymn for Returning the Injunctions *(Huan-chieh sung)*, sixteen verses. Lu Hsiu-ching offers no instructions for this act (HY 528, p. 50a–b).

40. Brahman Chanting *(Fan yung)*. The officiant and the ordinands circle the altar, Brahman chanting (HY 528, p. 50b).

41. The Activation of the Talismans for Ascending to Heaven, and Reclining on Earth *(Hsing teng-t'ien chieh-ti fu)*. The former is written on white silk in blue-green ink and the latter on jade-green silk in yellow ink. After the officiant activates the talismans, the ordinands are led [to the south] where they face north and bow four times as if at an audience with the Most Exalted Jade Dawn; [to the west] where they face east and bow twice as if at a visitation with the Great Sovereign Lord; [to the north] where they face south and salute the Eminent Exalted Perfected with two bows; and [to the east] where they face west and bow twice in worship of the Celestial Master Lord Chang (HY 528, p. 50b).

42. Exit. The officiant and the ordinands, Brahman chanting, leave the altar from the Gate of the Nine Heavens in the northwest corner, never looking back (HY 528, p. 50b).

*C. The Transmission of the Procedures (HY 1231, ch. 2, p. 20b).

    1. The Transmission of the Slip Writs?

    2. The Sealing of the Staff?

*IV. The Third Covenant: the Great Covenant of the Numinous Treasure.

  *A. The Conferral of the One Hundred and Eighty Injunctions of the Three Primes (HY 1231, ch. 1, p. 2a).

*V.   A retreat of thanksgiving for mercy (HY 528, p. 50b).
*VI.  The Casting of the Dragon Tablets (HY 528).

  A.  Lighting the Censer. The ordinands clack their teeth thrice, offer incense, and recite this invocation, which is basically the same as previously described (Section III, Part B, number 9 above) (HY 528, pp. 50b–51a).

 *B.  Reading the Slips. The ordinands face the direction of the Regal Gate, clack their teeth twelve times, read the inscriptions on the slips, and recite an invocation (HY 528, p. 51a–b).

  C.  Returning to the Censer. The ordinands offer incense and perform this rite as previously described (Section III, Part A, number 8 above) (HY 528, p. 51b).

# APPENDIX THREE
## The Works of Chang Wan-fu

1. *Tung-hsüan ling-pao wu-liang tu-jen ching-chüeh yin-i* (The Sound and Sense of the Scripture and Oral Instructions for the Immeasurable Salvation of Man, a Cavern-Mystery and Numinous Treasure Text) (HY 95), a treatise in nine folios (less four lines), compiled *(tsuan)* by Chang Wan-fu around A.D. 713. Five characters from one set of stanzas are missing (p. 6a9). This work has three parts.

   a) *Chüeh* (Oral Instructions) (pp. 1a–7b8). This section contains procedures and invocations for the recitation, as well as an interpretation of the terms in the title, of the *Tu-jen ching,* the most important scripture in the Ling-pao canon. It includes excerpts from:

   (1) the *Chin-lu chien-wen ching* (Scripture of the Slip Writ for the Gold Register) (p. 1a).

   (2) the *T'ai-chi pao-chüeh* (T'ai-chi's Treasure-Instructions) (p. 1a–b).

   (3) the *Tung-yüan ling-pao shih-pu ching hsü* (Preface to the Cavern-Prime and Numinous Treasure Scriptures in Ten Sections) (pp. 1b–3b).

   (4) the *Tung-hsüan ling-pao chai nei-shih hsin-yeh hsü* (Preface to the Mind Endeavor of Inner Worship for the Retreat of the Cavern-Mystery and Numinous Treasure) (p. 3b).

   (5) the *Ling-pao yü-tzu ching* (The Numinous Treasure Scripture of Jade Graphs) (pp. 3b–7b).

   b) *Yin-i* (Sound and Sense) (pp. 7b9–9a2). This is a short section in twenty-five lines, giving pronunciations and meanings for terms in the *Tu-jen ching.*

c)   The treatise concludes with a short bibliographical note (fourteen lines) describing the structure of the *Tu-jen ching* as it existed in Chang's day (pp. 9a3–9b6). The scripture was then divided into three *hsü* (prefaces), two *chang* (sections), and the *Ta-fan yin-yü* (Hidden Discourse of the Great Brahman). This format corresponds exactly to the versions of the *Tu-jen ching* in the *Yüan-shih wu-liang tu-jen shang-p'in miao-ching ssu-chu* (HY 87), a collection of the oldest annotations to the text, and to the Sung (960–1279) version of it in chapter one of the *Ling-pao wu-liang tu-jen shang-p'in miao-ching* (HY 1) (compiled between 1116 and 1119), except that a set of stanzas called the *T'ai-chi chen-jen sung* (Hymn of the Perfected, T'ai-chi) has been added to the latter work. A comparison of Chang's description with HY 1 yields the following internal divisions for the *Tu-jen ching:*

(1)  Front Preface:          HY 1, ch. 1, pp. 1a1–5b8.
(2)  Middle Preface:        HY 1, ch. 1, pp. 13b2–14b9.
(3)  Rear Preface:          HY 1, ch. 1, pp. 17b9–18a9.
(4)  Front Petition:         HY 1, ch. 1, pp. 6a2–10b5.
(5)  Rear Petition:          HY 1, ch. 1, pp. 10b6–13b1.
(6)  *Ta-fan yin-yü:*        HY 1, ch. 1, pp. 14b10–17b8.

At the end of this section (p. 9b4–5), Chang mentions the titles of two collections devoted to recording accounts of Taoist miracles:

(1)  *Hsüan-men ling-yen chi* (A Record of Miracles Experienced by the Followers of Mystery).
(2)  *Tao-men chi-yen chi* (A Record of Collected Miracles Experienced by the Followers of the Tao).

Neither of these texts survives today, but Tu Kuang-t'ing (850?–933) also mentions them in the preface (*hsü*, p. 2b9–10) to his work on miracles, the *Tao-chiao ling-yen chi* (HY 590). Tu adds that each of these texts was ten chapters in length and that the author of the latter was Su Huai-ch'u of Shih-p'ing while the author of the former was Li Ch'i-chih of Ch'eng-chi.

> *Note:* The last two sections, if not the entire text of this work, appear to have originally been parts of the *I-ch'ieh Tao-ching yin-i* (see Chapter One).

2.   *San-tung chung-chieh wen* (Writs of All Injunctions for the Three Caverns) (HY 178); two chapters with a preface, a short treatise in fif-

teen folios (less four lines), edited and recorded *(pien-lu)* by Chang
Wan-fu, Student of the Three Caverns *(San-tung ti-tzu)* and Priest of
the T'ai-ch'ing kuan (Supreme Purity Abbey) in the capital, and
completed between 710 and 713. Although the preface neatly lists
the sixteen sets of injunctions which were presented to students
from their first initiation to the final stage of ordination *(hsü,* pp.
1b–2a; the same list appears in ch. 1, pp. 1a–2a of HY 1231, number eight below), the text does not proceed according to that order,
describes extraneous matter, and omits most of the sets in the list.
This text has eleven parts.

Chang's preface, which has a citation from the *Ling-pao sheng-
hsüan pu-hsü chang* (A Numinous Treasure Petition for Pacing
the Void to Ascend to the Mystery) (p. 1a2–3).

a) *Shih ch'i-hsin ju-tao san-kuei-chieh wen* (Writ of the Injunctions for
Taking Refuge in the Three Presented when the Thought of
Entering Taoism First Arises in the Mind) (ch. 1, pp. 1a–2b).
These three precepts concern allegiance to the Tao, the Vener-
able Scriptures in Thirty-Six Titles, and the Grand Preceptors.
This set of injunctions was adopted from the Buddhist notion
of *trisarna* and adapted to Taoist needs. It was the first set given
to an initiate. There are two excerpts from scriptures.

b) *Ti-tzu feng-shih k'o-chieh wen* (Writ of the Rules and Injunctions
Governing the Student's Service to the Preceptor) (ch. 1, pp.
2b–5a). This is a set of thirty-six precepts that established standards of decorum for the student in his relations with his master. They have no particular reference to any of the phases of
instruction or ordination.

c) *Ling-pao ch'u-meng pi-sai liu-ch'ing chieh wen* (Writ of the Injunctions to Arrest the Six Sensations for the First Covenant of the
Numinous Treasure) (ch. 2, pp. 1a–2a). These six precepts for
controlling the senses, desires, the mind, and the hand (that is,
greed and theft) were transmitted to a student when he established the first covenant for receiving the Ling-pao scriptures.
The same set, with variant readings, can be found in HY 1130,
ch. 46, pp. 11b–12a, and in the *T'ai-shang tung-chen chih-hui
shang-pin ta-chieh* (HY 177, p. 6a–b). There is one excerpt from
scripture and a note by Chang Wan-fu.

d) *San-chieh wen* (Writ of the Three Injunctions) (ch. 2, pp. 2a–
3a). These three precepts were presented to the T'ai-shang ti-
tzu who were students of the *Tao-te ching.* See the HY 1117, ch.
4, p. 7a. They deal with karma. The same set, with variant

readings, can be found in HY 1130, ch. 46, pp. 14b–15a (citing the *Tung-shen ching*). There is one excerpt from scripture
and a comment.

e) *Wu-chieh wen* (Writ of the Five Injunctions) (ch. 2, p. 3a–b).
This set of precepts, which deal with control of the senses, was
presented to Register Pupils, children who had received the
second set of registers in Celestial Master initiations (see HY
1231, ch. 1, p. 1b and 3b; and HY 1117, ch. 4, p. 5b).
Although these injunctions are not related to the five *sila* or
commandments that were given to Buddhist laymen, the
notion that twenty-five spirits, five for each precept, would
protect the observer of the injunctions was related. The same
precepts, with variant readings, can be found in HY 1130, ch.
46, pp. 14b–15a (again citing the *Tung-shen ching*). They are not
the original Celestial Master injunctions set forth in the *Cheng-i
fa-wen* (Liturgical Writs of True-Unity). See HY 1130, ch. 46,
pp. 16b–18a. There is one excerpt from scripture and a comment.

f) *Pa-chieh wen* (Writ of the Eight Injunctions) (ch. 2, pp. 3b–4b).
A second set of precepts given to Register Pupils. The same
injunctions, with variant readings, can be found in HY 1130,
ch. 46, pp. 15b–16a (again citing the *Tung-shen ching*). There is
one excerpt from scripture and a comment.

g) *San-chüeh wen* (Writ of the Three Oral Instructions) (ch. 2, p.
5a–b). These all concern karma. There is one excerpt from
scripture and a comment.

h) *Pa-pai wen* (Writ of the Eight Defeats) (ch. 2, pp. 5b–6a). This
is a list of eight things to be avoided lest they cause setbacks in
the quest for longevity. These are the same as the eight *sila*
given to Buddhist laymen, except that the vow in the Buddhist
precepts not to eat after noon has been dropped in favor of
another injunction. There is one excerpt from scripture and a
comment.

i) *San-yao wen* (Writ of the Three Essentials) (ch. 2, p. 6a–b). This
writ ranks striving for longevity, seeking invisibility, and avoid-
ing worldly glory as the first, second, and third priorities in
self-cultivation.

j) *Shih-san-chin wen* (Writ of the Thirteen Interdictions) (ch. 2, pp.
6b–7a). If observed, these thirteen will prolong life.

k) *Ch'i-pai-erh-shih men yao chieh lü chüeh wen* (Writ of the Essentials,
Oral Instructions, Statutes, and Injunctions for the Seven
Hundred and Twenty Gates) (ch. 2, pp. 7a–10a). This section

contains a lengthy discussion of the items, described in its title, that were transmitted to ordinands seeking the *San-huang wen.* See HY 1231, ch. 1, p. 2a. None of the essentials, instructions, injunctions, or statutes are named, because they could only be transmitted orally. There is one excerpt from scripture and a note by Chang Wan-fu.

3. *Tung-hsüan ling-pao san-shih ming-hui hsing-chuang chü-kuan fang-so wen* (Writ for the Taboo Names, Vitae, and Locations of Home Abbeys for the Three Preceptors, a Cavern-Mystery and Numinous Treasure Text (HY 445), a short treatise in four folios and three lines, edited and recorded *(pien-lu)* by Chang Wan-fu, Student of the Three Caverns and Priest of the T'ai-ch'ing Abbey in the capital, written between 710 and 713. This text supplies a series of formulas which are marked at points where a preceptor was to fill in such particulars as the names, the locations and titles of home abbeys, the parishes of registration, and ages of the priest who was ordained and the officiants who presided at his investiture. The officiants were the three Canon Preceptors: the *Tu-shih* (Preceptor of Ordination), *Chi-shih* (Preceptor of Registration), and *Ching-shih* (Preceptor of Scripture). Thereafter the priest employed these documents whenever he conducted his offices. This treatise has nine parts devoted to seven formulas.

   *a)* Chang's prologue explaining the necessity of making obeisances to the officiants, reciting the formulas, and visualizing the preceptors before conducting rites. According to the *Wu-shang pi-yao,* these acts were performed immediately after reciting an incantation upon entering the altar at ordination rituals (HY 1130, ch. 35, pp. 2b–3a).

   *b)* Taboo Names for True-Unity Preceptors *(Cheng-i shih-hui)* (pp. 1a–2a): for those who received the Celestial Master Registers.

   *c)* Taboo Names for the Preceptors of the Classic of Five Thousand Words *(Wu-ch'ien-wen)* (pp. 2a–3a): for those who received the *Tao-te ching* and related matter.

   *d)* Taboo Names for the Preceptors of the Scripture of Divine Incantations *(Shen-chou)* (p. 3a): for those who received the *Tung-yüan shen-chou ching* (Cavern-Prime Scripture of Divine Incantations) and related matter.

   *e)* Taboo Names for the Cavern-Divine *(Tung-shen)* Preceptors (pp. 3b): for those who received the *San-huang wen* and related matter.

*f)* Taboo Names for the Preceptors of the Scripture for Ascension to the Mystery (pp. 3b–4a): for those who received the *Sheng-hsüan ching* and related matter.

*g)* Taboo Names for the Cavern-Mystery *(Tung-hsüan)* Preceptors (p. 4a): for those who received the corpus of Ling-pao scriptures and related matter.

*h)* Taboo Names for the Superior-Purity *(Shang-ch'ing)* Preceptors (p. 4a–b): for those who received the corpus of Shang-ch'ing scriptures and related matter.

*i)* Chang's postscript on the color of ink and paper to be used in writing the formulas with further remarks on obeisance and visualization.

With the exception of (f) above these stages of investiture correspond exactly to those given in HY 1117, ch. 4, p. 6a, to ch. 5, p. 2b. Under (c), Chang lists six categories of participants who officiated at the ordination rite for transmission of the *Tao-te ching,* giving their titles and numbers (a total of thirty-eight). Under (e), (g), and (h), he states that the same numbers of officiants with the same titles presided at investitures for the *San-huang wen,* Ling-pao, and Shang-ch'ing scriptures (see Chapter Three).

4. *Wu-shang huang-lu ta-chai li-ch'eng i* (Protocols for the Immediate Completion of the Great Retreat of the Peerless Yellow Register (HY 508), compiled by Liu Yung-kuang (1134–1206) and edited by his pupil Chiang Shu-yü (1156–1217), begun in 1202 and completed in A.D. 1223; chapter 16 augmented and corrected *(pu-cheng)* by Chang Wan-fu, Canon Preceptor of the Three Caverns *(San-tung fa-shih)* from the Ch'ing-tu [kuan] (Pure Capital Abbey) of the Great T'ang. This chapter is devoted to instructions for performing the *Su-ch'i* (Nocturnal Annunciation). In Sung times (960–1279) the protocols set forth in this chapter were considered to be the old version since they were based on a text written by Lu Hsiu-ching (406–477). Aside from his signature at the beginning of the chapter and a single reference to him in a note (p. 25a2–3), Chang has left no discernible mark on this text, and it is not at all clear what he accomplished when he edited it. Although his signature appears only at the beginning of chapter 16, the compiler and the editor of the compendium cited him, either as Chang Wan-fu or as Chang Ch'ing-tu (Chang of the Ch'ing-tu Abbey), elsewhere in their work (for example, see ch. 2, pp. 6b and 7a; and ch. 17, pp. 11b, 28b, and 38a).

5.  *San-tung fa-fu k'o-chieh wen* (Writ of the Injunctions and Regulations
    for the Liturgical Vestments of the Three Caverns (HY 787), one
    chapter in ten folios, edited and recorded *(pien-lu)* by Chang Wan-
    fu, Student of the Three Caverns and Priest of the T'ai-ch'ing
    Abbey in the capital, written between 710 and 713. This text takes
    the form of a dialogue between the Celestial Master Chang Tao-
    ling and T'ai-shang (Lord Lao or Lao Tzu Deified), in which the
    Celestial Master poses a few short queries about vestments and
    T'ai-shang gives lengthy replies. It is divided into two parts: the
    dialogue (pp. 1a–7a) and a commentary (pp. 7a–10b).

    *a)*  The dialogue.

        (1)  A description of the raiments for gods, Perfected, immor-
             tals, and other officials in the Nine Heavens, beginning
             with the highest *(Ta-lo)* and concluding with the Cavern
             Palaces beneath the Five Marchmounts and other famous
             mountains) (pp. 1a–4a).
        (2)  A discussion of why formless beings need clothing and
             which of the supernatural bureaucrats must wear gar-
             ments. This is followed by an enumeration of the seven
             types of vestments for mortal priests (pp. 4a–5b).

            *(a)*  *Ch'u-ju tao-men* (Those who first enter the gate of the
                   Tao, initiates) (p. 4b).
            *(b)*  *Cheng-i* (True-Unity or Celestial Master Priests)
                   (p. 4b).
            *(c)*  *Tao-te* (Recipients of the *Tao-te ching* and related matter)
                   (p. 4b).
            *(d)*  *Tung-shen* (Recipients of the *San-huang wen* and related
                   matter) (p. 4b).
            *(e)*  *Tung-hsüan* (Recipients of the Ling-pao corpus and
                   related matter) (pp. 4b–5a).
            *(f)*  *Tung-chen* (Recipients of the Shang-ch'ing corpus and
                   related matter) (p. 5a).
            *(g)*  *San-tung chiang fa shih* (Canon Preceptor for Lecturing
                   on the Doctrines of the Three Caverns) (p. 5a–b).

        (3)  A statement which establishes moral rectitude, purity,
             detachment, and ordination as prerequisites for wearing
             vestments (pp. 5b–6b).
        (4)  An account of various kinds of raiments that T'ai-shang
             dons to read scripture, transform mankind, travel in the
             heavens, conduct celestial audiences, and so forth (p. 7a).

*b)*   The commentary.

(1)   An enumeration of forty-six regulations that govern when, where, and how a Taoist priest should wear his vestments (pp. 7a–9b).

(2)   Lists of the ten kinds of beings who will lose respect for or scorn the priest who violates the rules governing clothing (pp. 9b–10b).

(3)   Admonitions which warn that penalties will be inflicted in hell on those who disobey the regulations governing vestments (p. 10b).

> *Note:* the section on the seven grades of vestments for mortal priests corresponds to the same types of costumes outlined in HY 1117, ch. 5, pp. 4a–5b, except that the latter does not include the first category and adds an intermediate one, between six and seven, called the *Ta-tung fa-shih* (Canon Preceptor of the Great Cavern). There are discrepancies and variant readings between these texts.

6.   *Chiao san-tung chen-wen wu-fa Cheng-i meng-wei lu li-ch'eng i* (Protocols for the Immediate Completion for the Sacrifice of the Registers for True-Unity and Covenantal-Authority, the Five Conjurations or Procedures, and the True Writs in the Three Caverns) (HY 1202), one chapter (twenty-five folios and seven lines), written *(chuan)* by Chang Wan-fu, Student of the Three Caverns. This is a thirteen-part manual for conducting a *chiao* ritual during which the officiant petitions the gods to have blessings bestowed on the souls of the dead, that is, to accrue merit for the salvation of ancestors (p. 1a and p. 21a). A diagram for arranging the altar of this rite appears on pp. 4b–5a.

Chang's prologue: p. 1a–b.

*a)*   *She-t'an tso-wei* (establishing the altar and its seats) (pp. 2a–5a). Here the term "seats" refers to the positions on the altar where various liturgical writs were placed. These writs were the *Shang-ch'ing fa-lu* (Liturgical Register of Superior-Purity), *Liu-chia fu, San-huang fu* (Talisman of the Three Sovereigns), *Wu-yüeh chen-hsing t'u, Wu-fu* (The Five Talismans), *Meng-wei fu* (The Talisman of Covenantal Authority), and the *Tung-hsi erh-chin fu* (Talisman of the Two Interdictions, East and West).

*b)*   *Chieh-t'an chieh-hui* (purifying the altar to free it from defilement) (pp. 5a–6a). This purification was accomplished by writing a talisman, sprinkling the altar and its accoutrements with holy water (clear spring water boiled with a bag into which peach bark, bamboo leaves, aloeswood, cloves, and cedar leaves had been placed), a visualization, an incantation, and a dance.

c) *Ju-hu chu* (incantation for entering the portal) (pp. 6a–b). After uttering this incantation the officiants circle the altar, assume their proper places, and visualize their three preceptors.

d) *Fa-lu* (lighting the censer) (pp. 6b–7a). This is an invocation of Lao Tzu Deified to summon forth thirty-six inner gods from the officiant's body so that those spirits can inform the local gods and Perfected that the rite is about to take place. At the end of it the priest requests the energies *(ch'i)* of the ten directions to enter his body. This invocation is followed by the lighting of incense.

e) *Ch'u ling-kuan* (externalizing the numinous officials) (pp. 7a–8a). The officiant externalizes a host of officials and a horde of soldiers from his body to carry his announcement to the gods. He then submits his credentials to the powers, supplying the date that he received the writs displayed in the altar's array and the name of the preceptor who transmitted them to him. Finally he says that the rite is occurring at such-and-such an abbey and requests that the numinous officials of the cosmos join the spirits of his body to assist in carrying out the ritual.

f) *Ch'ing-kuan ch'i-shih* (petitioning the officials to report the rite) (pp. 9a–23a). This part has two subsections.

(1) In the first, the officiant calls each of the gods represented in the liturgical writs by their names and requests that they descend to the altar (pp. 9a–18b). During the course of this litany the titles of the twenty-four Celestial Master registers are given (pp. 13a–16b).

(2) This is followed by the presentation of three declarations which constituted the core of the rite (pp. 19a–23a). The first is the officiant's address to the gods which concludes by asserting that he is qualified to undertake the duty of conducting the rite because he has received the scriptures, registers, talismans, and other matter. The second is a request that the gods be merciful and lenient toward ancestors to the seventh degree, who may have committed great sins (a list of specific transgressions is appended) during their lives, so that they may be released from hell and transferred to the Elysian Fields *(Fu-ti)*. The last expresses the fear and loathing of the sinner seeking divine

mercy, his desire for the protection of the gods and powers against external danger, and his wish that the energies (*ch'i*) of the gods and powers enter his body to destroy or suppress the agents of death so that he can attain immortality early.

g) *Sung shen-chen* (dispatching the gods and the Perfected) (p. 23a). The officiant calls on the gods to return to the Golden Portal (*Chin-ch'üeh*) in heaven.

h) *Ch'ih hsiao li shen* (commanding the lesser functionaries and gods) (pp. 23b–24a). This is a request for the inferior divine functionaries to return to their posts, where they are supposed to protect the blessings which have descended by virtue of this rite, and to eliminate catastrophes.

i) *Nei-kuan* (the inner gods) (p. 24a–b). Here the officiant asks the inner gods to return to their places in his body.

j) *Fu-lu* (returning to the censer) (p. 24b). The officiant asks the Jade Lads and Jade Maids of the Ten Directions to attend to the incense smoke so that it will convey his report to the Jade Emperor in heaven.

k) *Sung shen sung* (a hymn for dispatching the gods) (pp. 24b–25a). This is a set of sixteen verses sung to send the spirits on their way.

l) *Ch'u hu chu* (incantation for leaving the portal) (p. 25a). The utterance of this incantation closes the rite.

m) *Chiao hou chu-chi* (various taboos observed in the days after the sacrifice) (pp. 25b–26a). These taboos include injunctions against drinking wine, eating certain foods, and the like.

7. *Tung-hsüan ling-pao tao-shih shou san-tung ching-chieh fa-lu che-jih li* (A Calendar for Selecting the Days when Taoist Priests Should Receive the Scriptures, Injunctions, and Liturgical Registers of the Three Caverns, a Cavern-Mystery and Numinous Treasure Text) (HY 1230), a treatise in eight folios less three lines, written (*chuan*) by Chang Wan-fu, Student of the Three Caverns in the capital and Priest of the Ch'ing-tu Abbey, completed after 713. In the prologue to this text Chang says that he has been a Taoist and a priest for more than forty years. The work is divided into two parts.

Chang's prologue (pp. 1a–2a).

a) The first section is a kind of almanac whose purpose is to provide an instrument for choosing the proper days of initiation and investiture (pp. 1a–6a). The stages covered are:

(1) The Talismanic Register of the Immortals and Powers for True-Unity, and so forth (p. 2a–3a). Days for the trans-

mission of the Seventy-Five and One Hundred and Fifty Generals' Registers.

(2) Registration in the Twenty-Four Parishes—Yang-p'ing, Lu-t'ang, and so forth—and the Mobile-Dispersed Astral Parishes (pp. 3b–4b). Days for Registration in Celestial Master parishes. Source: *Cheng-i fa-wen tu-lu tu-chih i* (Protocols for the Register Ordination and Parish Ordination of the True-Unity Liturgical Writs).

(3) The Gold Knob of Lord Lao, List of Scriptures, Scriptures, and so forth (p. 4b). Days for the transmission of the *Tao-te ching* and other items associated with it. Source: *Lao-chün ch'uan-i chu-chüeh* (Commentary and Oral Instructions for Lord Lao's Protocols of Transmission).

(4) Talismans, Contracts, Illustrations, Scriptures, and so forth of the Divine Incantations (p. 4b). Days for the transmission of the *Shen-chou ching* and other items associated with it. On this level of investiture, see HY 1117, ch. 4, p. 6b.

(5) Talismans, Illustrations, Scriptures, and so forth of the Three Sovereigns in the Cavern-Divine (p. 4b). Days for the transmission of the *Tung-shen ching* in fourteen *chüan* and other items associated with it. Source: *Tung-shen ching.*

(6) The Self-Generating Tally, Scriptures of the Central Covenant, Two True Writ Registers, Inciting Staff of the Powers, and so forth for the Cavern-Mystery (p. 5a). Days for the transmission of the Ling-pao canon.

(7) *Wu-fa* (The Five Procedures or Conjurations) (p. 5a–b). Days for the transmission of the *Liu-chia fu, Chin-shan* (Mountain Interdictions), *Wu-yüeh chen-hsing t'u, San-huang fu,* and *Wu-fu* (p. 5a–b). Source: *T'ao-kung ch'uan i* (Duke T'ao [Hung-ching]'s Protocols for Transmission).

(8) *Ho-t'u pao-lu* (The River Chart and [The Nine Sovereigns', *chiu-huang*] Treasure-Register) (p. 5b). Days for the transmission of the River Chart and the Lo-shu. Source: *Chiu-huang chiao i* (The Nine Sovereigns' Protocols for Sacrifice). For the full title of the Lo-shu see HY 1117, chap. 4, p. 9b.

(9) The Seven Tallies of Superior-Purity, List of Scriptures, Scriptures, the Three Registers, Various Conjurations or Procedures, and the Girdle of Purple-Patterned Silk from the Mysterious Capital of the Grand Origin): Days for the transmission of the corpus of Shang-ch'ing scriptures and other items associated with it (pp. 5b–6a). Sources: *Shang-*

*ch'ing ching* (Scripture of Superior-Purity) and *Chen-kao* (HY 1010).

*b)*   A lengthy disquisition on (1) the necessity of strict adherence to the established order for transmitting different sets of scripture, (2) the corrupt practices in ordinations that existed in Chang's day, and (3) the superiority of rituals based on the Three Caverns (*San-huang wen,* Ling-pao and Shang-ch'ing) to those of the Libationers (*Chi-chiu,* Celestial Master priests) (pp. 6a–8b).

8.   *Ch'uan-shou san-tung ching-chieh fa-lu lüeh-shuo* (A Synopsis for Transmissions of Liturgical Registers, Scriptures, and Injunctions in the Three Caverns) (HY 1231): two chapters in thirty-eight and a half folios (the beginning of chapter one, which probably included Chang's signature, is missing), the colophon appended to the last chapter is dated January 1, 713, and signed Chang Wan-fu, Priest of the T'ai-ch'ing Abbey. The text has four parts. In all but the last section, the items under consideration are followed by excerpts from scriptures and/or Chang's own comments.

Chang's prologue (ch. 1, p. 1a).

*a)*   Inventories of the items transmitted at various stages of initiation and ordination in Taoism (ch. 1, pp. 1a–12b). The last step, transmission of the Shang-ch'ing scriptures, is conspicuously missing, probably indicating that Chang had yet to be ordained at that level.

(1)   *Chieh-mu* (ch. 1, pp. 1a–3b). This is an inventory of the titles for sixteen sets of injunctions given to students and priests, beginning with the set conferred when they first entered the religion and ending with that for Shang-ch'ing ordination. There is a disquisition on injunctions in general with a note by Chang and excerpts from scriptures.

(2)   *Cheng-i fa-mu* (ch. 1, pp. 3b–5a). This is a list of Celestial Master registers in two parts. The first embraces four registers that were given to children as a form of confirmation. The second encompasses twenty-four registers, which constitute all that remains of the Celestial Master corpus in this work. There is an excerpt from the *Cheng-i fa-wen k'o-chieh p'in* (Categories of Regulations and Injunctions from the Liturgical Writs of True-Unity) and a note by Chang.

(3)   *Tao-te ching mu* (ch. 1, pp. 5a–7a). This is an inventory of texts and other matter bestowed when the *Tao-te ching* was transmitted. There are excerpts from the *T'ai-chi tso-hsien*

*kung Tao-te ching hsü* (Preface to the *Tao-te ching* by the Immortal Duke of the Left in the Great Bourne) and the *T'ai-shang yü-ching yin-chu* (Hidden Annotations of the Most-Exalted Jade Scripture) as well as a note by Chang.

(4) *San-huang fa-mu* (ch. 1, pp. 7a–b). This is a list of texts and other matter transmitted with the *San-huang wen*. There are excerpts from the *Ling-pao ching* and *Tung-shen t'ai-ch'ing t'ai-chi kung ching* (A Cavern-Mystery Scripture of the Great Bourne in the Supreme-Purity Heaven) as well as a note by Chang.

(5) *Ling-pao fa-mu* (ch. 1, pp. 8a–12a). This is an inventory of the Ling-pao canon and other matter. There are excerpts from the *Chen-wen ch'ih-shu ching* (HY 22), *Erh-shih-ssu sheng ching* (HY 1396), and *Yü-tzu shang-ching* (The Superior Scripture in Jade Graphs) as well as a note by Chang.

*b)* Comments on five texts that were transmitted to ordinands in the last three stages of investiture (ch. 1, pp. 12b–19a).

(1) *Ling-pao wu-fu* (The Five Talismans of the Numinous Treasure) (ch. 1, pp. 12b–14a). This was part of the Ling-pao canon (HY 1117, ch. 4, p. 9b8). There are excerpts from the *T'ai-hsüan ching* (Scripture of the Grand Mystery) and *K'ai-yüan ching* (Scripture of the Opened Prime) as well as a note by Chang.

(2) *Tung-hsi chin-wen* (Writs of the Interdictions, East and West) (ch. 1, p. 14a–b). This was a text from the *San-huang wen* corpus. See HY 1117, ch. 4, p. 7b4. There is a note by Chang.

(3) *Wu-yüeh chen-hsing t'u* (Illustrations of the Five March-mounts' True Forms) (ch. 1, pp. 14b–18a). This was a scripture from the Ling-pao canon. See HY 1117, ch. 4, p. 9b7. There is an excerpt from the *Wu-yüeh chen-hsing t'u hsü* and a note by Chang.

(4) *San-huang nei-wen* (Esoteric Writs of the Three Sovereigns) (ch. 1, pp. 18b–19a). There is an excerpt from the *San-huang wen* and a note by Chang.

(5) *San-t'ien cheng-fa ch'u liu-t'ien yü-wen* (Jade Writ of the Three Heavens of True-Unity for Eliminating the Six Heavens) (ch. 2, pp. 1a–5a). This was part of the Shang-ch'ing corpus and appears to have been adapted from a Celestial Master scripture. There is an excerpt from the

*Kao-shang yü-ch'en feng-t'ai ch'ü-su shang-ching* (Superior Scripture of the Ch'ü-shu Contract from the Phoenix Terrace of his Highness, the Jade Dawn) and a note by Chang. At the end of this passage there is a disquisition on the nature of the mind in Taoism (ch. 2, pp. 5a–8a). There are excerpts from the *Lao-chün nei-kuan ching* (Scripture of Lord Lao's Inner Vision).

c) This section opens with a description of the six steps in initiation and investiture for Taoism and a statement on the necessity of expending wealth to acquire ordination in an age of decadence when transmission from mind to mind is no longer possible. This is followed by comments on twenty-six kinds of pledges, oaths, and other aspects of Taoist investitures (ch. 2, pp. 8a–15a).

(1)   The seven treasures.
(2)   Twenty-four ounces of gold and silver.
(3)   Nine ounces of superior gold.
(4)   Ten gold rings.
(5)   Three gold dragon plaques and twenty-seven gold knobs.
(6)   Slip-writs of the gold dragons and jade disks.
(7)   Gold rings and jade rings.
(8)   Breaking rings.
(9)   Fifty feet of plain thread or, if one-hundred feet, five and ten ounces.
(10)  Blue-green thread.
(11)  Cutting hair and smearing blood on the lips.
(12)  Scarlet kerchiefs and jade-green kerchiefs.
(13)  The Five Aromatics.
(14)  Silk of the directions.
(15)  Destiny silk.
(16)  Destiny rice.
(17)  Gold lambs.
(18)  Jade geese.
(19)  Gold fish and jade fish.
(20)  Polychrome brocade.
(21)  Blue-green net and purple net.
(22)  Blue-green bast fabrics.
(23)  Paper, pens, and ink.
(24)  Tallies and contracts.
(25)  Covenants.
(26)  Oaths.

Chang concludes with a statement on the importance of oaths and covenants and further remarks on pledges.

*d)* The last part of this text is Chang's account of the transmissions of the Ling-pao scriptures and Shang-ch'ing canon to Princesses Gold-Immortal and Jade-Perfected. The first took place between February 10 and 20, 711 and the second on December 19, 712 (ch. 2, pp. 18a–21a).

# NOTES

## Prelude

1. The full description of the investiture appears in chapter 2, pp. 18a9–21a1, of the *Ch'uan-shou san-tung ching-chieh fa-lu lüeh-shuo* (HY 1231), compiled by Chang Wan-fu, whose postscript is dated January 13, 713. The passage translated here can be found on p. 18a9–18b4. All texts from the *Cheng-t'ung Tao-tsang* (Repository of the Taoist Canon compiled in the Cheng-t'ung era, 1436–1450) cited in this study will be referred to by the numbers assigned them in the Harvard-Yenching (HY) index to the repository, *Tao-tsang tzu-mu yin-te*, compiled by Weng Tu-chien (Taipei, 1966).

## Chapter One

1. *Chiu T'ang shu* (hereafter *CTS*), compiled by a commission under the direction of Liu Hsü (887–946), submitted to the throne on July 12, 945 (Peking, 1975), ch. 61, p. 2176; and *Hsin T'ang shu* (hereafter *HTS*), compiled by Ou-yang Hsiu (1007–1072) and others, submitted to the throne in 1060 (Shanghai, 1975), ch. 76, p. 3489. On Jui-tsung's assumption of the throne in 684, Lady Tou received the title *Te-fei* designating her as his third consort. Since Jui-tsung's empress, that is his principal wife, did not fall into the hierarchy of imperial consorts, Lady Tou was actually his fourth wife. However, the use of *Te-fei* to refer to Lady Tou at this time is anachronistic because Jui-tsung's empress was demoted and the system of titles for his lesser consorts abolished when he was deposed. In their own day Princesses Gold-Immortal and Jade-Perfected were known as the eighth and ninth daughters of Jui-tsung, respectively, because his second daughter, who died in her youth, was not included in the count. In later sources, however, the second daughter was incorporated,

and consequently Princesses Gold-Immortal and Jade-Perfected were designated the ninth and tenth daughters, respectively (*HTS,* ch. 83, pp. 3656–3657,
and *T'ang hui-yao* [hereafter *THY*], final compilation made by Wang P'u [932–
982], completed in 961 [Taipei, 1968], ch. 6, p. 64). The *Chiu T'ang shu* records
Gold-Immortal's death on June 6, 732, and her epitaph, which Hsü Ch'iao
wrote, states that she was forty-three years of age at the time. This means that
she was born in 688 or 689 (*CTS,* ch. 8, p. 198, and *Chin-shih ts'ui-pien* [hereaf-
ter *CSTP*], compiled by Wang Ch'ang [1725–1806] and completed in 1805
[Shanghai, 1921], ch. 84, p. 12b). Although Wang Ch'ang was unaware of the
Princess's obituary in the *Chiu T'ang shu,* he accurately calculated the year of
her death by a series of complex deductions. According to one copy of an
inscription written by Ts'ai Wei, a priest from the Hung-tao Abbey in Ch'ang-
an, to commemorate auspicious portents that appeared during a rite which
Jade-Perfected conducted in 753, Yeh Fa-shan ordained her at the beginning of
the Ching-yün era (710–711) when she was eleven years of age (*Ch'üan T'ang
wen* [hereafter *CTW*], compiled under imperial auspices by a commission under
the direction of Tung Kao [1740–November 8, 1818], whose preface is dated
1814 [Taipei, 1961], ch. 927, p. 10a). This is manifestly impossible, because
her date of birth would have been 698 or 699, six or seven years after the death
of her mother. Copies of this inscription were recovered from a badly weathered
stele and were illegible, or nearly so, in a number of places. Another version of
it gives Jade-Perfected's age at this time as twenty-eight, which is also incorrect
because that would have made her older than Princess Gold-Immortal (*Chin-
shih hsü-pien,* compiled by Lu Yao-yü, whose preface is dated 1868 [appended to
the *CSTP*], ch. 8, p. 2b). It is possible that the first digit (two) in her age was
unreadable to the copyist who made the facsimile used by the editors of the
*Ch'üan T'ang wen.* If this was the case, then she was actually twenty-one in 710
or 711, and was born around 689.

   2. The account of Wei T'uan-erh's activities is based on the *T'ai-shang huang
shih-lu* (Veritable Record of the Retired Emperor, i.e., Jui-tsung), compiled by
Liu Chih-chi (661–721), who submitted the work to the throne on December 2,
716. This text is no longer extant, but Ssu-ma Kuang cites it in his *Tzu-chih
t'ung-chien k'ao-i,* which has been incorporated into the notes for the edition of
the *Tzu-chih t'ung-chien* used here. The narrative of the incident given in the
*Tzu-chih t'ung-chien* itself follows the *Tse-t'ien shih-lu* (Veritable Record of
[Empress Wu] Tse-t'ien), compiled by Wei Yüan-chung (d. ca. 710) and others, submitted to the throne between June 15 and July 14, 706. The latter,
which is also lost, was more elliptical than Liu Chih-chi's account. It stated only
that T'uan-erh held a grudge against Jui-tsung and accused his wives of practicing sorcery. Actually there was no contradiction between the two sources. Liu
Chih-chi's account was simply more detailed than Wei Yüan-chung's (*Tzu-chih
t'ung-chien* [hereafter *TCTC*], compiled under imperial auspices by Ssu-ma
Kuang [1019–1086] and others, completed January 1, 1085, annotated by Hu
San-hsing [1230–1287] whose preface is dated December 14, 1285 [Shanghai,
1976], ch. 205, p. 6488; and C. P. Fitzgerald, *The Empress Wu* [Melbourne,
1955], pp. 148–149). The annals of the *Hsin T'ang shu* date the murder of Lady

Liu and Lady Tou on January 25, 693, which was the third day of the *la* month. The *Tzu-chih t'ung-chien* dates it on December 15, 692, which was the second day of the *cheng* month. According to the *Ta T'ang liu-tien,* the national anniversary of Lady Tou's death as observed in Hsüan-tsung's reign fell on the second day of the *cheng* month. Consequently, the *Tzu-chih t'ung-chien's* date is preferable. (*Ta T'ang liu-tien* [hereafter *TTLT*], compiled under imperial auspices by a commission nominally under the direction of Li Lin-fu [d. December 22, 752] and completed in 738 or 739 [Taipei, 1968], ch. 4, p. 48a). On the gravity of sorcery as a crime during the T'ang see *T'ang lü shu-i,* first compiled in 618, revised in 624, 637, 651, and 653 (the present edition represents that completed in 653 by a commission under the direction of Chang-sun Wu-chi [d. 659], which also added the commentary) (Taipei, 1969), ts'e 1, ch. 1, p. 17; and *The T'ang Code,* trans. by Wallace Johnson (Princeton, 1979), vol. 1, p. 69.

3. On Wu Tse-t'ien's reign of terror see *THY,* ch. 41, pp. 740–744; *Ts'e-fu yüan-kuei* (hereafter *TFYK*), compiled under imperial auspices by a commission under the direction of Wang Ch'in-jo (962–1052) and Yang I (974–1020), begun in 1005 and submitted to the throne on September 20, 1013 (Taipei, 1967), ch. 521, pp. 12a–15a and ch. 522, pp. 16b–18a; *CTS,* ch. 186a, pp. 4836–4848; *HTS,* ch. 209, pp. 5903–5911; *T'ung-chien chi-shih pen-mo,* compiled by Yüan Shu (1131–1205), first printed in 1174 (Peking, 1979), ch. 30, pp. 2715–2774; *Wen-hsien t'ung-k'ao,* compiled by Ma Tuan-lin (1254–1325) and printed in 1339 (Taipei, 1963), ch. 166, pp. 1438b–1439c; Denis Twitchett and Howard Wechsler, "Kao-tsung (reign 649–83) and the Empress Wu: The Inheritor and the Usurper," and Richard Guisso, "The Reigns of Empress Wu, Chung-tsung and Jui-tsung (684–712)," in *The Cambridge History of China,* vol. 3, *Sui and T'ang China, 589–906,* part 1, ed. by Denis Twitchett and John K. Fairbank (New York, 1979), pp. 244–273 and 290–345; Fitzgerald, *The Empress Wu,* pp. 76–180; R. W. L. Guisso, *Wu Tse-t'ien and the Politics of Legitimation in T'ang China* (Bellingham, Washington, 1978), pp. 51–69 and 126–154; and Lin Yu-tang, *Lady Wu, a Novel* (New York, 1965), pp. 146–158. The officials executed for visiting Jui-tsung without permission were P'ei Fei-kung and Fan Yün-hsien (*CTS,* ch. 6, p. 123 and ch. 187a, p. 4885; *HTS,* ch. 4, pp. 93; and *TCTC,* ch. 204, p. 6490). On An Chin-ts'ang, see Liu Su (fl. 806–821), *Ta-T'ang hsin-yü,* Liu's preface is dated the first month (February 11 to March 12) 807, collated and punct. by Hsü Te-nan and Li Ting-hsia (Peking, 1984), ch. 5, p. 73; *CTS,* ch. 187a, p. 4885; and *TCTC,* ch. 204, p. 6490. In these sources Chin-ts'ang is called a *kung-jen* (workman, artisan, musician) in the Service of the Grand Standard-Bearer, an agency responsible for directing the activities of several bureaus that managed imperial temples, sacrifices, divination, medicine, music, and entertainment (*Traité des fonctionnaires et Traité de l'armée,* trans. by Robert des Rotours [San Francisco, 1974], vol. 1, p. 315). On Lai's conspiracy in 697 see *TCTC,* ch. 206, p. 6519; Fitzgerald, *The Empress Wu,* pp. 153–154; and Guisso, *Wu Tse-t'ien,* p. 143.

4. *CTS,* ch. 6, p. 126; *HTS,* ch. 4, pp. 98–99; *TCTC,* ch. 206, pp. 6529–6539; Fitzgerald, *The Empress Wu,* pp. 158–161; Guisso, *Wu Tse-t'ien,* pp. 145–146; and *The Cambridge History of China,* vol. 3, pt. 1, pp. 317–318. Li Ch'ung-fu

was the son who informed on his elder brother Li Ch'ung-jun, Princess Yung-t'ai, and her husband Wu Yen-chi (*HTS*, ch. 83, p. 3654; *TCTC*, ch. 207, pp. 6556–6557; and Fitzgerald, *The Empress Wu*, p. 170).

5. For the plot against Jui-tsung during Chung-tsung's reign see Liu Su, *Ta-T'ang hsin-yü*, ch. 5, p. 76. On the events in 710 and 713 see *CTS*, ch. 7, p. 152 and ch. 8, pp. 166 and 169; *HTS*, ch. 5, pp. 115–116 and 122; *TCTC*, ch. 209, pp. 6641–6646, and ch. 210, pp. 6683–6694; Howard Levy, "How a Prince Became Emperor," *Sinologica* 6, no. 2 (1959): 101–119; and *The Cambridge History of China*, vol. 3, pt. 1, pp. 326–327.

6. On Jui-tsung's commentary see *Wen-hsien t'ung-k'ao*, ch. 211, p. 1730c; and *Lao Lieh Chuang san-Tzu chih-chien shu-mu*, compiled by Yen Ling-feng (Taipei, 1965), vol. 1, p. 58.

7. For Jui-tsung's other daughters see *HTS*, ch. 83, p. 3656–3657.

8. The tomb inscription for Princess Gold-Immortal can be found in *CSTP*, ch. 84, p. 12b. On Jade-Perfected's ordination see Ts'ai Wei's inscription in the *CTW*, ch. 927, p. 10a; and the *Chin-shih hsü-pien*, ch. 8, p. 2b. From the Han dynasty (206 B.C.–A.D. 220) onward the marriageable ages were fixed at sixteen and fourteen for men and women, respectively (*T'ung-tien*, compiled by Tu Yu [735–December 23, 812], submitted to the throne between March 19 and March 26, 803 [Taipei, 1965], ch. 59, pp. 340b–341a; and Ch'ü T'ung-tsu, *Han Social Structure* [Seattle, 1972], p. 33). Yeh Fa-shan was one of the most prominent Taoists at Jui-tsung's court and during Hsüan-tsung's early years on the throne. Yeh knew Hsüan-tsung before he became emperor, when he was the Adjutant *(pieh-chia)* of Lu-chou (707–710), and is said to have accurately predicted the events of the Hsien-t'ien era (September 12, 712 to December 22, 713) at that time. On April 12, 710, an immortal (one source says three) appeared before the priest and instructed him to proceed to Ch'ang-an in the eighth month (August 29 to September 28), where he was to assist Jui-tsung as well as to transmit the doctrine of the Tao to Hsüan-tsung. There is a problem with the dating of this epiphany. Yeh's biography (HY 778) says that it occurred in the fourth year of the Ching-lung era (710), but gives *hsin-hai* as the cyclical designation for that year. *Hsin-hai* was actually the cyclical designation for the following year, and, consequently, if that was the true date, the epiphany would have occurred on May 2, 711. However, as Ts'ai Wei's note (*CTW*, ch. 927, p. 10a) on Jade-Perfected's ordination indicates, Yeh had to have been in the capital before February of 711, the month of the Princesses' Ling-pao ordination, because the only other investiture for the ladies in this period did not take place until December 1 of 712. The cyclical date *hsin-hai* must therefore be an error. Most sources on Yeh's life contend that he was 107 years of age at the time of his demise, but the epitaph which Hsüan-tsung wrote for him (dated April 8, 739) states that he was born in 616, and this would have made him 105 or 106 years old when he died. None of the priest's biographies in the *Tao-tsang* mentions his role in the Princess' ordination (*T'ang Yeh chen-jen chuan* [HY 778], the origin of this work is unknown; the preface, which is dated 1241 and was written by Ma Kuang-tsu [fl. 1226–1269], who was a governor of Kua-ts'ang, states that Ma received the text from Chang Tao-t'ung [fl. 1240], who was his cousin, pp.

10a–11b, 29a and 30b; *CTW*, ch. 41, pp. 25a and 26a; *TFYK*, ch. 53, p. 10a; *CTS*, ch. 191, p. 5108; *HTS*, ch. 204, p. 5805; *T'ai-p'ing kuang-chi*, compiled under imperial auspices by a commission directed by Li Fang [925–996], begun in March of 977 and completed in August of 978 [Taipei, 1969], ch. 26, p. 2a-b; *Hsüan-p'in lu* [HY 780], compiled by Chang Yü [1277–1350] whose preface is dated October 1, 1335, ch. 4, p. 10a; *Li-shih chen-hsien t'i-tao t'ung-chien* [HY 296], compiled by Chao Tao-i [fl. 1299–1307], ch. 39, p. 2a; and Judith Boltz, *A Survey of Taoist Literature, Tenth to Seventeenth Centuries* [Berkeley, 1987], pp. 96–97). See Chapter Four on the various stages and phases of initiation and investiture. There were a number of other ordinations which preceded that for the Ling-pao canon, but they do not appear to have been nearly as important as the vows and investitures noted here.

9. On Empress Wu's Buddhist ideology see Kenneth Ch'en, *Buddhism in China, a Historical Survey* (Princeton, 1964), pp. 219–222; Kenneth Ch'en, *The Chinese Transformation of Buddhism* (Princeton, 1973), pp. 110–111; Stanley Weinstein, "Imperial Patronage in T'ang Buddhism," in *Perspectives on the T'ang*, ed. by Arthur Wright and Denis Twitchett (New Haven, 1973), pp. 297–303; Antonio Forte, *Political Propaganda and Ideology in China at the End of the Seventh Century* (Naples, 1976), pp. 3–22 and 125–176; and Guisso, *Wu Tse-t'ien*, pp. 31–49 and 66–68. For T'ang Taoist ideology, see C. Benn, *Taoism as Ideology in the Reign of Emperor Hsüan-tsung (712–755)* (unpublished doctoral dissertation, University of Michigan, 1977).

10. On Princess T'ai-p'ing see *THY*, ch. 50, p. 877; *Ch'ang-an chih*, compiled by Sung Min-ch'iu (1019–1079), a preface by Chao Yen-jo is dated March 12, 1076, in vol. 1 of *Sung-Yüan ti-fang chih ts'ung-shu* (Taipei, 1980), ch. 7, p. 12b and ch. 10, p. 2a; *T'ang liang-ching ch'eng-fang k'ao* (hereafter *TLCCFK*), compiled by Hsü Sung (1781–1848) and completed in 1810 (Taipei, 1963), ch. 2, p. 12b and ch. 4, p. 9b; *TCTC*, ch. 202, p. 6402; and Fitzgerald, *The Empress Wu*, pp. 85–86. Fitzgerald's account of these events must be used with great caution. He does not recognize that the Princess was inducted into a Taoist order (as opposed to a Buddhist), claims that the investiture was undertaken to avert bad luck and to atone for Empress Wu's transgression when she broke her vow as a Buddhist nun to enter the imperial harem (neither of which was the case), and contends that the abbey for the Princess was constructed in the precincts of the palace (it was actually built in the outer city). The *Tzu-chih t'ung-chien* also errs in saying that the T'ai-p'ing Abbey was established when the Tibetans asked for the Princess' hand in 677. The imperial rescript (now lost) authorizing the Princess "to leave the family" (become a nun) was engraved on a stele dated 672 and erected in Ch'eng-tu (*Pao-k'o lei-pien*, compiled by an unknown author around 1279 [*Ssu-pu ts'ung-k'an:* Shanghai, 1919–1937], ch. 8, p. 268). The correct sequence of these events is given in the *Ch'ang-an chih* (reproduced verbatim in the *TLCCFK*). The *Ch'ang-an chih* was based largely on information taken from the *Liang-ching hsin-chi*, written by Wei Shu (cs. 708–d. 757 or 758) and completed in 722. Wei's text was still extant in Sung Min-ch'iu's time, though only a portion of its third chapter survives in Japan today. See *Chōan to Rakuyō, shiryō hen*, compiled by Hiraoka Takeo (Kyoto, 1965), pp. 181–196. Wei Shu

was a near contemporary of the Princess and, as an imperial academician, had access to primary historical materials on her affairs. Consequently, the statements found in the *Ch'ang-an chih* about her and the establishment of an abbey for her are more reliable than those made in other sources. The *T'ang hui-yao* (ch. 50, p. 877) errs in giving the title for the Princess' abbey as T'ai-ch'ing. This mistake appears to have resulted when part of the text was deleted by a copyist (see note 29 below for further comments on the relationship between the T'ai-p'ing and T'ai-ch'ing Abbeys). For an example of a Taoist rite whose function was to assist the souls of ancestors in obtaining release from hell see *Chiao san-tung chen-wen wu-fa Cheng-i meng-wei lu li-ch'eng i* (HY 1202), written by Chang Wan-fu, pp. 19a–23a (Appendix Three, number 6). There were many kinds of acts in medieval Buddhism and Taoism the performance of which was thought to accrue merit for ancestors. For examples involving the sponsoring of rituals, donation of land, and financing of statuary, see Kenneth Ch'en, *The Chinese Transformation of Buddhism,* pp. 53–55 and 128; Ōmura Seigai, *Shina bijutsu shi, chōsō hen* (Tokyo, 1915), pp. 116–612; and Alexander Soper, *Literary Evidence for Early Buddhist Art in China* (Ascona, 1959). One of the best pieces of evidence that Empress Wu supported the T'ang Taoist ideology before the death of her husband was her suggestion that questions on the *Tao-te ching* be added to civil service examinations (*THY,* ch. 75, p. 1373; *HTS,* ch. 76, p. 3477; Fitzgerald, *Empress Wu,* p. 78; Toyama Gunji, *Sokuten Bukō* [Tokyo, 1966], p. 83; "Une traduction juxtalinaire commente de la biographie officielle de l'Imperatrice Wou Tso-t'ien," trans. by Nghiem Toan and Louis Richard, *Bulletin de la Société des Études Indochinoises* 34, no. 2 [1959]: 122–123; and Guisso, *Wu Tse-t'ien,* pp. 30–31).

11. On the ages for various levels of initiation for the Taoist community see *Tung-hsüan ling-pao san-tung feng-tao k'o-chieh ying-shih* (HY 1117), compiled by Chin-ming Ch'i-chen (fl. 545–554) around A.D. 550, ch. 4, pp. 5a–b; and Chapter Four, numbers 1 to 3. For Princess T'ai-p'ing's marriage see *CTS,* ch. 5, p. 108; and *TCTC,* ch. 202, p. 6402.

12. Prince Shou, the Emperor's son, took Yang Yü-huan, an orphan from a prominent family and the most beautiful woman of her day, as a consort in the eleventh month (November 30 to December 29) of 734. His father later arranged for her ordination in order to avoid a scandal which an open divorce and remarriage would inevitably have created. Yang Kuei-fei left her convent to join Hsüan-tsung's seraglio in the same month that Prince Shou remarried (Yüeh Shih [930–1007], *Yang T'ai-chen wai-chuan,* probably written after 986, in *K'ai-yüan T'ien-pao i-shih shih-chung,* ed. by Ting Ju-ming [Shanghai, 1985], p. 131; *CTS,* ch. 51, p. 2178; and *HTS,* ch. 76, p. 3493).

13. In 721 Hsüan-tsung purportedly offered Princess Jade-Perfected's hand in marriage to Chang Kuo, a Taoist hermit who later became one of the most revered immortals. Chang laughed heartily and rejected the proposal (*CTS,* ch. 191, p. 5107; and *HTS,* ch. 204, p. 5810). The Emperor had summoned Chang to the capital, and he arrived there in March of this year. In the *Ts'e-fu yüan-kuei,* the year reads 720, but some copyist has dropped the last digit of the number, and it should read 721 (*TFYK,* ch. 53, pp. 12b and 13b; and *HTS,* ch. 204, p. 5810).

14. *TCTC*, ch. 210, p. 6659. It is quite apparent from the style and content of this passage that Ssu-ma Kuang did not take it from the Veritable Records or any other official source. He seems to be citing some collection of miscellaneous notes or an unofficial history.

15. The dates for the transmissions of Ling-pao and Shang-ch'ing scriptures to Princesses Gold-Immortal and Jade-Perfected are given in HY 1231, ch. 2, pp. 18a and 20b. The remainder of the chronology can be found in *THY*, ch. 50, pp. 871–875; *CTW*, ch. 278, pp. 2b–4a; and Chang Tsun-liu, "Sui T'ang Wu-tai Fo-chiao nien-piao," in Fan Wen-lan, *T'ang-tai Fo-chiao* (Peking, 1979), pp. 172–174. For other notices on these events see the *CTS*, ch. 7, p. 1517; and *TCTC*, ch. 210, pp. 6659 and 6665. Both of these sources erroneously group acts of different dates under single headings. C. Benn, *Taoism as Ideology in the Reign of Emperor Hsüan-tsung (712–755)*, vol. 1, p. 68, errs in stating that Jui-tsung granted permission in the third month of 711 for Princess Gold-Immortal to marry a foreign prince. The error is a misreading of the name for the Princess so betrothed, Gold-Mountain, for Gold-Immortal. Tu Kuang-t'ing (850?–933) erroneously dated the ordination of the Princesses and the establishment of abbeys for them in 749. He also mistakenly identified Princess Jade-Perfected as Jade-Magic-Mushroom *(yü-chih)* *(Li-tai ch'ung-tao chi* [HY 593], p. 11a; the author's postscript is dated January 4, 885). There is no record of either Princess occupying the temple built for her before 756. They may well have lived in their temples after their investitures, but not permanently (see the discussion of their later lives).

16. On the appanages and administrations *(fu)* created for princesses in Chung-tsung's reign and their subsequent abolition, see *TTLT*, ch. 29, p. 20a; *THY*, ch. 6, p. 69; *HTS*, ch. 82, p. 3615, and ch. 83, p. 3658; *TCTC*, ch. 208, p. 6597; *Traité des fonctionnaires et Traité de l'armée*, vol. 2, p. 645; and *The Cambridge History of China*, vol. 3, pt. 1, pp. 321–326. In 710 the throne replaced the princesses' administrations, which were equivalent to those for princes, with fief administrations that were smaller. It also abolished some of the appanages at that time, but it was not until sometime after 713 that the court reduced them all to the sizes that had been prescribed for them in the early T'ang. The memorials censuring Jui-tsung for constructing the abbeys can be found in the *THY*, ch. 50, pp. 871–875. See also *CTS*, ch. 98, pp. 3061–3063, ch. 100, pp. 3128–3129, ch. 101, pp. 3158–3161, ch. 178, p. 4626, and ch. 183, p. 4725; *HTS*, ch. 109, p. 4100; and *Ku-chin t'u-shu chi-ch'eng*, begun by Ch'en Meng-lei (1651–d. ca. 1723) who finished the first draft in 1706, reedited by a commission under the direction of Chiang T'ing-hsi (1669–1732) at imperial behest and first printed in 1728 (Taipei, 1979), *Shen-i tien*, ch. 214, p. 49a–b.

17. *CSTP*, ch. 84, p. 12b; *THY*, ch. 50, p. 876; and *CTS*, ch. 8, p. 198. The court left Ch'ang-an on November 24 and arrived in Loyang on December 14, 731. It returned to Ch'ang-an on December 24, 732, after a long detour to T'ai-yüan. In 731, just before Princess Gold-Immortal's death, Hsüan-tsung presented statues of her and her sister to the Ch'ang-tao Abbey on Mt. Ch'ing-ch'eng near Ch'eng-tu for some unspecified reason (*Tao-chiao ling-yen chi* [HY 590], compiled by Tu Kuang-t'ing, ch. 1, p. 4b).

18. *THY*, ch. 50, p. 876; *CTS*, ch. 86, p. 2826; *HTS*, ch. 81, p. 3587, ch.

134, p. 4559, and ch. 192, p. 5532. Princess Jade-Perfected's petition of October 20, 729, addressed the case of Li Wei, who was being persecuted by Chief Minister Yü-wen Jung (d. 730 or 731).

19. *CTS,* ch. 192, p. 5128; *HTS,* 196, p. 5606; *Hsü hsien chuan* (HY 295), compiled by Shen Fen (fl. 937–975), ch. 3, p. 2a; and Ch'en Kuo-fu, *Tao-tsang yüan-liu k'ao* (Peking, 1963), vol. 1, pp. 56–57. Curiously, the *Hsü hsien chuan* mentions the official, Wei T'ao, who accompanied the Princess on this mission, but not Jade-Perfected herself. Tu Kuang-t'ing claims that she studied with Ssu-ma Ch'eng-chen. *T'ien-t'an Wang-wu shan sheng-chi chi* (HY 967), p. 4a. For contemporary Taoist definitions of the Gold Register Retreat see the *Chai-chieh lu* (HY 464)—this text was probably compiled in the early eighth century during Hsüan-tsung's first years on the throne, p. 3a; and *Yao-hsiu k'o-i chieh-lü ch'ao* (HY 463), compiled by Chu Chün-hsü (alias Chu Fa-man, d. July 9, 720), ch. 8, p. 1b. On the dating of these texts see *Tung-hsiao t'u-chih,* compiled by Teng Mu (1247–1306) in 1302 (Shanghai: Ts'ung-shu chi-ch'eng, 1935), ch. 5, p. 43; Yoshioka Yoshitoyo, "*Saikairoku to Shigensō,*" *Taishō Daigaku kenkyū kiyō* 52 (1968): 283–301; and Wu Chi-yu, *Pen-tsi king (Livre de terme originel)* (Paris, 1960), pp. 18–19. For the contemporary official interpretation of the rite see *TTLT,* ch. 4, p. 42b.

20. *Chin-shih hsü-pien,* ch. 8, p. 2a–b; and *CTW,* ch. 927, pp. 7b–9b. This account is based on two copies of the inscription written by Ts'ai Wei (see note 2), who apparently accompanied the Princess on her journey to Ch'iao-chün, Mt. Sung, and Mt. Wang-wu. Of these versions the poorest is that in the *Ch'üan T'ang wen,* which begins by stating that Hsüan-tsung had been on the throne for forty years (i.e., 752) when the epiphany occurred, and ends by supplying 753 as the date for the completion of the inscription. This is patently false because the Heavenly Treasure was recovered in 742. However, while the copy in the *Chin-shih hsü-pien* is fuller and more accurate, it has lacunae and misreadings that the *Ch'üan T'ang wen's* does not. On February 17, 742, T'ien T'ung-hsiu, an official in the household of one of Hsüan-tsung's sons, was standing outside the main gate of the Ta-ming Palace when a purple cloud formed above his head. Beneath the cloud Lao Tzu appeared riding a white horse and informed T'ien that he had hidden a talisman in the home of Yin Hsi at the Han-ku Pass east of Ch'ang-an when he, Lao Tzu, left China on his way west. On learning of this development Hsüan-tsung sent a commission to investigate the matter. It unearthed a stone casket containing a jade tablet on which was inscribed in red script the talisman promised (HY 593, pp. 8b–9a; *Yu-lung chuan* [HY 773], compiled by Hsieh Shou-hao [1131–1212] and submitted to the throne in 1191, ch. 8, pp. 36b–38a; *Hun-yüan sheng-chi* [HY 769], compiled by Chia Shan-hsiang [fl. 1086–1101], ch. 5, pp. 23b–24a; Cheng Ch'i [ca. 889–904], *K'ai-T'ien ch'uan-hsin chi,* in *T'ang-tai ts'ung-shu* [Taipei, 1968], p. 130a; *CTS,* ch. 9, p. 214; *TFYK,* ch. 54, p. 1a–b; *THY,* ch. 50, p. 865; *T'ang ta chao-ling chi,* compiled by Sung Min-ch'iu [1019–1079] and completed in 1070 [Taipei, 1978], ch. 4, pp. 21–22; *Ta T'ang chiao-ssu lu,* compiled by Wang Ching [fl. 785–804] and completed in 793, in *Shih-yüan ts'ung-shu* [n.p., 1913–1917], ch. 9, p. 1a; *TCTC,* ch. 216, p. 6852; and Fan Tsu-yü, *T'ang chien* [Peking,

1958], ch. 9, p. 80). HY 593 and HY 773 erroneously date this incident in 741. When Emperor Kao-tsung visited Lao Tzu's temple in Po-chou during 666, he changed the name of its subprefecture, and apparently that of the temple complex as well, to Chen-yüan. (*T'ai-p'ing huan-yü chi*, compiled by Yüeh Shih [930–1007] and completed in 986 [Taipei, 1963], ch. 12, p. 19a). The retreat in which Jade-Perfected and Master Hu participated, was a rite for the transmission of specific texts, not an ordination as suggested by Edward Schafer, "The Capeline Cantos," *Asiatische Studien* 32 (1978): 8.

21. *Wang Mo-chieh ch'üan-chi chien-chu*, annotated by Chao T'ien-ch'eng, whose preface is dated February 26, 1736 (Taipei, 1966), ch. 11, pp. 153–154; *CTS*, ch. 9, p. 218; and *HTS*, ch. 83, p. 3657. According to an inscription written by Wang Shou-tao in 1308, the vestiges of Jade-Perfected's manor were located at Lou-kuan, a famous Taoist temple some sixty kilometers west of Hsian (Ch'ang-an in T'ang times). Another inscription by Liu T'ung-sheng, dated August 19, 742, says that Lou-kuan was the place where the Princess practiced pieties (*Ku Lou-kuan Tzu-yün yen-ch'ing chi* [HY 956], compiled by Chu Hsiang-hsien [1279–1308], ch. 2, p. 21b and ch. 1, p. 12a). Chao T'ien-ch'eng seems to have felt that the notion that her estate was located there was nothing more than a popular tradition.

22. *CTS*, ch. 184, p. 4760; and *HTS*, ch. 208, pp. 5880–5881. Hsüan-tsung founded the Pear Garden Troupe in 714, and it became the most famous in Chinese history (*THY*, ch. 34, p. 629; and Kishibe Shigeo, "Li-yüan," in *T'ang-tai yin-yüeh shih ti yen-chiu*, trans. by Liang Tsai-p'ing and Huang Chih-chiung [Taipei, 1973], vol. 1, p. 334). The actual offense for which the throne punished Hsüan-tsung was unauthorized liaison with officials who were not members of his circle. The court always took a dim view of such contacts during the T'ang because such intercourse often took place when cliques were being formed in opposition to the crown. Li Fu-kuo was the eunuch responsible for breaking up the coterie. Incidentally, Hsüan-tsung enjoyed the dubious distinction of abdicating after he had already been deposed (August 12, 756).

23. Chang Cho (657–730), *Ch'ao-yeh ch'ien-tsai*, completed sometime between 713 and 730 (Ts'ung-shu chi-ch'eng [Shanghai, 1936]), ch. 5, p. 64; *CTS*, ch. 7, p. 141; and *TCTC*, ch. 208, p. 6598. In the preface to his manual for conducting the liturgy of Ling-pao ordinations, Lu Hsiu-ching (406–March 31, 477) notes that the scriptures of all Three Caverns could be transmitted at the same time on the same altar under a single covenant (*T'ai-shang tung-hsüan ling-pao shou-tu i* [HY 528], compiled by Lu Hsiu-ching about 454, p. 2a). On the dating of this text see Michel Strickmann, *Le Taoisme du Mao chan, chronique d'une révélation* (Paris, 1981), p. 72. According to the "New Protocols Imperially Compiled (*Yü-chih hsin-i*)," which Emperor Wu-ti (r. 561–578) of the Northern Chou dynasty (557–581) had compiled, it was possible to receive the Ten Injunctions, *Tao-te ching*, *San-huang wen*, Ling-pao canon, and Shang-ch'ing scriptures together at the same time on the same altar (*Wu-shang pi-yao* [HY 1130], compiled under imperial auspices by a commission between 577 and 578, ch. 35, p. 1b; and John Lagerway, *Wu-shang pi-yao, somme Taoiste du VIe siècle* [Paris, 1981], pp. 4 and 125). See Chapter Four on the hierarchy of ordina-

tion. On the Three Caverns, see Ofuchi Ninji, "The Formation of the Taoist Canon," in *Facets of Taoism,* ed. by Anna Seidel and Holmes Welch (New Haven, 1979), pp. 253–267. The *Chiu T'ang shu* says only that Shih Ch'ung-hsüan and ten odd men were appointed to offices and conferred aristocratic titles as rewards for their assistance in establishing the Sheng-shan ssu. The *Tzu-chih t'ung-chien,* which errs in calling the prelate Shih Ch'ung-en, states that his rank was raised to the fifth grade and that he was appointed Libationer for the Directorate of the Sons of State as a supplementary official. On that office and Shih's appanage, see *TTLT,* ch. 2, p. 33b; and *Traité des fonctionnaires et Traité de l'armée,* vol. 1, pp. 43 and 442–443.

24. Chang Cho, *Ch'ao-yeh ch'ien-tsai,* ch. 5, p. 64; *HTS,* ch. 83, p. 3656; *TTLT,* ch. 18, pp. 11a–21b; *Traité des fonctionnaires et Traité de l'armée,* vol. 1, 408–417; and Yamazaki Hiroshi, "Tōdai ni okeru sōni sorei no mondai," *Shina Bukkyō shiseki* 3, no. 1 (1939): 1–4. On supernumerary offices see *The Cambridge History of China,* vol. 3, pt. 1, pp. 323–324.

25. Chang Cho, *Ch'ao-yeh ch'ien-tsai,* ch. 5, p. 64; *HTS,* ch. 83, p. 3656; *Ch'ang-an chih,* ch. 10, p. 6a–b; and *TLCCFK,* ch. 4, p. 19a. Wei Ts'ou, Vice-Minister in the Department of Justice, made the remark about the excessive expenditures laid out for the T'ai-ch'ing kuan in a remonstrance against the construction of the Princesses' abbeys. *THY,* ch. 50, p. 875.

26. *I-ch'ieh Tao-ching yin-i miao-men yu-ch'i* (HY 1115), Shih Ch'ung-hsüan's preface, pp. 4a–6a. The signature to this preface contains all of Shih's titles as given in HY 1231 (see the introduction to this study). The Sung texts that contain citations from the *I-ch'ieh Tao-ching yin-i* are the *Shang-ch'ing ta-tung chen-ching yü-chüeh yin-i* (HY 104), compiled by Ch'en Ching-yüan (1025–July 27, 1094); and the *Nan-hua chen-ching chang-chü yin-i* (HY 736), compiled by Ch'en Ching-yüan, whose preface is dated February 23, 1084. Yoshioka Yoshitoyo analyzed information provided in Shih Ch'ung-hsüan's and Hsüan-tsung's prefaces and arrived at the conclusion that the compilation consisted of two parts: the glossary and the catalog. He also determined that the entire work had a total of 253 chapters (*Dōkyō keiten shiron* [Tokyo, 1955], pp. 98–109). Hsüan-tsung's preface contains what was probably his earliest published recognition of the basic premise underlying the T'ang Taoist ideology, "revered is Lao Tzu, first ancestor of the state." On his search for lost texts, the formation of a new *Tao-tsang,* and dissemination of this library to the provinces, see C. Benn, *Taoism as Ideology in the Reign of Emperor Hsüan-tsung,* vol. 2, pp. 288–289.

27. *HTS,* ch. 83, pp. 3656–3657 and ch. 36, p. 954. These two passages are versions of the same incident, supplying different, but not contradictory, information. The first calls the intruder Tuan Hsien, discusses the Buddhist involvement in the affair, and describes the throne's response after Tuan's arrest. The second is a more detailed account of Tuan's actions at the T'ai-chi Hall, dating the incident in the T'ai-chi era (March 1 to June 21, 712).

28. *San-tung chung-chieh wen* (HY 178), p. 1a; *Tung-hsüan ling-pao san-shih ming-hui hsing-chuang chü-fang-so wen* (HY 445), p. 1a; *San-tung fa-fu k'o-chieh wen* (HY 787), p. 1a; HY 1231, ch. 1, pp. 1a–12a, and ch. 2, pp. 20b–21a and 21b; and HY 1115, Shih Ch'ung-hsüan's preface, p. 6a. The date for the abolition of the T'ai-ch'ing kuan is well fixed, but there is a certain amount of confusion about

the date of its establishment. The *Ch'ang-an chih* says that, when the property of
Princess An-lo was seized in 710, the throne ordered Shih Ch'ung-hsüan, a
priest of the T'ai-ch'ing kuan, to assume control. This may just be a slip of the
pen, and the passage should actually read something like the throne ordered
Shih Ch'ung-hsüan to take charge of the T'ai-ch'ing kuan. However, the literal
reading is clear: a T'ai-ch'ing kuan existed before 710. The implications are
that there was a temple of the same name elsewhere in the capital and that its
title was transferred to Princess An-lo's property in 711. There is a reference in
the same source to an earlier abbey with that name. Sometime after the Tibetans asked for the hand of Princess T'ai-p'ing in 677, her abbey was moved to
another ward in the capital, and the structure which it had previously occupied
was renamed T'ai-ch'ing kuan. However, in 687 the title of the latter was again
changed to Wei-kuo kuan (*Ch'ang-an chih*, ch. 7, p. 12b, and ch. 10, pp. 2a and
6a–b; and *TLCCFK*, ch. 2, p. 12b, and ch. 4, pp. 9b and 19a). There are no
further references to a T'ai-ch'ing kuan after 687. Perhaps another alteration of
the name for a capital abbey occurred in that period, references to which were
subsequently lost. Since the existence of such an abbey prior to 710 cannot be
ruled out, it is possible that some of those works which Chang Wan-fu signed as
a priest of the T'ai-ch'ing kuan were written prior to 710.

29. HY 508, ch. 16, p. 1a; and HY 1230, p. 1a and 1b. For Chang's comments about his years as a Taoist and as a priest see HY 1230, p. 1b. *Ching-yü* is
a variant reading for *Ching-t'u* (Pure Land), a Buddhist paradise. "Ascending
to the Pure Territory" refers to the salvation of souls in hell who rise to the Pure
Land by virtue of meritorious acts performed by their descendants. In this con-
text the phrase seems to be a euphemism for initiation, that is, for the first vows
which an ordinand took and which were apparently thought to ensure his salvation from the torments of hell. I have found no textual basis for this interpretation, which is therefore conjectural, but, as will be seen, certain rites of passage,
notably Ling-pao ordinations, included conferrals which were safe-conducts
that permitted the initiate or ordinand to bypass hell after death. Perhaps similar notions were attached to the swearing of the first vows. Yoshioka Yoshitoyo
says that Chang wrote HY 1230 as a priest of the Pure Capital Abbey *before* he
was transferred to the T'ai-ch'ing kuan. However, he did not take into account
the signature on chapter sixteen of HY 508 or the omission of the Shang-ch'ing
inventory in HY 1231. He also states that Chang swore his oath to his preceptor
between the ages of five and ten, and this would have made him around fifty-
five to seventy years of age at the time he composed HY 1231. I have been unable to find any regulation in Taoist protocols which permitted the taking of
vows at that tender age ("Sandō hōdō kakai gihan no kenkyū," in *Dōkyō to
Bukkyō* [Tokyo, 1976], p. 91).

## Chapter Two

1. HY 1231, ch. 2, p. 18b. On the Kuei-chen Abbey see *Ch'ang-an chih*, ch.
6, p. 2b; and *TLCCFK*, ch. 1, p. 4a. The Great Inner Palace served as quarters
for T'ang emperors from 618 until 664, when Kao-tsung moved into the Palace
of Great Brilliance. Although the latter eclipsed the former in importance there-

after, the Great Inner Palace continued to play a major role at various political, social, and ceremonial functions (*THY*, ch. 30, pp. 553–554; *Yü-hai*, compiled by Wang Ying-lin [1223–1296] [Taipei, 1964], ch. 157, p. 3a–b; and Howard Wechsler, *The Mirror to the Son of Heaven, Wei Cheng at the Court of T'ang T'ai-tsung* [New Haven, 1974], p. 136). In traditional China the front court or cloister of a home or abbey was generally reserved for public affairs and the rear for residence. The conversion of T'ang measures into modern metric and Anglo-American units is based on a table in Nathan Sivin, *Chinese Alchemy, Preliminary Studies* (Cambridge, Massachusetts, 1968), pp. 252–256. Sivin's table is devoted to apothecary measures: the small foot, small ounce, and small bushel. These units were used only for tuning musical instruments, making calculations on the sundial and mixing medicine. For all other measurements the large foot, ounce, and bushel, also given in his table, were employed (*TTLT*, ch. 3, p. 47b; and Stefan Balazs, "Beiträge zur Wirtschaftgeschichte der T'ang-Zeit," *Mitteilung des Seminars für Orientalische Sprachen* 36 [1933]: 42–44). *Ch'ing,* the term for the color of the silk cordon used in this citation, stands for three different hues in Chinese of which only blue or green applies in this case. Chang Wan-fu himself gives two conflicting glosses on the subject. He says that it is the color of heaven (blue), and the color of the east and virtue of spring (green) (HY 1231, ch. 2, p. 12b). The actual color was a hue of blue-green associated in traditional China with the color of kingfisher feathers. My thanks to Professor Michael Saso for clarifying this and several other points of confusion about Taoist rites. On tamped earth see Paul Wheatley, *The Pivot of Four Quarters* (Edinburgh, 1971), pp. 33–34 and 91. The dynastic history of the Sui dynasty contains an extremely brief discussion of a Taoist altar and a ritual of investiture which is overly simplified and erroneous in parts (*Sui shu,* compiled by Wei Cheng [580–643] and others, completed in 636 [Peking, 1973], ch. 35, p. 1092; and "The *Wei Shu* and *Sui Shu* on Taoism," trans. by James Ware, *Journal of the American Oriental Society* 53 [1933]: 245). The square, three-tiered, outdoor altar of tamped earth was also a standard fixture for the worship of the soil god, a cult which was ubiquitous in rural China from prehistoric times to the twentieth century. For a woodblock illustration of one see *Nung shu,* by Wang Chen, whose preface is dated April 11, 1313 (Taipei, 1975), ch. 11, p. 7a.

2. For Ennin's notes on Buddhist ordination platforms see *Ennin's Diary, the Record of a Pilgrim to China in Search of the Law,* trans. by Edwin O. Reischauer (New York, 1955), pp. 45–46, 207, 217, 222, and 228–229. While Ennin was in China, Buddhism was suffering from official persecution, and, as he says at the beginning of his diary, there were only two ordination platforms left in the empire, one in Loyang, which he did not see, and the other at Mt. Wu-t'ai. However, the first that he visited was one that had been recently opened in the K'ai-yüan Monastery of Pei-chou (modern Ho-ch'ing hsien in southern Hopei Province; Reischauer misreads the character Pei and gives Chü-chou as the name for the district; see note 797 on p. 206). This dais had two levels which were two and a half feet high each. The lower was twenty-five feet square and the upper fifteen feet square. It was constructed of brick and was blue-green in color. After Ennin reached Mt. Wu-t'ai he visited the Chen-yüan Cloister and

saw the Wan-sheng Ordination Platform. This fixture was octagonal in shape, made of "white jade [marble?]," and had a single tier three feet high. Its base was filled with a plaster made in part from incense, and it was covered with a polychrome silk carpet. John Lagerway contends that the great Taoist abbeys of ancient times often had permanent three-tiered altars of tamped earth. Such fixtures must, however, have been covered in some fashion because they could not have survived the elements otherwise (*Taoist Ritual in Chinese History and Society* [New York, 1987], p. 25).

3. For Chang's diagram see HY 1202, pp. 4b–5a (Appendix Three, number 6). In the prologue to his manual, Lu Hsiu-ching says that he constructed his liturgy from elements that he found in the *Chin-lu* (*chien-wen*, The Slip-Writs for the Gold Register), *Huang-lu* (*chien-wen*, The Slip-Writs for the Yellow Register), *Ming-chen k'o* (The Code of Perfection Clarified), the *Yü-chüeh* (Jade Instructions), and the *Chen-i tzu-jan ching chüeh* (Instructions from the Spontaneously Generated Scripture of True Unity). The first two of these texts are now lost except for excerpts cited in other works. Ōfuchi Ninji has tentatively identified three Tun-huang manuscripts (P. 2356, P. 2403, and P. 2452) in the Pelliot collection as fragments from the last scripture that Lu mentions (*Tonkō Dōkei, mokuroku hen*, compiled by Ōfuchi Ninji [Tokyo, 1978], pp. 77–79; and *Tonkō Dōkei, zuroku hen*, compiled by Ōfuchi Ninji [Tokyo, 1979], pp. 116–121). "S." stands for the Stein collection of Tun-huang manuscripts in the British Museum and "P." for the Pelliot collection in the Bibliothèque Nationale in Paris. The remaining texts, the *Yü-chüeh* and the *Ming-chen k'o*, have survived in the *Tao-tsang* under the titles *T'ai-shang tung-hsüan ling-pao ch'ih-shu yü-chüeh miao-ching* (HY 352), and *Tung-hsüan ling-pao ch'ang-yeh chih fu chiu-yu yü-kuei ming-chen k'o* (HY 1400). Together with the *Shang-ch'ing T'ai-chi yin-chu yü-ching pao-chüeh* (HY 425), the latter constitute the most important scriptures in the Ling-pao corpus relative to the arrangement of altars for the ritual of investiture. On the original corpus of Ling-pao scriptures see *Tonkō Dōkei, mokuroku hen*, compiled by Ōfuchi Ninji, pp. 17–76 and 365–369; Ōfuchi Ninji, "On *Ku Ling-pao ching*," *Acta Asiatica* 27 (1974): 34–56; and Stephen Bokenkamp, "Sources of the Ling-pao Scriptures," in *Tantric and Taoist Studies in Honour of R. A. Stein*, ed. by Michel Strickmann (Brussels, 1983), pp. 434–486. The chapters relevant to Ling-pao ordinations in the *Wu-shang pi-yao* are 34 and 39. For synopses in French of all the extant chapters from this compendium see John Lagerway, *Wu-shang pi-yao, somme Taoiste du VIe siècle*. The most important illustrations of Taoist alters vis-à-vis Ling-pao ordinations are in HY 508, ch. 2, pp. 2a–4b.

4. HY 1130, ch. 39, p. 1a.

5. HY 352, ch. 2, pp. 21a–22a; and HY 528, pp. 2b–3b. HY 352 states that five gates should be erected, but it is clear from its directives regarding the placards that the altar actually had only four. The use of one of the seasonal gates to stand for the center as well was an accommodation that attempted to solve one of the perennial problems of traditional Chinese cosmologists: having predicated the existence of five elements/phases/directions, where did the fifth fall in space and time? The interpretation for the meaning of the term "main portal" in HY 352 is based on the notion of Regal Gate as found in HY 1130, ch. 39, p.

1b–3a. For Lu Hsiu-ching's directions, which indicate the existence of a second four-gate enclosure called the Capital altar, see HY 528, pp. 8b5 and 9a4.

6. HY 1130, ch. 39, pp. 1a–2a. Like HY 352 (preceding note), this text states that five gates should be erected. However, later on when it addresses the question of where to place the gates according to the points of the compass, it is clear that the gates for the center and the Perfected had their own openings in the enclosure and that there were six gates in all. The regulations governing the design of altars for the transmission of the *San-huang wen* canon required three gates: one in the north for the Celestial Sovereign, one in the west-south-west for the Terrestrial Sovereign, and one in the east-north-east for the Human Sovereign. Those for the arrangement of altars used at Shang-ch'ing ordinations called for four gates, one in each corner of the structure (HY 1130, ch. 38, p. 1a; and ch. 40, p. 1a).

7. HY 528, p. 8a; HY 1130, ch. 39, p. 1b, and HY 508, ch. 2, pp. 1a–2a. An earlier description of this altar appears in the *Wu-shang pi-yao* (HY 1130), ch. 54, pp. 1a–2a. John Lagerway gives a synopsis of the account in *Taoist Ritual in Chinese Society and History,* pp. 35–36. The description in HY 508 is far more detailed and concise than that in HY 1130. This may reflect an evolutionary development that occurred between 578 and 1223. HY 508 cites Chang Wan-fu and other T'ang liturgists who edited the protocols for the Yellow Register Retreat. However, the compilers of the *Wu-shang pi-yao* often shortened or abbreviated the investiture liturgies. A comparison of their ritual for the Ling-pao ordination in chapter 39 with Lu Hsiu-ching's in HY 528, or their rite for the transmission of the *San-huang wen* canon in chapter 38 with that provided in the *T'ai-shang tung-shen san-huang i* (HY 802), which possibly dates from the T'ang period, reveals omissions and simplifications in the *Wu-shang pi-yao* that can only be accounted for if one assumes that the compilers made large excisions. I have found no basis in HY 1130 for Lagerway's conclusion that the outer enclosure of this altar had eight gates. To my knowledge no dictionary defines *tsuan* as pole, but the meaning is clear from a passage in HY 508, ch. 2, p. 7a. At that point the text describes the construction of the outermost enclosure. It says that "the taller poles of it should extend one *chang,* nine *ch'ih* (5.6 meters or 23.2 feet) out of the ground and the shorter should be seven *ch'ih,* six *ts'un* (2.21 meters or 7 feet) in length, of which six *ts'un* (15 centimeters or 5.7 inches) should be sunk into the ground." The ten gates represented the deities of the Ten Directions, a cluster of gods that was apparently adopted from Buddhism (Stephen Bokenkamp, "Sources of the Ling-pao Scriptures," p. 462).

8. Part of the basis for interpreting the description of the altar for Ling-pao investitures as a tiered structure is the phrase "a layered altar of ten gates," which follows the account of the six-gate altar in the *Wu-shang pi-yao.* However, the wording is ambiguous and could be construed to mean that three enclosures were erected on flat terrain (HY 1130, ch. 39, p. 1b). John Lagerway interprets another passage from the *Wu-shang pi-yao* that gives directions for constructing an altar used in the Retreat of the Three Primes *(San-yüan chai)* to mean that the outlines of its three steps were merely traced with red mud and not built of tamped earth (HY 1130, ch. 52, p. 1a; and *Taoist Ritual in Chinese History and*

*Society,* p. 31). Finally, Ennin visited an ordination platform for nuns at the Shan-kuang Monastery in Pei-chou, which was simply laid out on the floor and roped off from the rest of the hall. This measure was probably adopted as an expedient. Permanent platforms may well have been proscribed during the persecution of Buddhism in the mid-ninth century (*Ennin's Diary, the Record of a Pilgrim to China in Search of the Law,* p. 207). It seems that both religions made concessions to suit circumstances. On the altar as a symbol for the mountain, see HY 528, pp. 8a9 and 9a2.

9. The table for this paragraph shows that in the second source (HY 528) Lu Hsiu-ching simply altered the annotations to the portal inscriptions which appeared in the first source (HY 352) from the Ling-pao canon, amplifying them by specifying the hues of the fields, but not contradicting the basic regulation. In the third source (HY 1130), however, the rules reverse the relationship of the colors of the scripts and tablets, indicating that some form of deviation from the canonical standard had occurred in the century or more between Lu Hsiu-ching's time and that of the *Wu-shang pi-yao*'s compilation. The size of the placards given in the *Wu-shang pi-yao* appears to be too small, but that text abandoned the lengthy gate inscriptions given in earlier sources in favor of five character titles (HY 352, ch. 2, pp. 21a–22a; HY 528, pp. 2b–3b; and HY 1130, ch. 39, p. 1a–b). The term purple-gold, *tzu-chin,* also refers to a kind of gold which had traces of iron in it that turned purple under heat. See Edward Schafer, *The Golden Peaches of Samarkand* (Berkeley, 1963), pp. 254–255. It would not have been totally out of the question for the throne to have had placards manufactured from this rare metal, but it seems more likely that it would have had them made of painted wood.

10. HY 1231, ch. 2, pp. 19b–20a. In Chin-ming Ch'i-chen's collection of excerpts from regulations on liturgical paraphernalia (ca. A.D. 550) there is a list of twenty-one varieties of banners classifed according to the materials, decorations, and processes used in their fabrication. The last six *(lou-fan)* of those enumerated in Chang's work appear to fall into the tenth category in that list. The liturgical rules prescribed fixed lengths from three *ch'ih* (73.8 centimeters or 2 feet 10.5 inches) to 1,000 *ch'ih* (246 meters or 958 feet) for the pennons as well. Only four of these—73.8 centimeters (2 feet 10.5 inches), 57.5 centimeters (4 feet 9.5 inches), 172.2 centimeters (6 feet 9.5 inches), and 221.4 centimeters (8 feet 7.5 inches)—could possibly have been used on altars, because the others were too long for the poles. The regulations in Chin-ming Ch'i-chen's text also divide banners into three classes on the basis of their functions: those for the dead, whose titles reflect a desire for the salvation of the soul of the deceased; those for the ill, whose names allude to dispelling misfortune and prolonging life; and those for normal households, whose titles express longings for prosperity, good fortune, and longevity. These pennons were to be suspended from poles erected in courtyards or beside statues of the gods (HY 1117, ch. 3, p. 2a–b).

11. HY 1231, ch. 2, p. 18b. Dragon-beard mats were a product of north China, especially the area around the capitals. A phoenix-pinion mat is mentioned as a tribute product of Ho-pei Circuit which was the northeastern divi-

sion of the empire in the T'ang (*TTLT,* ch. 3, pp. 7b, 11a–b, and 13a; and Edward Schafer and B. E. Wallacker, "Local Tribute Products of the T'ang Dynasty," *Journal of Oriental Studies* 4 [1957–1958]: 230 (no. 329) and map 15. The terms "dragon beard" and "phoenix pinion" probably refer to the appearance of the pattern in the weave of the mats.

12. HY 1231, ch. 2, p. 20a. In Taoism the seven treasures were yellow gold and white silver, red coral, amber, agate, carnelian, true pearls, and blue-green jade (HY 1231, ch. 2, p. 9a). The seven treasures *(sapta ratna)*—the term as well as many of the objects—was a notion adopted from Buddhism *(Fo-hsüeh ta-tz'u-tien,* compiled by Ting Fu-pao from a Japanese dictionary of the same name which Oda Tokumo compiled [Taipei, 1969], vol. 1, p. 116). For the protocols governing the numbers of lanterns to be lit to dispel calamities, see HY 352, ch. 1, pp. 18b–19a. The citation from the *Chin-lu chien-wen* can be found in HY 463, ch. 8, pp. 17b–18a. This text lists only fifteen groups of lanterns, in contrast to HY 508, which lists sixteen. The title Tao-hu teng (Lanterns of the Portal of the Tao) from the latter compendium is missing in the former work.

13. HY 1231, ch. 2, pp. 18b and 19a–b. Curiously, Chang's account of the tables and their kerchiefs is broken into three entries inserted at three different points in the text. Chin-ming Ch'i-chen's collection of excerpts from statutes on liturgical paraphernalia contains a list for six types of tables placed before statues of the Celestial Venerables or used for reciting scripture: jade, gold, silver, stone, aromatic [wood], and wood. Although it says that the size of them varied according to circumstances, it also provides the measurements for scripture recitation tables: one *ch'ih,* eight *ts'un* (49 centimeters or 19 inches) long; one *ch'ih,* two *ts'un* (34.4 centimeters or 13.4 inches) wide; and one *ch'ih,* five *ts'un* (41.8 centimeters or 16.3 inches) high. The height of these tables is consistent with that depicted in the illustration (Figure 5) from the *Wu-shang pi-yao* and means that Taoist rites in pre-T'ang and T'ang times were conducted from a kneeling position. Chin-ming Ch'i-chen also supplies an enumeration of kerchiefs, eight in number, for covering the tables. Those used at the investiture of 711 fall into the first of those categories, assorted brocades (HY 1117, ch. 3, pp. 4b–5a and 3a).

14. HY 1130, ch. 39, p. 2b; and HY 1231, ch. 2, p. 19a. The passage from the Ling-pao canon can be found in HY 352, ch. 2, pp. 23a–24b. The officiant was supposed to read the inscriptions and make obeisances to bring the energies down to the altar. In Chin-ming Ch'i-chen's work there is a list for fifteen varieties of braziers classified according to the materials or processes used in their manufacture and the character of their decorations. Three of the designs that Chang describes (numbers one, two and five) are described in it (HY 1117, ch. 3, pp. 2b–3a).

15. HY 1231, ch. 2, p. 13a; HY 352, ch. 2, p. 23a; and HY 528, p. 2a. On imported aromatics see Edward Schafer, *The Golden Peaches of Samarkand,* pp. 163–165, 166–168, and 171–172; and Chi Han, *Nan-fang ts'ao-mu chuang, a Fourth Century Flora of Southeast Asia,* trans. by Li Hui-lin (Hong Kong, 1979), pp. 79–80 and 89. *Ch'ing-mu,* number four, is now identified with Birthwort, a Chinese plant. In the T'ang, the identity of the plant was the subject of some

confusion, but all of the commentators at that time agreed that it was imported, and this would make it Putchuk, a plant native to Kashmir and Ceylon (*Pen-ts'ao kang-mu,* compiled by Li Shih-chen [1518–1593] and completed in 1596 [Hong Kong, 1976], ch. 14, p. 19; and G. A. Stuart, *Chinese Materia Medica, the Vegetable Kingdom* [Taipei, 1979], pp. 49–50 and 380).

16. HY 1130, ch. 39, p. 11a; HY 1202, p. 21b; and Joseph Needham and Lu Gwei-djen, *Science and Civilization in China,* vol. 5, *Chemistry and Chemical Technology,* pt. 2 (Cambridge, England, 1974), pp. 128 ff. On the role that true, not symbolic, alchemy played in religious Taoism, see Michel Strickmann, "On the Alchemy of T'ao Hung-ching," in *Facets of Taoism,* pp. 123–192. Cinnabar was also a form of pledge at Taoist investitures (HY 802, p. 1b; and HY 508, ch. 3, p. 4a).

17. HY 1231, ch. 2, p. 13a; HY 1130, ch. 39, pp. 5b–6a and 11a; and Michael Saso, *The Teachings of Taoist Master Chuang* (New Haven, Connecticut, 1978), pp. 218–219.

18. HY 1130, ch. 39, p. 2b; and HY 1231, ch. 2, p. 19a–b. On the symbolism of the cloths' colors, see HY 352, ch. 2, pp. 22b–23a; and HY 528, pp. 1b and 2a. Both brocade and embroidered wrappers appear in Chin-ming Ch'i-chen's list of five, and two of Chang's cases seem to correspond to the carved jade and pure gold in his enumeration of twelve varieties (HY 1117, ch. 3, p. 3b).

19. On the concept that these gages served as collateral for vows, see HY 352, ch. 2, p. 29b; HY 1400, pp. 37b–38a; HY 528, p. 1b; and HY 1130, ch. 34, p. 7b. For Chang's remarks see HY 1231, ch. 2, pp. 18a and 13a. The *Wu-shang pi-yao* calls for only five lengths. The size of the *p'i* (bolt) as a measure of cloth is given in Stefan Balazs, "Beiträge zur Wirtschaftgeschichte der T'ang-Zeit," pt. 3, p. 44. The Anglo-American and metric equivalents plugged into this formula are, however, based on Nathan Sivin's table (see note 1, Chapter Two). On the placement of the silk under the tables see HY 528, p. 3b.

20. On the numerology of the five directions, see HY 528, pp. 52b–53a; Michael Saso, *The Teachings of Taoist Master Chuang,* p. 215; and Lagerway, *Taoist Ritual in Chinese Society and History,* p. 104.

21. The list of pledges submitted at the Princesses' ordination can be found in HY 1231, ch. 2, pp. 18b–19a. On the regulations governing "Destiny Silk" see *T'ai-shang tung-hsüan ling-pao chih-hui ting-chih t'ung-wei ching* (HY 325), a text from the original Ling-pao canon, p. 17b; HY 1400, p. 37a–b; HY 528, p. 2a; HY 1130, ch. 39, p. 2a–b; and HY 1231, ch. 2, p. 13a–b. On turning purple or blue-green net into liturgical vestments, see HY 1231, ch. 2, p. 14b. Net, an openwork fabric favored for light summer clothing in traditional China, does not appear in the lists of sureties for Ling-pao ordinations, but was an element at Shang-ch'ing transmissions of texts (HY 1130, ch. 34, pp. 14a, 14b, 15a, and 15b). On the character of net and all other fabrics mentioned in this study, see *Chung-kuo li-tai chih-jan-hsiu t'u-lu,* ed. by Kao Han-yü (Hong Kong, 1986), pp. 14–19 and 242–244; and *Chung-kuo ta pai-k'o ch'üan-shu, Fang-chih,* ed. by Hu Ch'iao-mu (Peking, 1984).

22. HY 802, p. 1b; *T'ai-shang chiu-ch'ih pan-fu wu-ti nei-chen ching* (HY 1318),

p. 32a; *Shang-ch'ing t'ai-shang pa-su chen-ching* (HY 426), p. 25a; *Shang-ch'ing kao-shang yü-ch'en feng-t'ai ch'ü-su shang ching* (HY 1361), p. 11b; and HY 1130, ch. 34, pp. 13b, 14b, and 11b. See HY 1361, p. 11b for the statement about using this cloth as a substitute for smearing blood on the lips.

23. HY 352, ch. 2, p. 19b; HY 1400, p. 38a; HY 528, p. 1a; and HY 1130, ch. 34, p. 7b. Chang Wan-fu does not mention this form of gage in his discussion of pledges.

24. HY 1400, p. 38a; HY 352, ch. 2, p. 19b; HY 528, pp. 1a and 1b; and HY 1130, ch. 34, p. 7b.

25. HY 1231, ch. 2, p. 14b.

26. On the role of incense as a pledge in the Shang-ch'ing tradition, see HY 1130, ch. 34, pp. 11a, 11b, 12a, 13b, and 14a.

27. HY 1231, ch. 2, p. 12a–b. Chang's symbolic interpretation is based on the notion that blue-green represents Heaven and the spring as well as their life-sustaining powers.

28. HY 1231, ch. 2, p. 15a. According to the protocols for the transmission of the *Tao-te ching,* in a text which probably dates from the late Nan-pei ch'ao or early T'ang, ordinands were given three days to complete their copying of the scriptures (*Ch'uan-shou ching-chieh i-chu chüeh* [HY 1228], p. 7b). On the dating of this text see Kusuyama Haruki, "Kajokō chu no seiritsu," in *Rōshi densetsu no kenkyū* (Tokyo, 1979), p. 128.

29. One of the Shang-ch'ing scriptures requires a book knife (*shu-tao*) as a pledge, claiming that its function is "to sever the path of the death vapors (*ch'i*)" (*Tung-chen t'ai-shang tzu-tu yen-kuang shen-yüan pien ching* [HY 1321], p. 16a; and HY 1130, ch. 34, p. 11b).

30. For the titles to the sets of Ling-pao injunctions, see HY 1231, ch. 1, p. 2a. The thirty-eight officiants are discussed in the following chapter of this study. On the division of tallies and rings, see HY 802, pp. 7a. This text calls for pledges of nine common knives and one gold knife (HY 802, pp. 1b and 2a).

31. HY 1231, ch. 2, pp. 10b and 19a. The Casting of the Dragon Tablets was an ancillary rite at Ling-pao investitures. See the end of Chapter Three below for a description of it.

32. HY 352, ch. 1, pp. 5a–b, 6a, and 7a; and HY 1231, ch. 2, p. 10b.

33. For Ko Hung's remark, see *Pao-p'u Tzu,* the *nei-p'ien* in 20 ch. completed in A.D. 317 and the *wai-p'ien* in 50 ch. sometime later, collated and corrected by Sun Hsing-yen (1753–1818), whose preface is dated A.D. 1813 (Taipei, 1969), ch. 19, p. 97; and *Alchemy, Medicine and Religion in the China of A.D. 320,* trans. by James Ware (Boston, 1966), p. 314. For the theory that sacrifice of wealth is necessary in a decadent age, see *T'ai-shang tung-hsüan ling-pao san-yüan p'in-chieh kung-te ch'ing-chung ching* (HY 456), a scripture from the original Ling-pao canon, p. 37a; HY 1130, ch. 34, p. 8b; and HY 1231, ch. 2, p. 8b.

34. The distribution of pledges was the subject of rules set down in the original Ling-pao canon (HY 456, p. 37a; and HY 1130, ch. 34, p. 8a–b). Another text from the canon supplies the percentages (HY 1400, p. 39a; and HY 1130, ch. 34, p. 8a). A third scripture (now lost) said that the Canon Preceptor may not use the pledges for his private needs (cited in HY 1130, ch. 34, p. 9a).

35. HY 1130, ch. 38, p. 1b; ch. 39, p. 2a; and ch. 40, p. 1b. The protocols also speak of deviations from the norm when pledges were offered for the transmission of the *Tao-te ching* (HY 1130, ch. 37, p. 1a).

36. It is possible that the Princesses paid the bill for the ordination out of their own pockets, but, given the huge cost, it seems more likely that it was the throne that paid.

## Chapter Three

1. The *Wu-shang pi-yao* contains the only other datable pre-T'ang or T'ang liturgy for Ling-pao ordinations known to me. Like Lu Hsiu-ching's work, it contains directions for both the Reading of the Petition on Yellow Silk and the Nocturnal Revelation. However, the *Wu-shang pi-yao*'s account has been drastically abridged. More importantly, certain aspects of the rite are missing, notably the procedures for transmitting the True Writs, the True Writ Registers, Slip-Board Writs, and Staffs. I suspect that its liturgy was never intended for use at ordinations, but was, instead, meant to supply its patron, Emperor Wu-ti of the Northern Chou, with a synopsis of the rite, perhaps for his edification.

2. The protocols for performing the primitive version of the *Su-ch'i* in the Ling-pao canon required ablution *(mu-yü)*, pure fasting *(ch'ing-chai)*, and burning incense *(shao-hsiang)* before the rite could be conducted (HY 352, ch. 2, pp. 24b–25a). By the end of the sixth century, if not earlier, these three acts were standard prerequisites for the transmissions of all scriptures (HY 1130, ch. 35, p. 1a). The canon also prescribed ablutions as preliminaries for celebrations on the Days of the Three Primes *(San-yüan jih)*, Taoist holy days that fell on the fifteenth days of the first, seventh, and tenth months in the lunar calendar (*T'ai-shang ta-Tao san-yüan p'in-chieh hsieh-tsui shang-fa* [HY 417], a Ling-pao text of the Nan-pei ch'ao period, but not part of the original corpus, p. 14b; and HY 1130, ch. 66, p. 1a–b). HY 417 is the text which recommends the use of the Five Aromatics in bath water. For the list of religious activities that required fasting, see *Shang-ch'ing T'ai-chi yin-chu yü ching pao-chüeh* (HY 425), a scripture from the original Ling-pao canon, p. 15b. The regulations governing the construction of oratories *(ching-shih)* were given in the *T'ai-chen k'o*, an ancient Celestial Master code which is now lost (cited in the *Chen-kao* [HY 1010], compiled by T'ao Hung-ching [456–April 18, 536] and completed in 499 or shortly thereafter, ch. 18, pp. 6b–7a; and Ch'en Kuo-fu, *Tao-tsang yüan-liu k'ao,* vol. 2, pp. 333–335).

3. The protocols fixing the dates for the transmission of the canon can be found in HY 352, ch. 20b; HY 528, p. 2b; and *Tung-hsüan ling-pao tao-shih shou san-tung ching-chieh fa-lu che-jih li* (HY 1230), compiled by Chang Wan-fu sometime after 713, p. 5a. As the latter source indicates, these regulations were still effective in the early eighth century.

4. The original figure for the number of officiants was set forth in the *Chin-lu chien-wen,* which is now lost, but this passage is cited in HY 463, ch. 8, p. 7b; *T'ai-shang chen-jen fu ling-pao chai-chieh wei-i chu-ching yao-chüeh* (HY 532), a scripture from the original Ling-pao canon, p. 20b; and HY 1130, ch. 35, p. 8a. Although the second source quotes the *Chin-lu chien-wen,* its wording is different

from the text in HY 463, and it includes a code of forbidden acts no longer extant in HY 532. The titles and numbers of officiants given here is based on Chang Wan-fu's *Tung-hsüan ling-pao san-shih ming-hui hsing-chuang chü-fang-so wen* (HY 445), p. 2b.

5. HY 1130, ch. 35, pp. 8a, 9a, and 10a. Originally HY 532 listed four duties for the cantors—consulting with the Canon Preceptor, understanding the intentions of the retreat's sponsors, prearranging the schedule for the rite, and striking the bell and the drum. This passage is no longer extant in the version of the scripture that survives in the *Tao-tsang* today, but it is cited in HY 463, ch. 8, p. 9b.

6. HY 1130, ch. 35, pp. 8a–10a. The remarks on the Directors acting as liaisons are based on a list of ten tasks which was part of the *Sheng-hsüan ching,* a Ling-pao text that was not one of the original scriptures in the canon and which is no longer extant (cited in HY 463, ch. 8, pp. 13b–14a). On the permanent posts for Directors of Retreats in T'ang abbeys, see *TTLT,* ch. 4, p. 42a.

7. HY 1130, ch. 35, p. 8a.

8. HY 1130, ch. 35, pp. 8b, 9a, and 10a.

9. HY 1130, ch. 35, pp. 8b and 9a. This source lists a seventh category of officiants, the Attendants of the Seats *(shih-tso),* but these posts appear to have disappeared by the early eighth century.

10. HY 445, p. 2b. It is possible that Chang Wan-fu was himself one of the officiants at the Princesses' ordination because he was one of Shih Ch'ung-hsüan's subordinates at the T'ai-ch'ing kuan.

11. HY 1130, ch. 35, p. 1a–b. The title of this section in the *Wu-shang pi-yao* is "The Nocturnal Annunciation's Protocols for the Statement of the Retreat for Transmission of the Canon," and the chapter is devoted to providing rules for ordinations during which more than one canon was conferred on a single occasion. It begins with a citation from the "New Protocols Imperially Compiled," commissioned by Emperor Wu-ti of the Northern Chou. Another form of the ritual appears in a manual for transmitting the *Tao-te ching.* In that account the visit occurs the day before the investiture, and the format of the statement is different (HY 1228, pp. 12a–13a).

12. According to the *Huang-lu chien-wen,* three attempts could be made to schedule an ordination facing unfavorable winds. After that the investiture had to be cancelled because the adverse conditions were ominous signs that the aspirants were without merit and that the gods would not promote or protect them (cited in HY 528, pp. 3b–4a). A period of seven days is also given as the rule for the duration of this ordination in the "New Protocols Imperially Compiled" of Emperor Wu-ti (HY 1130, ch. 35, p. 1a).

13. Chang Wan-fu defines these three stages in his inventory of injunctions (HY 1231, ch. 1, p. 2a). In his hierarchy of initiation and ordination, Chin-ming Ch'i-chen lists two phases, the first of which includes the transmission of the *Tzu-jan ch'üan.* He does not, however, indicate that it was associated with the breaking of the tally (HY 1117, ch. 4, p. 8a). The notion of the Three Covenants may have originated with the Celestial Master sect. There is a manual in the *Tao-tsang* devoted to "Protocols for Ascending the Altar to [Submit] the Yel-

low Silk Petition and to [establish] the Three Covenants." It is part of the *fa-wen* (liturgical writs) that were transmitted to Celestial Master priests (*Cheng-i fa-wen fa-lu pu-i* [HY 1232]). If Ch'en Kuo-fu is correct, the text dates from the Nan-pei ch'ao and is a vestige of a much larger scripture (*Tao-tsang yüan-liu k'ao,* vol. 2, p. 309). On the character of tallies as used by the state in the T'ang, see *TTLT,* ch. 8, pp. 37a–41a; and Robert des Rotours, "Les insignes en deux parties *(fou)* sous la dynastie des T'ang (618–907)," *T'oung Pao* 41, nos. 1–3 (1952): 44–60. On their functions in Taoism see Max Kaltenmark, "*Ling-pao:* note sur un terme du Taoisme religieux," *Mélanges publié par l'Institut des Hautes Études Chinoises* (Paris, 1960), pp. 573–576; and Anna Seidel, "Imperial Treasures and Taoist Sacrements—Taoist Roots in the Apocrypha," in *Tantric and Taoist Studies in Honour of R. A. Stein,* ed. by Michel Strickmann (Brussels, 1983), p. 310.

14. For the place of tallies and contracts in ordination inventories see HY 1117, ch. 4, pp. 6a–10a. The description of the rending of the tally can be found in HY 802, p. 7a. The text which contains the protocols for rending the Ling-pao tally is the *Tung-hsüan ling-pao tzu-jan ch'üan i* (HY 522).

15. The oldest version of these injunctions appears in one of the scriptures from the original Ling-pao canon, *T'ai-shang tung-chen chih-hui shang-p'in ta-chieh* (HY 177), p. 6a–b. They have been copied verbatim into one of Chang Wan-fu's works (HY 178, ch. 2, p. 1a–b).

16. HY 1231, ch. 1, p. 2a; and HY 528, p. 4a. In his manual, Lu employs only the term *shih* (preceptor) for the officiant who directs the investiture. It is translated in the singular throughout this study even though there is no question that three preceptors and a total of thirty-eight officiants presided at such rituals by the early eighth century.

17. HY 1130, ch. 39, pp. 3b–4a. The *Ming-k'o* referred to here is probably the *Ming-chen k'o* (HY 1400).

18. HY 528, p. 6b. The Six Heavens and stale emanations or stale emanation from the Six Heavens were Celestial Master buzzwords for "excessive local cults," which constituted that sect's main competition at its inception. See Rolf Stein, "Religious Taoism and Popular Religion from the Second to the Seventh Centuries," in *Facets of Taoism,* pp. 59–65.

19. HY 528, p. 7a. The *Shang-huang pao-p'ien* may be another name for the Jade Slats, which, in turn, was an alternative title for the True Writs.

20. HY 1231, ch. 2, p. 20a.

21. HY 528, pp. 21b–23b and 23b–25a; and HY 1231, ch. 2, p. 20a–b.

22. HY 528, p. 25a–b. The text of Lu's manual appears to be defective at this point. It reads, "the ordinands acknowledge reception of the oral instructions for the True Writ of the East." There are no further notes describing the actions which the officiant and the ordinands were to take for the transmission of the remaining writs.

23. The account of the True Writs' origin and celestial transmission given here is a brief paraphrase of the opening section in the first revealed scripture of the Ling-pao canon (HY 22, ch. 1, pp. 1a–7a).

24. HY 22, ch. 1, p. 10a–b. This translation and others involving Ling-pao

writs given in this study are tentative. More research needs to be done to uncover all of the allusions and references in these texts. The glosses on the True Writs in HY 352 describe their use in the ritual for expunging sins recorded in celestial ledgers which priests performed on the Days of the Eight Segments *(Pa-chieh jih):* the solstices, equinoxes, and first days of the four seasons. Lu Hsiu-ching compiled a separate manual for this rite in which he simplified the procedure that he found in the scripture. In it he preserved only the first sections of the writs (in both secret seal script and standard Chinese calligraphy), which appropriately dealt with summoning the gods for altering numinous ledgers (*T'ai-shang tung-hsüan ling-pao chung-chien wen* [HY 410], pp. 7a–12a).

25. HY 352, ch. 1, pp. 8b–9b. I have not been able to find the invocations, the intonation of which was part of the rites described in these passages.

26. HY 22, ch. 1, pp. 10b–11b. For the original versions of the Five Ling-pao Talismans, see HY 388, ch. 3, pp. 9b–11b. On the legend of the revelation of the talismans to Yü the Great, which is only partially recorded in HY 388 (ch. 1, p. 6a–b), see Kaltenmark, "*Ling-pao:* note sur un terme du Taoisme religieux," pp. 561–563.

27. For the characterization of the first half of the talismans as *ling,* celestial, and the second as *pao,* terrestrial, see the gloss on the *Tu-jen ching* in *Yüan-shih wu-liang tu-jen shang-p'in miao-ching ssu-chu* (HY 87), ch. 2, p. 2b. On the role of the True Writs in the Retreat of the Gold Register, see HY 1130, ch. 53, p. 1a–b; and Lagerway, *Wu-shang pi-yao, somme Taoiste du VIe siècle,* pp. 161–162.

28. HY 528, p. 28a. The *Tu-jen ching* declares that the Five Monarchs of the Demons are leaders of all spirits and command the demon troops (HY 1, ch. 1, p. 10a5–7). On the magic powers derived from knowledge of a god's names, see Seidel, "Imperial Treasures and Taoist Sacraments," p. 322. Professor Seidel's conclusions are based on the Han apocrypha, but apply equally well to Taoism.

29. HY 528, pp. 28b–29a; and HY 1396, pp. 29b–30a, 38b–39a, and 47b–48a. For an explanation of the Eight Effulgent Spirits, see Robinet, *La révélation du Shangqing,* vol. 1, pp. 129–130.

30. HY 528, pp. 29a–31b. In his notes for the last three writs, Lu says only that the officiant transmits the tiny graphs. However, the text may be corrupt at these points. The word "transmit" has been substituted for the character for "read," and there appears to be no reason for conferring the later writs by a procedure different from that for the first. The sum of the ethers' numbers in the titles of the writs is twenty-four, and this corresponds to the numbers of cosmic ethers, internal spirits of the human body, and the astral deities of the zodiac. The Eight Assemblies refers to the Days of the Eight Segments.

31. For the Hidden Discourse of the Great Brahman, see HY 1, ch. 1, pp. 16b, 16–17a, 17a–b, and 17b; and HY 97, ch. 1, pp. 1b–12b. Only that portion of the discourse cited in Lu's liturgy is the authentic passage from the original *Tu-jen ching.* The remainder is an interpolation probably introduced to the text around A.D. 1100. For the sections of HY 97 on procedures for activating the writs and on explanations of them, see ch. 1, p. 15b, to ch. 2, p. 16b; and ch. 3, p. 7a, to ch. 4, p. 21a. The invocations can be found in HY 97, ch. 3, p. 17a;

ch. 3, pp. 27b–28a; and ch. 4, p. 10b; and ch. 4, p. 21a (Bokenkamp, "Sources of the Ling-pao Scriptures," pp. 462–465).

32. HY 528, pp. 31b–33a.

33. HY 352, ch. 1, pp. 24b–26a; and HY 1231, ch. 2, p. 18b.

34. HY 528, pp. 33b–35b.

35. HY 1231, ch. 2, p. 18b; and HY 352, ch. 1, pp. 23a–24a.

36. HY 22, ch. 1, pp. 35b–36a. The powers ascribed to the staffs in the Jade Instructions are virtually the same as those ascribed to the Slip-Board Writs (HY 352, ch. 2, p. 23b).

37. A version of the *Ssu-chi ming-k'o* survives in the *Tao-tsang*. However, it is a syncretic text which evolved after A.D. 400 and not to be confused with that which Lu cites (*T'ai-chen yü-ti ssu-chi ming-k'o ching* [HY 184], 5 ch.; and Isabelle Robinet, *La révélation du Shangqing dans l'histoire du Taoisme* [Paris, 1984], vol. 2, pp. 428–430).

38. HY 528, pp. 37a–38a.

39. For Ko Hung's remark see *Pao-p'u Tzu, nei-p'ien*, ch. 4, p. 12; and *Alchemy, Medicine and Religion in the China of A.D. 320*, p. 70.

40. HY 1130, ch. 39, p. 8a.

41. On the genesis of the canon and its revelation to Ko Hsüan, see HY 22, ch. 1, pp. 1a7–9, and ch. 3, p. 15a6–9; and *San-tung chu-nang* (HY 1121), compiled by Wang Hsüan-ho (fl. 666–683), ch. 2, p. 6b8–9. On Ko Ch'ao-fu as the actual author of the texts, see the *Chen kao* (HY 1010), compiled by T'ao Hung-ching (456–April 18, 536), completed in A.D. 499 or shortly thereafter, ch. 19, p. 11b; Ch'en Kuo-fu, *Tao-tsang yüan-liu k'ao*, vol. 1, p. 67; Max Kaltenmark, "*Ling-pao*, note sur un terme du Taoisme religieux," p. 560; Michel Strickmann, "The Mao Shan Revelations, Taoism and the Aristocracy," *T'oung Pao* 63, no. 1 (1977): 19 and 46; and Bokenkamp, "Sources of the Ling-pao Scriptures," pp. 436–442.

42. For the note on the ten divisions of the scriptures in the Ling-pao canon, see HY 22, ch. 3, p. 15a10–15b1. Lu Hsiu-ching's dated preface survives in the *Yün-chi ch'i-ch'ien* (HY 1026), compiled by Chang Chün-fang (fl. 1008–1029) and completed in A.D. 1028 or 1029, ch. 4, pp. 4a–6a. The Tun-huang manuscripts, two fragments from a single scroll, containing the corrupt version of Lu's catalog are preserved in the Pelliot collection at the Bibliothèque Nationale in Paris. Photographic reproductions of the manuscripts (P. 2861b and P. 2256) can be found in *Tonkō Dōkei, zuroku hen*, compiled by Ōfuchi Ninji (Tokyo, 1978), pp. 725–728 (the list occupies columns 1–13 of the first and columns 1–37 of the second manuscript). Sung Wen-ming, if he was the author, copied Lu's catalog and added his own notes to it. Ōfuchi Ninji, who proposed the identification of the text and its author, has reconstructed the list (the beginning portion of it is missing) from the manuscripts and works in the *Tao-tsang*. Ōfuchi Ninji, "On *Ku Ling-pao ching*," and *Tonkō Dōkei, mokuroku hen*, pp. 365–368.

43. HY 1117, ch. 4, pp. 8a7–9b6. There is one piece of evidence which invalidates the absolute assertion that the canon which the Princesses received can be identified with Chin-ming Ch'i-chen's inventory. Two titles—the *Ling-pao san-yüan chai i* in one *chüan* and the *Ling-pao fu wu-ya li-ch'eng* in one *chüan*—listed at

the end of the catalog in the *Tao-tsang* version of his text are missing from the enumeration in the Tun-huang copy of it (HY 1117, ch. 4, pp. 9b1–2 and 9b4–5; and *San-tung feng-tao k'o-chieh i-fan* [P. 2337], photographically reproduced in *Tonkō Dōkei, zuroku hen,* pp. 228–229). One is inclined to give greater weight to the evidence from the Tun-huang manuscript because it probably dates from the T'ang dynasty. However, the text was hand-copied, and it is quite possible that the copyist omitted the titles.

44. HY 528, p. 38a–b.

45. HY 1117, ch. 4, p. 4b, to ch. 5, p. 2b; and Ch'en Kuo-fu, *Tao-tsang yüan-liu k'ao,* vol. 2, pp. 351–359. In a masterful study of Taoist registers, Professor Anna Seidel has made a profound contribution to our understanding of the origins and character of investitures. As she has shown, tokens—registers, writs, talismans, contracts, tallies, and the like—were instruments for transferring charisma and authority from the spiritual hierarchy to the mortal priest, who thereafter became the administrator of the gods on earth. The analysis of registers given here owes a great deal to her work, "Imperial Treasures and Taoist Sacrements," esp. pp. 323–333.

46. HY 528, pp. 38b–41a; HY 1427, pp. 3b–5b; and HY 532, pp. 6b–7a. For some unexplained reason, Lu's directives calling for the ordinands to sing praises after each stanza of the Pu-hsü tz'u actually appear after the Chanting of the Hymn for the Salute to the Canon.

47. HY 528, p. 41a–b.

48. HY 528, p. 41b. On the *triratna* as a loan from Buddhism, see E. Zürcher, "Buddhist Influence on Early Taoism," *T'oung Pao* 66, nos. 1–3 (1980): 115.

49. HY 528, pp. 41b–42b; and HY 1231, ch. 1, p. 2a. This set of injunctions was part of a scripture in the original Ling-pao canon (*T'ai-shang tung-hsüan ling-pao chih-hui tsui-ken shang-p'in ta-chieh ching* [HY 457], ch. 1, pp. 5b–6b).

50. HY 528, p. 43a–b.

51. HY 528, p. 43b.

52. HY 1231, ch. 2, p. 20b.

53. HY 1231, ch. 2, p. 20b; and HY 1130, ch. 39, p. 8a.

54. HY 1231, ch. 1, p. 2a; HY 528, p. 4a; and Appendix Two, section III, part B, numbers 18 and 22. I have not been able to identify the One Hundred and Eighty Injunctions of the Three Primes in the *Tao-tsang.*

55. HY 528, pp. 50b–51b.

56. This paragraph is a paraphrase of the oldest set of protocols for conducting the Casting of Dragon Tablets as found in a scripture from the original Ling-pao canon (HY 352, ch. 1, pp. 5a–7b). These regulations have been copied verbatim into HY 1131, ch. 2, pp. 6a–12a. This rite appears to be an elaborate variation of an older form of penance that the Celestial Master sect originated. That sect required sinners to write confessions on three sheets of paper, the first of which was then supposed to be placed on a mountain top, the second cast into a river, and the third buried in the ground. Afterward, the gods would grant remission for sins (Holmes Welch, *Taoism, the Parting of the Way* [Boston, 1966], p. 115; and Ōfuchi Ninji, *Dōkyō shi no kenkyū* [Tokyo, 1964], p. 7).

Edouard Chavannes made the only full-length study of the Casting of Dragon Tablets in a Western language as an offshoot of his work on Mt. T'ai. He translated a number of inscriptions relevant to the topic, but was unaware of the primary sources for the rite. See "Le jet des dragons," in *Mémoirs concernant l'Asie Orientale* (Paris, 1919), vol. 3, pp. 51–220.

## Chapter Four

1. On the dating of HY 1117 see Yoshioka Yoshitoyo, "Sandō hōdō kakai gihan no kenkyū," in *Dōkyō to Bukkyō* (Tokyo, 1976), pp. 75–160; and Yoshioka Yoshitoyo, "Sandō hōdō kakai gihan no seiritsu ni tsuite," in *Dōkyō kenkyū* (Tokyo, 1965), vol. 1, pp. 5–108. In 1963 and 1964, Ōfuchi Ninji and Akizuki Kan'ei challenged Yoshioka's dating of this text to the late sixth century. Ōfuchi contended that it was written in the late seventh century while Akizuki favored A.D. 600. In the articles cited here, Yoshioka marshaled new evidence and raised new arguments which convincingly refuted the objections of his critics. Like many other works of medieval times, HY 1117 has not survived intact. The version in the *Tao-tsang* is about two-thirds the size of the original and has different chapter divisions. There are two fragments from the lost portions (P. 3682 and S. 809) as well as a copy of the section which includes Chin-ming Ch'i-chen's hierarchy of initiation and ordination (P. 2337), among the Tun-huang manuscripts. The latter is particularly important because it can be used to supply omissions that exist in HY 1117 (*Tonkō Dōkei, mokuroku hen,* pp. 115–121; and *Tonkō Dōkei, zuroku hen,* pp. 219–242). The second volume of Ōfuchi's work, the *zurokuhen,* contains photographic reproductions of the manuscripts analyzed in the first. Chang Wan-fu's short list (ch. 2, p. 8a) categorizes initiations and investitures as follows:

*a)*  The presentation of injunctions.
*b)*  The conferral of registers.
*c)*  The transmission of the *Tao-te ching.*
*d)*  The bestowal of the *San-huang wen.*
*e)*  The conferral of the Ling-pao corpus.
*f)*  The transmission of the Shang-ch'ing canon.

His inventories (ch. 1, pp. 1a–8a) follow the same order except for the last stage, which is missing. In the enumeration of injunctions (ch. 1, pp. 1a–2a), he incorporates further stages and phases of initiation and investiture that he does not mention in his short list or elsewhere in this text. Chin-ming Ch'i-chen begins with a short discussion of eight titles (ch. 4, pp. 5a–b) and then proceeds to outline a hierarchy with three levels of initiation and seven tiers of ordination (ch. 4, p. 5b, to ch. 5, p. 2b). He discusses a total of nineteen stages and phases.

2. HY 1117, ch. 4, p. 5b. According to the *T'ai-chen k'o* (Statutes of the Grand Perfected, now lost except for excerpts in other works), a code of Taoist regulations that may date as early as the late second or early third century A.D., the transmission of the *Keng-ling* had two phases. In the first, the parents

received the register, standing in for the child. The second was a period of instruction in the commands during which the child was taught to repent his sins and faults so that he could abandon evil and pursue good (cited in HY 463, ch. 10, p. 5b). The "Register of One General" was a roster of supernatural beings over which the recipient had control and which he could use to protect himself, promote his salvation, and perform other religious acts by summoning these gods. The version which survives today in the *Tao-tsang* also has illustrations and talismans (HY 1199, ch. 1, pp. 1b–4a). The *T'ai-chen k'o* stipulated that this register should be conferred between the ages of seven and eighteen, and this probably represents an older tradition than that reported in HY 1117 (HY 463, ch. 10, p. 5b). Chang Wan-fu's only comment on this register is that it and the "Register of Ten Generals" (see the next stage) were transmitted to children (HY 1231, ch. 1, p. 3b).

3. HY 1117, ch. 4, p. 5b. According to the *T'ai-chen k'o* this title was to be conferred when the recipient reached the age of nineteen (adulthood), a regulation which again probably reflects practices predating the middle of the sixth century A.D. (cited in HY 463, ch. 10, p. 5b). Chang Wan-fu mentions a Register of Three Generals in his inventory of registers, but this is clearly not the one that was conferred on children. It may be the title for another register or perhaps it was no longer transmitted to the *Lu-sheng* in Chang's time (HY 1231, ch. 1, p. 4a). Versions of it and the "Register of Ten Generals" have survived in HY 1199, ch. 1, pp. 4a–7a and 12b–15a. A set of injunctions called the "Five Precepts of True-Unity *(Cheng-i wu-chieh)*, which may be the five referred to here, is preserved in the *Wu-shang pi-yao*. This text cites the *Cheng-i fa-wen*, which was purportedly one of the scriptures in the original Celestial Master canon (HY 1130, ch. 46, pp. 16b–18a). Chang Wan-fu asserts that Register Pupils received the "Eight Injunctions." In Chin-ming Ch'i-chen's hierarchy that set was bestowed in the following stage of initiation (number three).

4. HY 1117, ch. 4, p. 5b. This source mentions only the "Register of Seventy-Five Generals" and "Register of One Hundred and Fifty Generals." Chang Wan-fu explains the relationship between the two (HY 1231, ch. 1, p. 3b). A version of the "Register of One Hundred and Fifty Generals" survives in HY 1199, ch. 1, pp. 7a–12a. In the first part of it (pp. 7b–9b) the titles of the deities all begin with the prefix *shang-hsien* (superior immortal) or *ch'ih-t'ien* (red heaven), in the second half (pp. 10a–11b) with the prefix *shang-ling* (superior power). Presumably the former constituted the "Register of Seventy-Five Generals," which was conferred on young men while the latter was that given to young women. Much of the analysis on the early stages of initiation and the transmission of Celestial Master registers given here is based on Ch'en Kuo-fu's masterful study of the sect in the Nan-pei ch'ao ("Nan-pei ch'ao T'ien-shih tao k'ao ch'ang-pien," in *Tao-tsang yüan-liu k'ao*, vol. 2, pp. 308–369). Chin-ming Ch'i-chen's account of these three stages appears to be a simplification of earlier practices. One Celestial Master text, which probably dates from the Nan-pei ch'ao, says that initiates received the "Register of One General" five years (at the age of eleven or twelve?) after the conferral of the "Keng-ling," the

"Register of Ten Generals" four years later (age fifteen or sixteen), the "Register of Seventy-Five Generals" three years after that (age eighteen or nineteen), and the "Register of One Hundred and Fifty Generals" two years later (age twenty or twenty-one) (*Cheng-i fa-wen t'ai-shang wai-lu i* [HY 1233], p. 11a). *Kuan* (mandarin) is homophonous with *kuan,* which was the term for the capping ceremony performed at nineteen years of age to mark the attainment of manhood in ancient China. The use of the first term in Taoism for titles conferred at the same age suggests that the notion for this stage of initiation was based on the older manhood rites. Changes in the system of confirmation continued into the Sung dynasty (960–1279). According to a text on initiation and investiture from that period, confirmation began at the age of six for boys and nine for girls. The boys received the title *Lu-sheng ti-tzu* (Students and Register Pupils) and the girls *Nan-sheng ti-tzu* (Students and Southern Pupils). A preceptor transmitted the Three Injunctions and Five Injunctions, the initiates gradually ceased eating strong-smelling vegetables (onions, garlic, etc.) and meat, and accepted an interdiction never to marry. At the age of fourteen these aspirants could request permission to leave the family (become a member of the celibate priesthood) from their preceptors. They then took vows of celibacy and oaths to their preceptors (three in number) and were given the titles *Chih-hui shih-chieh ti-tzu* (Students of the Ten Injunctions for Wisdom), apparently having received these precepts through oral transmission. The preceptor then conferred the *Ch'u-chen pa-shih-i chieh* (Eighty-one Injunctions for Beginning Perfection). From this point on the ordinands were allowed to enter the oratory to recite scripture, visualize the gods, and conduct rituals. At no time in their progress did they receive registers (*San-tung hsiu-tao i* [HY 1227], compiled by Sun Chung-i, whose preface is dated September 28, 1003, p. 3a–b).

5. On registration in Celestial Master parishes during the T'ang, see Tu Kuang-t'ing, *Tung-t'ien fu-ti yüeh-tu ming-shan chi* (HY 599), pp. 11a–15a; *Tao-chiao ling-yen chi,* compiled by Tu Kuang-t'ing (HY 590), ch. 2, p. 11a; *Cheng-i hsiu-chen lüeh i* (HY 1229), p. 10b; and Ch'en Kuo-fu, *Tao-tsang yüan-liu k'ao,* vol. 2, pp. 337–338. On the existence of a separate ritual for registration, see HY 1230, pp. 3a–4b. In this text this rite appears immediately after that for the conferral of the *Hsien-kuan* and *Ling-kuan* registers. Chang supplies no specific age for either the investiture or registration, but if the older Cheng-i regulations were followed, the aspirant could not undergo the latter until he was at least nineteen years old.

6. HY 1231, ch. 2, p. 8a. In Chang's inventory, numbers one to six and eight were the sets of precepts reserved for initiation. The remaining precepts, those for investitures, are examined in note 14 below.

7. HY 1231, ch. 1, p. lb. These precepts have been preserved in another text written by Chang Wan-fu (*San-tung chung-chieh wen* [HY 178], ch. 1, pp. 1a–2b). On the Three Treasures and Three Formulas of Refuge as Buddhist loans to Taoism, see E. Zürcher, "Buddhist Influence on Early Taoism," p. 115. Zürcher based his analysis of the Three Formulas of Refuge on the *T'ai-shang tung-hsüan ling-pao chen-wen yao-chieh shang-ching* (HY 330), p. 8b. This was one of the

texts in the original corpus of Ling-pao canon. It interprets the three injunctions as applying to aspects of self in contrast to Chang's statement, which is closer to the original Buddhist notion.

8. HY 1231, ch. 1, p. 1b. For Chang's set, see HY 178, ch. 2, p. 3a–b. For the Celestial Master set, see HY 1130, ch. 46, pp. 16b–18a. Each of the precepts in Chang's list begins with a warning not to become attached to one of the senses and is followed by a vow to pursue a proper endeavor. This accounts for Chang's characterization of them in HY 1231. The same set, with variant readings, can be found in HY 1130, ch. 46, pp. 14b–15a. This passage is an excerpt from the *Tung-shen ching.* On the Five Turbities, which is another Buddhist loan, see *Tao-chiao i-shu* (HY 1121), compiled by Meng An-p'ai (fl. 684–704) around A.D. 700, ch. 9, pp. 4a–b.

9. HY 1231, ch. 1, p. 1b. A copy of these injunctions can be found in HY 178, ch. 2, pp. 3b–4b. In this text Chang says that if one maintains the precepts for three years, the gods of the eight directions will arrive to protect the observer. The same set, with variant readings, can be found in HY 1130, ch. 46, pp. 15b–16a. This passage was also taken from the *Tung-shen ching.* Another T'ang source contains an excerpt from an early Celestial Master text which states that those who become adherents of Taoism "received a talisman for protecting the body and the Three Injunctions. Then they progress to the Five Injunctions and Eight Injunctions. Afterward they receive registers. If they receive registers before receiving precepts, then they receive the precepts after they receive the registers" (HY 1131, ch. 6, p. 3b). The text cited here is the *Cheng-i fa-wen,* part of the original Celestial Master canon which Lao Tzu purportedly revealed to Chang Tao-ling (see the discussion of Cheng-i ordination that follows). This excerpt can now be found in the HY 1233, pp. 11b–12a.

10. HY 1231, ch. 1, p. 1b. A set of ten injunctions for laymen was part of a scripture in the original Ling-pao canon (*T'ai-shang tung-hsüan ling-pao chih-hui ting-chih t'ung-wei ching* [HY 325], p. 7b). The first five correspond to the five *sila* given to Buddhist laymen (Bokenkamp, "Sources of the Ling-pao Scriptures," pp. 470–471). However, this scripture does not mention the ten abominations or ten virtues. These are enumerated in the T'ang compendium *Tao-chiao i-shu* (HY 1121), ch. 3, pp. 6a–7a, and ch. 4, pp. 7a–8b. In this text the Ten Virtues (injunctions) are only partially similar to those given in HY 325. One of the difficulties in dealing with injunctions in pre-T'ang and T'ang times is that different texts of different schools from different epochs give different contents for sets of precepts with the same title. Part of the problem is that Taoists adopted many of their injunctions from Buddhism, and Buddhism presented them with variant versions of the precepts as different sutras, or different editions of sutras, were translated into Chinese. My thanks to Professor David Chappell for clarifying this and other points about Buddhist theories on precepts.

11. HY 1231, ch. 1, p. 1b. The *Ch'u-chen chieh* can be found in the *T'ai-shang tung-hsüan ling-pao ch'u-chia yin-yüan ching* (HY 339), pp. 4b–5a and 5b–6a. Shih Ch'ung-hsüan cites eleven passages (one twice) from this text in HY 1113, pp. 13a–b, 15a–17b, 30a–b, and 32a. Consequently, 713 is the latest possible year for the date of HY 339's composition. However, some form of the *Ch'u-chen*

*chieh* must have existed in the fifth or sixth century, when celibacy was introduced to the priesthood. In the *T'ai-shang Lao-chün chieh ching* (HY 783), a text of unknown date, the oath of celibacy was one of the Five Injunctions, p. 7a. According to a Sung set of protocols for taking the vow of celibacy, part of the rite required the initiate to take off his secular clothing after which the officiant dressed him in vestments (*T'ai-shang ch'u-chia ch'uan-tu i* [HY 1226], compiled by Chia Shan-hsiang [fl. 1086], pp. 6b–8a). The ten injunctions transmitted on this occasion were not the *Ch'u-chen chieh*. In fact the contents of the *Ch'u-chen chieh* do not appear to have been fixed. The set that appears in HY 1026 (ch. 40, pp. 7a–8b) is not the same as that in HY 339, and another Sung text mentions a set of Eighty-One Injunctions for Beginning Perfection (*Ch'u-chen pa-shih-i chieh*) (HY 1227, p. 3b).

12. HY 1231, ch. 1, p. 1b.

13. HY 1231, ch. 2, p. 8a, and ch. 1, p. 1b.

14. The remaining sets of injunctions in Chang's inventory of precepts—those conferred at ordinations, not initiations—recognized the following degrees of achievement:

*a)* Cheng-i Priest (no. 7),
*b)* Student of the *Tao-te ching* (no. 9),
*c)* Canon Preceptor of the *Tao-te ching* (no. 10),
*d)* Student of the *San-huang wen* (no. 11),
*e)* Student of the *Sheng-hsüan nei-chiao ching* (no. 12),
*f)* Ling-pao, the Beginning Covenant (no. 13),
*g)* Ling-pao, the Middle Covenant (no. 14),
*h)* Ling-pao, the Grand Covenant (no. 15), and
*i)* Shang-ch'ing Priest (no. 16).

Chin-ming Ch'i-chen supplies no injunctions for students of the Cheng-i canon, the *Shen-chou ching,* the *Sheng-hsüan nei-chiao ching,* Ling-pao scriptures, or the Shang-ch'ing canon, five of his seven levels of ordination. In contrast, registers were part of all preliminary phases of ordination except for the transmission of the *Tao-te ching.* The statement about probationary periods is conjecture on my part. I have found no regulations which required a waiting period between the bestowal of injunctions and the investiture of the canon.

15. HY 1117, ch. 4, p. 5a; *T'ai-shang tung-chen chih-hui shang-p'in ta-chieh* (HY 177), pp. 1b–5b; HY 1130, ch. 35, p. 1a–b; and John Lagerway, *Wu-shang pi-yao, somme Taoiste du VIe siècle,* p. 125. Stephen Bokenkamp has misread the title for these initiates, giving it as Students of Pure Heart ("Sources of the Ling-pao Scriptures," p. 481).

16. HY 1231, ch, 1, p. 1b.

17. On the early Ling-pao hierarchy of scriptural transmissions, see the *Shang-ch'ing T'ai-chi yin-chu yü-ching pao-chüeh* (HY 425), pp. 2a–3b. This text supplies separate rituals for the conferral of the texts named, but they are all essentially the same. For the lengths of various investiture rituals at the end of the Nan-pei ch'ao, see HY 1130, ch. 35, p. 1a.

18. HY 1117, ch. 4, p. 6a–b. In the interest of brevity the third and fourth titles, respectively twenty-four and forty-two characters in length, have been abbreviated. "The One Hundred and Eighty Injunctions of Lord Lao," which were composed some time before A.D. 550, are preserved in the *T'ai-shang Lao-chün ching-lü* (HY 785), pp. 2a–12b. See also Yoshioka Yoshitoyo, "Tonkō Taiheikyō ni tsuite," in *Dōkyō to Bukkyō* (Tokyo, 1970), p. 70. They can also be found in HY 1026, ch. 39, pp. 1a–14b. There is a *T'ai-shang Lao-chün hun-yüan san-pu fu* (HY 673), in three chapters, which may be the *Lao Tzu san-pu chen-fu* (*d,* number seven).

19. This list of revealed scripture can be found in the *Ch'ih-sung Tzu chang-li* (HY 615), ch. 1, p. 1a. This text was compiled in the twelfth century A.D., but it quotes the *T'ai-chen k'o* and the *Ch'ih-sung Tzu li* (Almanac of Master Ch'ih-sung) both of which dated from the second or third centuries A.D. A different list is given in a T'ang compendium, which also cites the *T'ai-chen k'o:*

 *a)* the *Cheng-i meng-wei chih ching* (Scripture of True-Unity and Covenantal Authority) in 930 chapters,

 *b)* the *Fu-t'u* (Talismans and Illustrations) in seventy chapters, and

 *c)* the *Ta-tung chen-ching* in twenty-one chapters.

HY 463, ch. 1, p. 2a; and Ch'en Kuo-fu, *Tao-tsang yüan-liu k'ao,* vol. 2, p. 351. The number of chapters ascribed to the first scripture appears to be an exagger-ation, and this undermines the validity of the inventory. The *Tao-chiao i-shu,* another T'ang text, which cites the *Cheng-i ching,* claims that Lao Tzu Deified also revealed the *T'ai-p'ing tung-chi ching* (Scripture of the Great Peace Penetrat-ing the Outer Limits) in 144 chapters during A.D. 142 (HY 1121, ch. 2, p. 9b). The same excerpt from the *Cheng-i ching* appears in the *Yün-chi ch'i-ch'ien,* which cites the *Hsüan-men ta-i* (Grand Purport of the Mysterious Gate) that was com-piled in the Sui dynasty (589–618) (HY 1026, ch. 6, p. 15b). This passage is translated in B. J. Mansvelt Beck, "The Date of the *Taiping jing,*" *T'oung Pao* 64, nos. 4–5 (1980): 163–164. For a fifth-century version of Lao Tzu's epiphany and revelations, see the *San-t'ien nei-chieh ching* (HY 1196), written by a Master Hsü (Hsü Shu-piao? fl. 470–479), ch. 1, pp. 5b–6b. On this text see Rolf Stein, "Religious Taoism and Popular Religion from the Second to the Seventh Centuries," in *Facets of Taoism,* p. 55n6; and Michel Strickmann, *Le Taoisme du Mao chan, chronique d'une révélation,* p. 71. Tu Kuang-t'ing's remark was originally made in the *Huang-lu hsü-shih i,* which is no longer extant but is cited in the *Tao-men ting-chih* (HY 1214), compiled by Lü Yüan-su (fl. 1188–1201) and edited and collated by Hu Hsiang-lung, Lu's preface dated 1188, ch. 6, p. 2b.

20. HY 1268, p. 7a–b; HY 463, ch. 8, pp. 1b–2a; HY 464, p. 3a–b; and Liu Chih-wan, "Chung-kuo hsiu-chai k'ao," in *Chung-kuo min-chien hsin-yang lun-chi* (Taipei, 1974), pp. 22–23. A note to a passage from the *T'ai-chen k'o* quoted in a T'ang compendium mentions the liturgies of the *T'u-t'an chai* and *Chih-chiao chai* (HY 1131, ch. 1, p. 23a). One of the scriptures from the original Ling-pao canon noted that the *San-t'ien chai* (Retreat of the Three Heavens) "was the lit-

urgy which the three Celestial Masters [Chang Tao-ling, his son Chang Heng, and his grandson Chang Lu] received, and it was called the *Chih-chiao ching* (Scripture for Instruction in the Teachings)" (cited in HY 1130, ch. 47, p. 2a). For a description of the *T'u-t'an chai,* see Henri Maspero, *Taoism and Chinese Religion,* trans. by Frank Kierman (Amherst, Massachusetts, 1981), pp. 381–186. Two sets of protocols, dates unknown, for performing the *Chih-chiao chai* survive in the *Tao-tsang (Cheng-i chih-chiao chai i* [HY 797] and *Cheng-i chih-chiao chai ch'ing-tan hsing-tao i* [HY 798]).

21. HY 1117, ch. 4, p. 6b.

22. HY 464, pp. 12a–14b; HY 335, Tu Kuang-t'ing's preface; and HY 295, ch. 28, pp. 1a–2b. On the dating of HY 335 see Ōfuchi Ninji, "Dōen shinju kyō no seiritsu," in *Dōkyō shi no kenkyū* (Tokyo, 1964), pp. 435–487. On its contents see Ōfuchi Ninji, "Dōen shinju kyō no naiyō ni kansuru kenkyū," in *Dōkyō shi no kenkyū,* pp. 435–487. A substantial number of manuscript copies for chapters of this text have survived among the Tun-huang manuscripts (*Tonkō Dōkei, mokuroku hen,* pp. 251–295; and *Tonkō Dōkei, zuroku hen,* pp. 519–564). For the examples of the text's applications in the T'ang, see HY 590, ch. 10, p. 8a; ch. 12, pp. 9b–10a; and ch. 15, pp. 1b and 4b.

23. HY 445, p. 3a; and HY 1230, p. 4b. In these texts, Chang places this investiture after that for the *Tao-te ching.*

24. HY 1117, ch. 4, pp. 6b–7a.

25. The two sets of injunctions which make up HY 459 were taken from the *T'ai-shang tung-hsüan ling-pao chih-hui ting-chih t'ung-wei ching* (HY 325), p. 7b; and *T'ai-shang tung-hsüan ling-pao tsui-ken shang-p'in ta-chieh ching* (HY 457), ch. 1, p. 5a. For the Tun-huang manuscripts, see *Tonkō Dōkei, mokuroku hen,* pp. 108–110 and 197–199; and *Tonkō Dōkei, zuroku hen,* pp. 197–199 and 411. In HY 783 (p. 6a–b) Student of Pure Faith is a title reserved for men and women who have received the Five Injunctions. By the Sung dynasty (960–1279) the meaning of *Ch'ing-hsin ti-tzu* changed again. Adult females received this title and adult males the title *Ch'ing-chen ti-tzu* (Students of Pure Perfection) (HY 1227, p. 3a).

26. HY 1117, ch. 4, pp. 6b–7a; and HY 1231, ch. 1, p. 5a–b. A set of injunctions called *Lao Tzu erh-shih-ch'i chieh* (Lao Tzu's Twenty-Seven Precepts) appears in the *T'ai-shang ching-chieh* (HY 786), pp. 17a–19a. These seem to be the set referred to as the Twenty-Seven Injunctions for the Hsiang-erh Commentary. There is a short passage under the title *Tao-te tsun-ching Hsiang-erh chieh* (The Hsiang-erh Precepts for the Venerable *Tao-te ching*) in HY 785 (p. 1a–b) which is identical to the introduction for Lao Tzu's Twenty-Seven Precepts in HY 786. The precepts themselves, however, are missing in HY 786.

27. For the account of the encounter between Lao Tzu and Yin Hsi, see Ssu-ma Ch'ien, *Shih chi* (Peking, 1972), ch. 63, p. 197; and Max Kaltenmark, *Lao Tzu and Taoism,* trans. by Roger Greaves (Stanford, 1969), p. 9. By the end of the Han dynasty the story had changed significantly. Yin Hsi is portrayed as a Taoist adept and accompanies Lao Tzu into the deserts of Central Asia (*Lieh-hsien chuan chiao-cheng pen,* attributed to Liu Hsiang [ca. 79–ca. 6 B.C.], but probably first written about A.D. 200; the text contains interpolations made in the

third and fourth centuries A.D., collated and annotated by Wang Chao-yüan [1763–1851], whose preface is dated March 12, 1804; in *Li-tai chen-hsien shih-chuan*, ed. by Hsiao T'ien-shih [Taipei, 1970], ch. 1, p. 2b; and *Le Lie-sien tchouan*, trans. by Max Kaltenmark [Peking, 1953], pp. 65–66). On the deification of Lao Tzu in the second century A.D. and his avatars, see the *Lao Tzu pien-hua ching* (S. 2295), reproduced in Anna Seidel, *La divinisation de Lao Tseu dans le Taoisme des Han* (Paris, 1969), pp. 133–134 (lines 41–58), and Professor Seidel's remarks on pp. 92–109. For the T'ang myths of revelation see *T'ai-shang hun-yüan chen-lu* (HY 953), pp. 5a–b, 10b, 13a–b, 15a, and 15a–19a; and Kusuyama Haruki, "Kankoku ni okeru Rōshi to In Ki," in *Rōshi densetsu no kenkyū* (Tokyo, 1979), p. 395. Kusuyama dates HY 953 as a late seventh- or early eighth-century text ("*Taijō kongen shiroku ko*," in *Dōkyō kenkyū ronshū, Yoshioka Yoshitoyo Festschrift* [Tokyo, 1977], pp. 457–476). According to this myth, Lao Tzu also transmitted two texts on alchemy at this time. HY 783 (p. 1a–b) claims that Lao Tzu also revealed the Five Injunctions to Yin Hsi.

28. HY 1231, ch. 1, p. 5a–b.

29. HY 1117, ch. 4, p. 7b. One line with three titles is missing from P. 2337, *Tonkō Dōkei, zuroku hen*, p. 227b.

30. On the revelation of the *San-huang wen*, see HY 1121, ch. 2, pp. 6b–7a; HY 1026, ch. 6, pp. 11a–12a; HY 640, p. 12a–b; *Shen-hsien chuan*, the original compiled by Ko Hung, but the present version greatly altered by later hands, in *Li-tai chen-hsien shih-chuan*, ch. 7, pp. 28b–29a; Ko Hung, *Pao-p'u Tzu nei-p'ien*, ch. 19, p. 97; *Alchemy, Medicine and Religion in the China of A.D. 320*, trans. by James Ware, p. 314; Ch'en Kuo-fu, *Tao-tsang yüan-liu k'ao*, vol. 1, pp. 71–76; and Ōfuchi Ninji, "*Sankōbun* yori *Tōshinkyō* e," in *Dōkyō shi no kenkyū*, pp. 277–297. The table of contents for the *Tung-shen ching* can be found in HY 802, p. 5a–b. On the character of the *Tung-shen chai*, see HY 1268, pp. 6b–7a; HY 464, pp. 3b and 5b; HY 463, ch. 8, p. 1b; and Liu Chih-wan, "Chung-kuo hsiu-chai k'ao," pp. 20, 22, and 23. This rite was also known as the *San-huang tzu-wu chai* (The Three Sovereigns Retreat of Midnight and Noon), midnight and noon referring to the mealtimes prescribed by the scripture. The retreat was performed at midnight on three successive days, though it was permissible to execute it on a single night (HY 1130, ch. 49, p. 2a–b). This chapter of the *Wu-shang pi-yao* is a liturgy for the retreat. Fa-lin (572–August 15, 640) says the rite's purposes were the search for immortality and the protection of the nation (*Pien-cheng lun*, completed in 629 or shortly thereafter, in *Taishō shinshu Daizokyō* [Tokyo, 1922–1936), vol. 52, ch. 2, p. 497a–b).

31. HY 1231, ch. 1, p. 7a.

32. HY 1117, ch. 4, p. 8a; and P. 2337, in *Tonkō Dōkei, zuroku hen*, p. 227b. The former source reads "register," the latter "tally."

33. *Tonkō Dōkei, mokuroku hen*, pp. 122–128.

34. HY 445, pp. 3b–4a.

35. HY 1117, ch. 4, pp. 8a–9b.

36. On the revelation of the Ling-pao canon to Ko Hsüan, see HY 1427, p. 8a; *T'ai-shang tung-hsüan ling-pao chen-i ch'üan-chieh fa-lun miao-ching* (HY 346), a scripture from the original Ling-pao canon, pp. 1b–5a; Lu Hsiu-ching, "Ling-

pao ching-mu hsü," in HY 1036, ch. 4, p. 4b; HY 1121, ch. 2, p. 6b; Ch'en Kuo-fu, *Tao-tsang yüan-liu k'ao,* vol. 1, pp. 66–67; and Stephen Bokenkamp, "Sources of the Ling-pao Scriptures," pp. 437–440. The character of HY 388 is analyzed in Ch'en Kuo-fu, *Tao-tsang yüan-liu k'ao,* vol. 1, pp. 64–66; and Stephen Bokenkamp, "Sources of the Ling-pao Scriptures," pp. 500 and 483–484. On Ko Ch'ao-fu, see HY 1010, ch. 19, p. 11b; Ch'en Kuo-fu, *Tao-tsang yüan-liu k'ao,* vol. 1, p. 67; Max Kaltenmark, *"Ling-pao,* note sur un terme du Taoisme religieux," vol. 2, p. 560; and Michel Strickmann, "The Mao Shan Revelations, Taoism and the Aristocracy," pp. 19 and 46. Lists of Ling-pao retreats can be found in HY 1268, pp. 5b–6b; HY 463, ch. 8, p. 1b; HY 464, pp. 3a–b and 5a–6; *TTLT,* ch. 4, pp. 42b–43b; Fa-lin, *Pien-cheng lun,* ch. 2, p. 497a–b; and Liu Chih-wan, "Chung-kuo hsiu-chai k'ao," pp. 20–23. Fa-lin lists a Yü-lu chai (Retreat of the Jade Register), but as nearly as I can tell this rite was not performed in the late Nan-pei ch'ao or early T'ang.

37. HY 1231, ch. 1, pp. 8a and 12b–14a, and ch. 2, p. 18b.

38. HY 1117, ch. 4, p. 9b; and HY 1230, p. 5a–b.

39. HY 1117, ch. 4, pp. 9b–10b, and ch. 5, pp. 1a–2b.

40. On the Shang-ch'ing revelations, see Michel Strickmann, "The Mao Shan Revelations, Taoism and the Aristocracy," pp. 3 and 41–42; Michel Strickmann, *Le Taoisme du Mao chan, chronique d'une révélation,* pp. 82–88; and Isabelle Robinet, *La révélation du Shangqing dans l'histoire du Taoisme,* vol. 1, pp. 107–109ff. Volume two of Professor Robinet's monumental contribution to Taoist studies is an analysis of the various lists of Shang-ch'ing scriptures from this period and the works from them that survive today. The description of Shang-ch'ing retreats given here can be found in HY 1268, p. 5a; HY 464, p. 3a; and Liu Chih-wan, "Chung-kuo hsiu-chai k'ao," pp. 22–23. On the citation from the *Chuang Tzu,* see *Chuang Tzu chi-shih,* assembled by Kuo Ch'ing-fan (1844–1896) and Wang Hsien-ch'ien (1842–1918), first printed in 1894 (Peking, 1978), ch. 7b, p. 741; and *The Complete Works of Chuang Tzu,* trans. by Burton Watson (New York, 1968), p. 238.

41. K'ou Ch'ien-chih derived the authority to eliminate the "abuses" of the Cheng-i sect from Lao Tzu Deified, who revealed a text of "injunctions from a new code" to him on November 22, 415. On his complaints about hereditary succession in the priesthood, see the remnants of his new code in the *Lao-chün yin-sung chieh-ching* (HY 784), pp. 1b–2b, 8b, and 12b–13a; Yang Lien-sheng, *"Lao-chün yin-sung chieh-ching* chiao-shih," *Chung-yang yen-chiu yüan Li-shih yü-yen yen-chiu-so chi k'an* 28, no. 1 (1956): 39, 44, and 48; T'ang Yung-t'ung and T'ang I-chieh, "K'ou Ch'ien-chih ti chu-tso yü ssu-hsiang," *Li-shih yen-chiu* 5 (1961): 70; and Richard Mather, "K'ou Ch'ien-chih and the Taoist Theocracy," in *Facets of Taoism,* p. 109. On the survival of the *chi-chiu* in Szechuan and the south during the T'ang, see Shih Ch'ung-hsüan's preface to HY 1113, p. 3a. For the hierarchies of priests constructed in the Nan-pei ch'ao, see HY 1115, pp. 17a–18b. The relevant passages on this question are excerpts from two earlier texts. The first, which appears to have been a Ling-pao work from the Nan-pei ch'ao, still contains the section cited (HY 339, p. 10b). The second, which has only six ranks (the third step as given in HY 339 is missing), is

HY 1117, but the excerpt quoted is no longer extant in that text. The seven classes of *tao-shih* given in HY 339 and Shih's preface to HY 1115 (pp. 2b–3a), are:

a)  the heavenly perfected *(t'ien-chen)*,
b)  the divine immortals *(shen-hsien)*,
c)  the retired *(yu-i)*,
d)  the mountain dwellers *(shan-chü)*,
e)  the celibate *(ch'u-chia)*,
f)  the familial *(tsai-chia)*, and
g)  the libationers *(chi-chiu)*.

The first two categories were classes of ethereal beings, and their inclusion in this hierarchy testifies to the strength of Taoist beliefs that the mortal clergy held inferior posts in a single bureaucratic order that governed both the natural and the supernatural, the celestial and the terrestrial, spheres of the cosmos. On the nature of precepts in Buddhism, see Sato Tatsugen, *Chūgoku Bukkyō ni okeru kairitsu no kenkyū* (Tokyo, 1986), pp. 1–22 and 113–131. On the functions of precepts in the life of the laity during the sixth century, see Whalen Lai, "The Earliest Folk Buddhist Religion in China," in *Buddhist and Taoist Practice in Medieval Chinese Society*, vol. 2 of *Buddhist and Taoist Studies,* ed. by David Chappell (Honolulu, 1987), pp. 16–32. On Buddhist ordinations in modern times, see Holmes Welch, *The Practice of Chinese Buddhism, 1900–1950* (Cambridge, Massachusetts, 1967), pp. 285–301.

## Finale

1. Lu Hsiu-ching mentions only bells and drums in his manual, but Chang Wan-fu notes the presence of musical instruments at the Princesses' investiture (HY 1231, ch. 2, p. 20b).

2. *T'ai-shang tung-hsüan ling-pao chen-i ch'üan-chieh fa-lun miao-ching* (HY 346), pp. 2bff; and *T'ai-shang tung-hsüan ling-pao pen-hsing yin-yüan ching* (HY 1107), pp. 5aff. The transcript of the Perfected's visitations to Yang Hsi can be found in HY 1010, ch. 1 to 3.

3. Anna Seidel, "Imperial Treasures and Taoist Sacrements," pp. 291–371.

4. The description of the retreats given here is based on a Sui dynasty codification of ritual that appeared in the *Tao-men ta-lun* (also known as the *Hsüan-men ta-lun*), which is now lost, but this passage is cited in HY 464, p. 3a–b. Ōfuchi Ninji dates the *Tao-men ta-lun* to the very beginning of the T'ang ("The Formation of the Taoist Canon," p. 255). Another hierarchy from the *Sheng-chi ching*, nearly the same as the first, can be found in HY 463, ch. 8, pp. 1b–2a. See also Fa-lin, *Pien-cheng lun*, ch. 2, p. 497a–b; Li Hsien-chang, "Tao-chiao chiao-i ti k'ai-chan yü hsien-tai ti chiao," *Chūgoku gakushi* 5 (1969): 10; and Liu Chih-wan, "Chung-kuo hsiu-chai k'ao," pp. 22–23. For the official version see *TTLT,* ch. 4, pp. 42b–43b.

5. For the data collected in this chart see *THY,* ch. 6, pp. 64–66, and ch. 50,

pp. 875 and 877; *HTS,* ch. 83, pp. 3658–3659, 3663, 3665, 3666–3668, and 3670; *Ch'ang-an chih,* ch. 3, p. 8a, and ch. 8, pp. 3a and 5b; and *TLCCFK,* ch. 3, pp. 6b and 10a, and ch. 4, p. 3a. Also see P'u-jen (pseud. for Wang Chia-yu), *Ti-wang sheng-huo* (Taipei, 1968), pp. 243–245; Wang Shu-nu, *Chung-kuo ch'ang-chi shih* (Shanghai, 1935), pp. 161–162; and Sun K'o-k'uan, "T'ang-tai tao-chiao yü cheng-chih," in *Han-yüan Tao-lun* (Taipei, 1977), pp. 132–137.

6. On T'ang Taoist ideology, see C. Benn, *Taoism as Ideology in the Reign of Emperor Hsüan-tsung.* For Princess Tai-kuo see *CSTP,* ch. 78, pp. 7b–8a.

7. HY 773, ch. 5, pp. 11a–14a, 15b–16b, 18a–b, 23a, and 25b; HY 769, ch. 8, pp. 4a–8a, 12a–b, 14b–15a, 30b, and 31a–b, and ch. 9, p. 2a–b; HY 593, pp. 4a–b, 5b, 10a–b, and 10b; HY 590, ch. 6, p. 2b; *T'ai-shang Lao-chün nien-p'u yao-lüeh* (HY 770), compiled by Hsieh Shou-hao (1131–1212) and collated by Li Chih-tao, pp. 9b, 10a, 10b, 10b–11a, and 11a–b; *Lung-shan shan chi* (HY 966), ch.1, pp. 1b–3a; *THY,* ch. 50, p. 865; *TFYK,* ch. 53, pp. 17a–18a and 19a–20b, and ch. 54, p. 12b; *CTW,* ch. 165, p. 11b; *Ta T'ang chiao-ssu lu,* ch. 9, p. 1a; J. J. L. Duyvendak, "The Dreams of Emperor Hsüan-tsung," in *India Antiqua* (Leiden, 1947), pp. 104 and 105; and C. Benn, *Taoism as Ideology in the Reign of Emperor Hsüan-tsung,* vol. 1, pp. 29–31, 51–52, 185–186, 191, and 228–229, and vol. 2, pp. 332–333, 339, 377–378, 379, and 391.

8. For the comment from the Shang-ch'ing scripture see *Shang-ch'ing t'ai-shang huang-su ssu-shih-ssu fang ching* (HY 1369), composed sometime between A.D. 400 and 550, p. 11b; HY 1130, ch. 34, p. 17a–b; and Isabelle Robinet, *La révélation du Shangqing dans l'histoire de Taoisme,* vol. 2, pp. 229–232. The remark from the Ling-pao canon can be found in HY 425, p. 17b; and HY 1130, ch. 47, p. 1a–b.

9. HY 1231, ch. 2, p. 20b. The *Wu-fa* is described in HY 1230, p. 5a–b. Chang cites the *T'ao-kung ch'uan i* (now lost), a work by T'ao Hung-ching, on the question of the proper times for its conferral.

# GLOSSARY

an 安
An Chin-ts'ang 安金藏
An-k'ang kung-chu (Princess) 安康公主
An-kuo kuan (Abbey) 安國觀
An-lo kung-chu (Princess) 安樂公主
An Lu-shan 安祿山

Chai-chüeh 齋訣
*Chai-i* 齋儀
chang 章
Chang Hsüan-pien 張玄辯
Chang Jen-sui 張仁邃
ch'ang-kuei 長跪
Chang Kuo 張果
Ch'ang-lung kung-chu (Princess) 昌隆公主
Ch'ang san-li 唱三禮
Ch'ang shih-fang t'ien-tsun fang 十方天尊方
Ch'ang-tao kuan (Abbey) 常道觀
ch'ang tu chih 唱度之
Chang Wan-fu 張萬福

Ch'ao Ssu-chi 朝四極
chen (suppress; ward off) 鎮
*Chen-i tzu-jan ching chüeh* 真一自然經訣
chen-jen fan 真人旛
*Chen-wen (erh lu)* 真文二籙
Chen-yüan kung 真源宮
Chen-yüan yüan 貞元院
Ch'eng-chi 成紀
*Cheng-i chai i* 正一齋儀
*Cheng-i (chen-chüan, ching)* 真卷經
*Cheng-i fa-wen (k'o-chieh p'in, tu-lu tu-chih i)* 法文科戒品度籙度治儀
*Cheng-i meng-wei fu-lu* 盟威符籙
Cheng-i meng-wei ti-tzu yüan-ming chen-jen 弟子元明真人
*Cheng-i pa-chieh wen* 八戒文
Cheng-i shih-hui 師諱
Cheng-i wu-chieh 五戒
Ch'eng-t'ien men (Gate) 承天門
ch'i (annunciation) 啟
ch'i (contract) 契
ch'i (energy, ether) 氣
Chi-chiu 祭酒

Ch'i-feng 啟奉

Ch'i-pai-erh-shih men yao chieh lü chüeh wen 七百二十門要戒律訣文

ch'i-pao (han, chou-tsu ch'ing-ssu) 七寶函周足青絲

Chi-shih 籍師

Ch'i-shih 啟事

Ch'i-shih-erh chieh 七十二戒

*Ch'i-shih-wu chiang-chün lu* 七十五將軍籙

Chiang Shu-yü 蔣叔輿

chiao 醮

Ch'iao-chün 譙郡

chiao hou chu-chi 醮後諸忌

Ch'iao-ling 橋陵

chieh (-mu, -t'an, -wen) 戒目壇文

Chieh-t'an chieh-hui 澳壇解穢

chien 簡

Chien-chai 監齋

*Ch'ien-erh-pai (kuan i, ta-chang)* 千二百官儀大章

Chien-shou ti-tzu fa-wei 簡授弟子法位

Chih-chiao chai 指教齋

*Chih-chiao ching* 經

Ch'ih chung fu 勅衆符

Ch'ih hsiao li shen 小吏神

Chih-hui shih-chieh ti-tzu 智慧十戒弟子

Ch'ih-shu 赤書

*Ch'ih-sung Tzu li* 赤松子曆

ch'ih (-t'ien, -tzu) 赤天字

chin (interdiction) 禁

chin (brocade) 錦

chin-ch'üan 金券

Chin-ch'üeh 金闕

Chin-hsien kung-chu (Princess) 金仙公主

*Chin-kang t'ung-tzu lu* 金剛童子籙

chin-lien (hua-tsuan, hua-shu) 金蓮華篹花樹

Chin-lu chai 金籙齋

*Chin-lu chien-wen* 簡文

Chin-ming Ch'i-chen 金明七真

chin-niu 金鈕

Chin-shan 禁山

Chin-tzu kuang-lu tai-fu 金紫光祿大夫

chin-tzu t'i-pang 金紫題牓

ching 精

ch'ing-chai 清齋

Ch'ing-chen ti-tzu 清真弟子

ch'ing-chin chih nang 青錦之囊

Ch'ing-ho hsien 清河縣

Ch'ing-hsin ti-tzu 清信弟子

Ch'ing-hua yüan-yang men 青華元陽門

ch'ing-kuan ch'i-shih 請官啟事

ch'ing-kuang chih teng 青光芝燈

ch'ing (-lo, -sheng, -ssu) 青羅繩絲

ching-shih 靜室

Ching-shih 經師

Ching-t'u 淨土

Ch'ing-tu kuan (Abbey) 清都觀

Ch'ing-wei 清微

ch'iu chin-lung 虬金龍

Chiu-hsien fan-hsing men 九仙梵行門

*Chiu-huang (chiao-i, pao-lu, t'u)* 九皇醮儀寶籙圖

Chiu-ling huang-chen men 九靈皇真門

Chiu-t'ien ch'ao 九天朝

*Chiu-t'ien (fa-ping fu, pao-ching, yin)* 發兵符寶經印

chu 祝

Chu Ch'ang-chung 祝昌中

Ch'u-chen (pa-shih-i) chieh 初真八十一戒

ch'u-chia 出家

Chü-chou 具州

Chu-hsia shih 柱下史

Ch'u hu chu 出戶祝

Ch'u-ju tao-men 初八道門
Ch'ü Keng-sheng 區更生
Ch'u-kuo kung-chu (Princess) 楚國公主
Ch'u (-ling) kuan 出靈官
Ch'u-meng 初盟
*Chu-shih fu* 竹史符
ch'u-su 出俗
chuan (written) 撰
ch'üan-chen 全真
ch'üan (-ch'i) 券契
ch'uan (-fa, -shou) 傳法授
*Ch'uan-i* 傳儀
chüeh 訣
Chung-chen men 眾真門
Chung-meng 中盟
*Chung-meng pa-chih ching* 八帙經
ch'ung-t'an shih-men 重壇十門
Chung-yüeh ch'ih 重約勑

erh-shih-pa hsiu teng 二十八宿燈
*Erh-shih-ssu chih cheng-i ch'ao-i* 法正一朝儀

fa (-chü, -hsin, -ku, -lu, -mu, -shih, -wen) 法具信鼓爐目師文
Fan Yün-hsien 范雲仙
Fan-yung 梵詠
fang-ts'ai 方綵
Fen-ch'üan 分券
Feng chang 封杖
feng-ho 奉和
feng-ko 鳳閗
fu 符
Fu (-kuan, -lu) 復官爐
Fu (-ti, t'ien) 福地田
Fu-yang chih ko 俯仰之格

Han-ku kuan (Pass) 函谷關
hang-t'u 行土
*Heng-hang yü-nü chou yin-fa* 橫行玉女呪印法
heng tu chih 橫讀之

Ho-nei chün k'ai-kuo kung 河內郡開國公
*Ho-shang Kung chen-jen chu* 河上公真人注
Ho-t'u pao-lu 河圖寶籙
Hsi-ch'eng kung-chu (Princess) 西城公主
Hsi-ling chen-jen 西靈真人
*Hsiang-erh (chu, erh-shih-ch'i chieh)* 想爾注二十七戒
Hsiang wang (Prince) 相王
hsieh (shih-fang) pan 謁十方版
Hsien-i kung-chu (Princess) 咸宜公主
*Hsien-kuan (Ling-kuan) ch'i-shih-wu chiang-chün lu* 仙官靈官七十五將軍籙
Hsin chai 心齋
Hsin-ch'ang kung-chu (Princess) 新昌公主
Hsin-yang kung-chu (Princess) 潯陽公主
hsing 形
Hsing-ch'ing kung (Palace) 興慶宮
hsing Tao (li) 行道禮
Hsing teng-t'ien chieh-ti fu 行騰天藉地符
hsiung 雄
hsü 序
Hsü Ch'iao 徐嶠
Hsü Hui, Hsü Mi 許謐許翽
Hsüan-k'o 玄科
*Hsüan-men ling-yen chi* 玄門靈驗記
*Hsüan-men ta-i (ta-lun)* 大義大論
Hsüan Yin-feng 玄尹豐
hu-chieh tao-chin 護戒刀巾
Hu hsien-sheng (Master Hu) 胡先生
Hua-yang kung-chu (Princess) 華陽公主
Huai-chou 懷州
Huan-chieh sung 還戒頌

*Huang-jen san-i piao-wen* 皇人三一
表文
Huang-lu chai 黃籙齋
*Huang-lu* (*chien-wen, ching*)
簡文經
*Huang-nü shen-fu* 黃女神符
*Huang-shen ch'ih-chang* (*yüeh-
chang*) 黃神赤章越章
*Huang-ti tan-shu nei-wen* 黃地
丹書内文
Hung-lu ch'ing 鴻臚卿
Hung-tao kuan (Abbey) 宏道觀

I-ch'ang kung-chu (Princess)
義昌公主
*I chiang-chün lu* 一將軍籙
*I-ch'ieh Tao-ching yin-i* 一切道經
音義
I-shih t'ou-tz'u 詣師投辭

*Jen-huang nei-wen* 人皇内文
Ju Ching-ssu san-shih 入精思
三師
Ju Ch'ü-cheng 辱曲正
Ju-hu chu 入戶祝

k'ai-shu 楷書
*K'ai-yüan ching* 開元經
K'ai-yüan kuan (ssu) (Abbey)
觀寺
Kao-ch'en 高晨
Kao-hsüan ti-tzu 高玄弟子
*Kao-shang Lao Tzu nei-chuan*
高上老子内傳
*Kao-shang yü-ch'en feng-t'ai ch'ü-su
shang-ching* 玉晨鳳臺曲素上經
Kao tan-shui wen 告丹水文
*Keng-ling* (*chiu-kuan*) *lu* 更令九
官籙
Ko Ch'ao-fu, Ko Hsüan, Ko
Hung 葛巢甫葛玄葛洪
K'ou Ch'ien-chih 寇謙之

k'ou-shou tu-tu 口授讀度
kuan (capping) 冠
*Kuan-ling nei-chuan* 關令内傳
Kuei-chen kuan (Abbey)
歸真觀
kuei-men 鬼門
kung 宮
kung-jen 工人
K'ung-tung 空洞
Kuo-tzu chi-chiu 國子祭酒

Lai Chün-ch'en 來俊臣
lan 欄
*Lao-chün ch'uan-i chu-chüeh* 老君
傳儀注訣
*Lao-chün i-pai-pa-shih chieh* 一百
八十戒
*Lao-chün liu-chia pi-fu* 六甲祕符
*Lao-chün nei-kuan ching* 内觀經
*Lao Tzu chieh-chieh* 老子節解
Lao Tzu ch'ing-ssu chin-niu
ti-tzu 青絲金鈕弟子
*Lao Tzu chung-ching* 中經
Lao Tzu erh-shih-ch'i chieh
二十七戒
*Lao Tzu miao-chen ching* 妙真經
*Lao Tzu nei-chieh* 内解
*Lao Tzu san-pu shen-fu* 三部神符
Li An-kuo 李安國
Li Ch'i-chih 李齊之
Li-ching sung 禮經頌
Li Ch'ung-fu, Li Ch'ung-jun
李重福李重潤
Li Fu-kuo 李輔國
Li I-hsin 李義琿
Li-pai chou shih-fang 禮拜
周十方
Li (pen-shih, san-shih) 禮本師
三師
Li Shang-chin 李上金
*Li-tsang ching* 歷藏經
Li Wei 李褘

Li Wu-shang 李无上
Li-yüan ti-tzu 梨園弟子
*Liang-ching hsin-chi* 兩京新記
lien-hua lou-fan 蓮華鏤幡
ling (-kuan) 靈官
Ling-hsien k'o-p'in 靈仙科品
Ling-nan 嶺南
*Ling-pao chen-wen fu t'u yü-tzu* 靈寶真文符圖玉字
*Ling-pao ching (mu)* 經目
Ling-pao ch'u-meng pi-sai liu-ch'ing chieh wen 初盟閉塞六情戒文
*Ling-pao chung-meng ching-mu* 中盟經目
*Ling-pao fu wu-ya li-ch'eng* 服五牙立成
*Ling-pao san-yüan chai i* 三元齋儀
*Ling-pao sheng-hsüan pu-hsü chang* 昇玄步虛章
*Ling-pao tung-hsüan ching fu t'u yü-tzu* 洞玄經符圖玉字
Ling-pao tzu-jan (ching-) ch'üan 自然經券
*Ling-pao yü-tzu ching* 玉字經
*Ling-pao yüan-shih wu-lao ch'ih-shu chen-wen pao-fu* 元始五老赤書真文寶符
Ling-t'ung chin-shang men 靈通禁上門
ling-wai 嶺外
Liu-chia fu 六甲符
Liu Chih-chi 劉知幾
Liu-huo chih t'ing 流火之庭
Liu shih (Lady) 劉氏
Liu T'ung-sheng 劉同昇
Liu Yung-kuang 留用光
Lo shu 洛書
Lou-kuan 樓觀
lu 籙
Lu chen-wen 露真文
Lu-chou 潞州

Lu Hsiu-ching 陸修靜
Lu-sheng 籙生
*Lu-sheng san-chieh wen* 三戒文
Lu-t'ang 鹿堂
Lung-ch'ang kung-chu (Princess) 隆昌公主
lung-hsü 龍鬚

Ma Yu-? 馬遊災
man-tseng 縵繒
meng (-shou, -wen) 盟受文
Meng-wei fu 盟威符
Ming-chen chai 明真齋
*Ming-chen k'o* 科
Ming (-chi, tseng) 命籍繒
ming (T'ien-) ku 鳴天鼓
Mou chih-ch'i cheng-i meng-wei ti-tzu 某治氣正一盟威弟子
Mou chih-ch'i nan-kuan nü-kuan 男官女官
Mt. Ch'ing-ch'eng 青城山
Mt. E-mei 峨眉山
Mt. Heng 恒山
Mt. Ho-ming 鶴鳴山
Mt. Ma-chi 馬跡山
Mt. Mao 茅山
Mt. Pao 苞山
Mt. Pei-mang 北邙山
Mt. Sung 嵩山
Mt. T'ai 泰山
Mt. T'ien-t'ai 天台山
Mt. Wang-wu 王屋山
Mt. Wu-t'ai 五臺山
Mt. Yü 虞山
mu-yü 沐浴

Nan-sheng nü-sheng 男生女生
Nan-sheng ti-tzu 南生弟子
nei (-kuan, -t'an, -yin) 內官壇音

*Pa-ch'eng (wei) wu-sheng shih-san fu* 八成威五勝十三符

Pa-chieh chai (jih) 八節齋日
Pa-chieh (wen) 八戒文
*Pa-ching nei-yin* 八景內音
pa-hui 八會
Pa (-lu, -nan) 八籙難
Pa-pai wen 八敗文
*Pa-shih lu* 八史籙
*Pa-ti ling-shu nei-wen* 八帝靈書
  內文
*Pa-ti (miao-ching, hsüan-pien,*
  *shen-hua) ching* 妙精玄變神化經
*Pa-wei ts'e-wen* 八威策文
Pai (-piao, -tu) 拜表都
Pai-pa-shih chieh chung-lü
  百八十戒重律
*Pai-wu-shih chiang-chün lu* 百五
  十將軍籙
pai-yin mu 白楬木
pan 版
p'an-lung hsiang-lu 盤龍香爐
*P'an-tai* 鞶帶
Pao Ching 鮑靚
*Pao-wen shih-pu miao-ching* 寶文
  十部妙經
Pei-chou 貝州
P'ei Fei-kung 裴匪躬
P'ei-fu 佩符
Pen-ming tseng 本命繒
pi chuan wen 祕篆文
piao 表
Pieh-chia 別駕
pien-lu 編錄
P'ing-en kung-chu (Princess)
  平恩公主
Po-chou 亳州
Po Ho 帛和
p'o Tzu-jan ch'üan 破自然券
pu-cheng 補正
*P'u-hsia pan* 普下版

*San chiang-chün t'u* 三將軍圖
San-chieh wen 三戒文

San-chüeh wen 三訣文
*San-huang (fu, wen)* 三皇符文
*San-huang (chai-i, ch'ao-i, ch'uan-*
  *shou i)* 齋儀朝儀傳授儀
*San-huang chen-hsing nei-hui pan*
  真形內諱版
*San-huang chiu-t'ien chen-fu ch'i-*
  *ling* 九天真符契令
*San-huang ch'uan-pan* 傳版
*San-huang nei-chen hui* 內真諱
*San-huang nei-ching fu* 內精符
*San-huang piao* 表
*San-huang san-chieh wu-chieh*
  *pa-chieh wen* 三戒五戒八戒文
*San-huang san-i chen-hsing nei-hui*
  *pan* 三一真形內諱版
*San-huang t'ien-wen ta-tzu* 天文
  大字
San-huang tzu-wu chai 子午齋
*San-huang yin* 印
*San-huang yü-ch'üan* 玉券
San-i ti-tzu, Ch'ih-yang chen-
  jen 三一弟子赤陽真人
San-kuan 三官
*San-kuei (wu-) chieh* 三歸五戒
San-meng 三盟
*San-pai-liu-shih chang* 三百六十章
*San-pai ta-chang* 三百大章
San-pao 三寶
*San-pu pa-ching tzu-jan chih-chen*
  *yü-lu* 三部八景自然至真玉籙
*San-t'ien chai* 三天齋
*San-t'ien cheng-fa ch'u liu-t'ien*
  *yü-wen* 正法除六天玉文
*San-t'ien t'ai-shang chao-fu chiao-*
  *lung hu-pao shan-ching wen*
  太上召伏蛟龍虎豹山精文
San-t'ien ts'ao 曹
San-tung (chiang, ta) fa shih
  三洞講大法師
San-tung ti-tzu 弟子
*San-tung tzu-wen ling-shu* 紫文靈書

San-wu ta-chai chih chüeh
三五大齋之訣
San-yao wen 三要文
San-yüan (chai, jih) 三元齋日
San-yüan pai-pa-shih chieh
百八十戒
sha 砂
sha-hsüeh 雨血
shan-chü 山居
shan-chuang 山莊
Shan-kuang ssu (Monastery)
善光寺
*Shang-ch'ing ching* 上清經
Shang-ch'ing fa-lu 法籙
Shang-ch'ing hsüan-tu ta-tung
san-ching ti-tzu, Wu-shang
san-tung fa-shih 玄都大洞三
景弟子無上三洞法師
*Shang-ch'ing pei-ti shen-chou wen*
北帝神呪文
*Shang-ch'ing p'in ching fu* 品經符
Shang chu-kuo 上柱國
*Shang-fa chiu-t'ien ling-wen* 上法
九天靈文
Shang-hsien chung-chen men
上仙眾真門
*Shang-huang pao-p'ien* 上皇寶篇
shao-hsiang 燒香
Shao-yang kung-chu (Princess)
邵陽公主
she-chai hsieh-en 設齋謝恩
she-t'an (su-lu fa, tso-wei)
設壇宿露法座位
Shen-chang 神杖
*Shen-chou (ch'üan, lu)* 神呪券籙
*Shen-hsien chin-chou ching* 神仙
禁呪經
Shen-pao chün 神寶君
shen-tsu ti-tzu 神足弟子
sheng-ch'i 生氣
*Sheng-chi ching* 聖紀經
sheng Ching-yü 昇淨域

*Sheng-hsüan ch'i-shih-erh tzu ta-lu
(ch'üan)* 昇玄七十二字大籙券
*Sheng-hsüan ching* 經
Sheng-hsüan fa-shih 法師
Sheng-shan ssu 聖善寺
*Sheng-t'ien ch'üan* 昇天券
shih 師
Shih (-ching, -hsiang, -teng,
-tso) 侍經香燈座
shih (-e, -shan) 十惡善
Shih ch'i-hsin ju-tao
san-kuei-chieh wen
始起心八道三歸戒文
*Shih chiang-chün fu-lu* 十將軍符籙
*Shih-chieh ching* 十戒經
Shih-chieh shih-ssu ch'ih-shen
chieh 十四持身戒
Shih Ch'ung-hsüan 史崇玄
Shih-erh k'o-ts'ung liu-ch'ing
chieh 十二可從六情戒
Shih-p'ing 始平
Shih-san chin wen 十三禁文
Shih-yang sheng-ch'i men
始陽生氣門
shou 授
Shou chen-wen (lu) 真文籙
shou-chieh 守戒
Shou (ching, tao) 受經道
Shou (ch'üan, liu-shih wen)
授券六誓文
shou-tao 守道
Shou wang (Prince) 壽王
shu-tao 書刀
Shuo-fa shou shih-chieh
說法授十戒
Shuo yüan-shih chin-chieh
說元始禁戒
So Ch'ung-shu 索崇術
*Ssu-chi ming-k'o* 四極明科
Ssu Ching 司精
ssu-fang 四方
Ssu-ma Ch'eng-chen 司馬承禎

*Ssu-shen t'u* 思神圖
Su (-ch'i, -lu) 宿啟露
Su Huai-ch'u 蘇懷楚
Sun Yu-yüeh 孫遊嶽
Sung (chen-wen hsü, chih-hui)
　誦真文序智慧
Sung Chin-chen t'ai-k'ung
　chang 金真太空章
Sung (feng-chieh sung, piao)
　奉戒頌表
Sung san-t'u wu-k'u tz'u 三徒
　五苦辭
sung shen (-chen, sung) 送神
　真頌
Sung wei-ling-shen chu 誦衛靈
　神祝
Sung Wen-ming 宋文明
Sung-yung wu chen-jen sung
　誦詠五真人頌


Ta-ch'ih 大赤
Ta-fan yin-yü 大梵隱語
Ta-hsieh 大謝
Ta-lo (fei-fan men) 大羅飛梵門
Ta-meng 大盟
Ta-ming kung (Palace) 大明宮
Ta-nei 大內
ta-te 大德
*Ta-ts'un t'u* 大存圖
*Ta-tung chen-ching* 大洞真經
*Ta-yu lu-t'u (T'ien-huang, Ti-*
　*huang, Jen-huang) nei-wen*
　大有籙圖天皇地皇人皇內文
T'ai-ch'ang ssu 太常寺
*T'ai-chen (i-) k'o* 太真儀科
T'ai-chen meng chüeh 盟訣
T'ai-chi (tien) (Hall) 太極殿
*T'ai-chi (chen-jen sung, pao-chüeh)*
　真人頌寶訣
*T'ai-chi tso-hsien kung Tao-te ching*
　*hsü* 左仙公道德經序

*T'ai-ch'ing chung-ching shen-tan*
　*fang* 太清中經神丹方
T'ai-ch'ing kuan (chu) 觀主
*T'ai-ch'ing yin-yang chieh* 陰陽戒
*T'ai-hsüan (ching, ho-t'u)* 太玄經
　河圖
*T'ai-i pa-t'ieh t'un-chia hsien-lu*
　太一八牒遁甲仙籙
Tai-kuo kung-chu (Princess)
　代國公主
T'ai-p'ing kung-chu (Princess)
　太平公主
*T'ai-p'ing tung-chi ching* 洞極經
*T'ai-shang huang shih-lu* 太上皇
　實籙
T'ai-shang kao-hsüan fa-shih
　高玄法師
T'ai-shang Lao-chün 老君
T'ai-shang ling-pao tung-hsüan
　ti-tzu 靈寶洞玄弟子
T'ai-shang Tao-chün 道君
T'ai-shang ti-tzu 弟子
T'ai-shang ts'ao 曹
*T'ai-shang tung-hsüan ling-pao*
　*chu-t'ien nei-yin lu* 洞玄靈寶
　諸天內音籙
*T'ai-shang tung-hsüan ling-pao*
　*erh-shih-ssu sheng t'u* 二十四
　生圖
*T'ai-shang tung-hsüan ling-pao*
　*sheng-hsüan nei-chiao ching*
　昇玄內教經
*T'ai-shang tung-hsüan ling-pao*
　*yü-chüeh* 玉訣
*T'ai-shang yü-ching yin-chu* 玉經
　隱注
T'ang Chen-chieh 唐真戒
T'ang P'ing 唐平
T'ao Hung-ching 陶弘景
*T'ao-kung ch'uan i* 陶公傳儀
*Tao-men (chi-yen chi, ta-lun)*
　道門集驗記大論

Tao-shih (priest) 道士

Tao-shih (chamber) 道室

Tao-te tsun-ching Hsiang-erh chieh 道德尊經想爾戒

Te-fei 德妃

T'e-ying 特盈

t'i 體

Ti-hu 地戶

*Ti-huang chi-shu wen* 地皇記書文

Ti-tzu feng-shih k'o-chieh wen 弟子奉師科戒文

Ti-tzu tzu meng-wen 自盟文

t'ien (-chen, -men, -pao, -shu, -t'ang) 天真門寶書堂

*T'ien-huang nei-hsüeh wen* 天皇内學文

*T'ien-shui fei-teng fu* 天水飛騰符

T'ien-tsun shih-chieh shih-ssu ch'ih-shen chieh 天尊十戒十四持身戒

T'ien T'ung-hsiu 田同秀

T'ien-yin yü chin-ko 天音於金格

t'ing-shu tao 挺書刀

T'ou lung-chien 投龍簡

Tou shih (Lady) 竇氏

*Tsa-shuo* 雜說

tsai-chia 在家

Ts'ai Wei 蔡瑋

Ts'e-chang 策杖

*Tse-t'ien shih-lu* 則天實錄

tso-wang 坐忘

tsuan 纂

ts'ung-shih chieh-shih 從師結誓

tu 度

Tu-chiang 都講

Tu-chien 讀簡

T'u-fu 土府

tu hsi tzu 讀細字

Tu huang-tseng chang 黃繒章

*Tu-jen ching* 度人經

Tu Kuang-t'ing 杜光庭

Tu meng-wen 讀盟文

Tu-pan 版

Tu piao-wen 表文

Tu-shen ts'ao 都神曹

Tu-shih 度師

Tu-t'an 都壇

T'u-t'an chai 塗炭齋

Tu ts'e-wen 讀策文

Tu-yang kung (Palace) 杜陽宮

tuan-fa 斷髮

Tuan (Wan-) Hsien 段萬謙

t'ui-chai 退齋

t'ung 同

Tung-chen fa-shih 洞真法師

tung-fang ch'ing-chin 東方青錦

Tung-hsi erh-chin (fu) 東西二禁符

t'ung-hsin chih teng 同心之燈

*Tung-hsüan ling-pao chai nei-shih hsin-yeh hsü* 洞玄靈寶齋内事心業序

*T'ung-hsüan lun* 通玄論

*Tung-hsüan wu-p'ien chen-wen wu-fu* 洞玄五篇真文五符

Tung-ling kung 洞靈宮

*Tung-shen ching* 洞神經

*Tung-shen san-tung yao-yen wu chieh shih-san chieh ch'i-pai erh-shih chieh men* 三洞要言五戒十三戒七百二十戒門

*Tung-shen t'ai-ch'ing t'ai-chi kung ching* 太清太極宮經

Tung-tou 東斗

t'ung-tzu 童子

Tung-yang chih kuan 洞陽之館

Tung-yang t'ai-kuang men 太光門

T'ung-yin chin-ch'üeh men 通陰金闕門

*Tung-yüan ling-pao shih-pu ching hsü* 洞元靈寶十部經序

*Tung-yüan shen-chou ching* 神呪經

Tung-yüan shen-chou ta-tsung

san-mei fa-shih hsiao-chao
chen-jen 大宗三昧法師小兆真人
tzu-chin (t'i-pang) 紫金題牓
*Tzu-hsü lu* 紫虛籙
Tzu-jan chai (ch'üan) 自然齋券
*Tzu-kung i-tu ta-lu* 紫宮移度大籙
tzu-t'ao lan teng 紫焰蘭燈
tzu-tzu chieh-shuo 字字解說
tz'u-wen 辭文

Wan-an kung-chu (Princess)
萬安公主
Wan-sheng 萬聖
Wang Fang-p'ing (Pao) 王方
平褒
Wang Shou-tao 王守道
Wang Tsuan 王纂
Wang Wei 王維
Wang Yü-chen 王玉真
Wei Cheng 魏徵
Wei hou 韋后
Wei-kuo kuan 魏國觀
Wei Shu 韋述
Wei T'ao 韋縚
Wei Tsou 韋湊
Wei T'uan-erh 韋團兒
Wei Yüan-chung 魏元忠
Wen-an kung-chu (Princess)
文安公主
Wu (-cho, -fa, -hsiang, -pao,
-tao) 五濁法香保道
*Wu-ch'ien wen (ch'ao-i)* 五千文
朝儀
*Wu-fu (hsü, ch'uan-pan)* 五符序
傳版
wu-hsing teng 五星燈
Wu-lao 五老
Wu mo (wang, yü-hui) 五魔王
玉諱
wu-se hua-chu 五色花燭
*Wu-shang chen-jen chuan* 無上
真人傳

*Wu-shang chih-chen wu-p'ien
ta-ching p'o-ch'üan ch'ih-su
chang* 至真五篇大經破券赤素章
Wu-shang shih chieh 十戒
Wu-shang (tung-hsüan, tung-
shen) fa-shih 洞玄洞神法師
Wu-shih pan 五師版
Wu-ti (chen-fu li) 五帝真符吏
Wu Tse-t'ien 武則天
wu-yao teng 五耀燈
Wu Yen-chi 武延基
*Wu-yüeh chen-hsing t'u (hsü)*
五嶽真形圖序
*Wu-yüeh kung-yang t'u* 供養圖

Yang Hsi 楊義
Yang Kuei-fei 楊貴妃
Yang-p'ing 陽平
Yang shih (Lady) 楊氏
Yang-t'ai kuan (Abbey) 陽臺觀
Yang Yü-huan 楊玉環
yao-chieh 要戒
Yeh Fa-shan 葉法善
Yen-kung fu-kuan 言功復官
Yen Lü-ming 閻履明
Yin Hsi 尹喜
*Yin-i* 音義
Yin kuan-ts'ao 陰官曹
yin-mu 椻木
Yin-sheng kuang-ling men
陰生廣靈門
Yü-chen kung-chu (Princess)
玉真公主
*Yü-chih hsin-i* 御製新儀
Yü-chüeh (cheng-yin) 玉訣正音
yu-i 幽逸
*Yü-li (chung-) ching* 玉曆中經
Yü-lu chai 玉籙齋
yü-pi 玉璧
Yü-p'ien 玉篇
*Yü-tzu shang-ching* 玉字上經
Yü-wen Jung 宇文融

Yü-yü 禹餘
Yüan-huang kao-ch'en men
   元黃高晨門
Yüan-shih ling-pao wu-ti
   chiao-chi chao-chen 元始
   靈寶五帝醮祭招真
*Yüan-shih ling-ts'e* 靈策
Yüan-shih wu-lao yin 五老印
Yüan-tu kuan 元都觀
yüeh chao ch'ien-yeh teng
   月照千葉燈

Yüeh-men 月門
Yung-an kung-chu (Princess)
   永安公主
Yung-chia kung-chu (Princess)
   永嘉公主
Yung-mu kung-chu (Princess)
   永穆公主
Yung Pu-hsü tz'u 詠步虛辭
Yung-t'ai kung-chu (Princess)
   永泰公主

# BIBLIOGRAPHY

## 1. Works from the *Tao-Tsang*
(see Appendix Two for texts written by Chang Wan-fu)

*Chai-chieh lu* (HY 464). This text was probably compiled in the early eighth century during the first years of Hsüan-tsung's reign (711–756).

*Chen kao* (HY 1010). Compiled by T'ao Hung-ching (456–April 18, 536) and completed in A.D. 499 or shortly thereafter.

*Cheng-i chih-chiao chai ch'ing-tan hsing-tao i* (HY 798). Date unknown.

*Cheng-i chih-chiao chai i* (HY 797). Date unknown.

*Cheng-i fa-wen fa-lu pu-i* (HY 1232). A possible remnant of the *Fa-wen* dating from the Nan-pei ch'ao (316–589).

*Cheng-i fa-wen t'ai-shang wai-lu i* (HY 1233). A possible remnant of the *Fa-wen* that was written in the Nan-pei ch'ao (316–589).

*Cheng-i hsiu-chen lüeh i* (HY 1229). Date unknown.

*Ch'ih-sung Tzu chang-li* (HY 615). Compiled in the twelfth century A.D.

*Ch'uan-shou ching-chieh i-chu chüeh* (HY 1228). This text probably dates from the late Nan-pei ch'ao or early T'ang dynasty (618–907).

*Hsü hsien chuan* (HY 295). Compiled by Shen Fen (fl. 937–975).

*Hsüan-p'in lu* (HY 780). Compiled by Chang Yü (1277–1350). His preface is dated October 1, 1335.

*Hun-yüan sheng-chi* (HY 769). Compiled by Hsieh Shou-hao (1131–1212).

*I-ch'ieh Tao-ching yin-i miao-men yu-ch'i* (HY 1115). Compiled by Shih Ch'ung-hsüan (d. A.D. 713), probably in A.D. 713.

*Ku Lou-kuan Tzu-yün yen-ch'ing chi* (HY 956). Compiled by Chu Hsiang-hsien (1279–1308).

*Lao-chün yin-sung chieh-ching* (HY 784). This is a remnant of a text purportedly revealed to K'ou Ch'ien-chih (d. 448) by Lao Tzu Deified on November 22, 415.

*Li-shih chen-hsien t'i-tao t'ung-chien* (HY 296). Compiled by Chao Tao-i (fl. 1299–1307).

*Li-tai ch'ung-tao chi* (HY 593). Compiled by Tu Kuang-t'ing (850?–933). His postscript is dated January 4, 885.

*Ling-pao wu-liang tu-jen shang-p'in miao-ching* (HY 1). Only the first chapter of this text was part of the original Ling-pao canon (ca. A.D. 400).

Lu Hsiu-ching (406–March 31, 477). "Ling-pao ching-mu hsü." In *Yün-chi ch'i-ch'ien* (HY 1036), ch. 4.

*Lung-chiao shan chi* (HY 966). A collection of documents dating from A.D. 713 to 1171.

*Nan-hua chen-ching chang-chü yin-i* (HY 736). Compiled by Ch'en Ching-yüan (1025–July 27, 1094). His preface is dated February 23, 1084.

*San-t'ien nei-chieh ching* (HY 1196). Written by a Master Hsü (Hsü Shu-piao? fl. 470–479).

*San-tung chu-nang* (HY 1131). Compiled by Wang Hsüan-ho (fl. 664–684).

*San-tung hsiu-tao i* (HY 1227). Compiled by Sun Chung-i. His preface is dated September 28, A.D. 1003.

*Shang-ch'ing kao-shang yü-ch'en feng-t'ai ch'ü-su shang ching* (HY 1361). Composed prior to A.D. 577.

*Shang-ch'ing ta-tung chen-ching yu-chüeh yin-i* (HY 104). Compiled by Ch'en Ching-yüan (1025–July 27, 1094).

*Shang-ch'ing T'ai-chi yin-chu yü-ching pao-chüeh* (HY 425). A scripture from the original Ling-pao canon (ca. A.D. 400).

*Shang-ch'ing t'ai-shang huang-su ssu-shih-ssu fang ching* (HY 1369). Composed sometime between A.D. 400 and 550.

*Shang-ch'ing t'ai-shang pa-su chen-ching* (HY 426). A text revealed to Yang Hsi between 364 and 370.

*T'ai-chen yü-ti ssu-chi ming-k'o ching* (HY 184). Composed sometime between 400 and 425.

*T'ai-chi chen-jen fu Ling-pao chai-chieh wei-i chu-ching yao-chüeh* (HY 532). A scripture from the original Ling-pao canon (ca. A.D. 400).

*T'ai-shang ching-chieh* (HY 786). Date unknown.

*T'ai-shang chiu-ch'ih pan-fu wu-ti nei-chen ching* (HY 1318). Composed prior to A.D. 577.

*T'ai-shang ch'u-chia ch'uan-tu i* (HY 1226). Compiled by Chia Shan-hsiang (fl. 1086–1101).

*T'ai-shang hun-yüan chen-lu* (HY 953). This text probably dates from the late seventh or early eighth century A.D.

*T'ai-shang Lao-chün chieh ching* (HY 783). Date unknown.

*T'ai-shang Lao-chün ching-lü* (HY 785). Date unknown.

*T'ai-shang Lao-chün hun-yüan san-pu fu* (HY 673). 3 ch., date unknown.

*T'ai-shang Lao-chün nien-p'u yao-lüeh* (HY 770). Compiled by Hsieh Shou-hao (1131–1212) and collated by Li Chih-tao.

*T'ai-shang san-wu cheng-i meng-wei lu* (HY 1199). This text probably dates from the late T'ang dynasty.

*T'ai-shang ta-Tao san-yüan p'in-chieh hsieh-tsui shang-fa* (HY 417). A Ling-pao text of the Nan-pei ch'ao period, but not part of the original canon.

*T'ai-shang tung-chen chih-hui shang-p'in ta-chieh* (HY 177). A scripture from the original Ling-pao canon (ca. A.D. 400).

*T'ai-shang tung-hsüan ling-pao chen-i ch'üan-chieh fa-lun miao-ching* (HY 346). A scripture from the original Ling-pao canon (ca. A.D. 400).

*T'ai-shang tung-hsüan ling-pao chen-wen yao-chieh shang-ching* (HY 330). A scripture from the original Ling-pao canon (ca. A.D. 400).

*T'ai-shang tung-hsüan ling-pao chih-hui ting-chih t'ung-wei ching* (HY 325). A scripture from the original Ling-pao canon (ca. A.D. 400).

*T'ai-shang tung-hsüan ling-pao chih-hui tsui-ken shang-p'in ta-chieh ching* (HY 457). A scripture from the original Ling-pao canon (ca. A.D. 400).

*T'ai-shang tung-hsüan ling-pao ch'ih-shu yü-chüeh miao-ching* (HY 352). A scripture from the original Ling-pao canon (ca. A.D. 400).

*T'ai-shang tung-hsüan ling-pao ch'u-chia yin-yüan ching* (HY 339). A Ling-pao scripture that dates from the late Nan-pei ch'ao period.

*T'ai-shang tung-hsüan ling-pao chung-chieh wen* (HY 410). Compiled by Lu Hsiu ching.

*T'ai-shang tung-hsüan ling-pao pen-hsing su-yüan ching* (HY 1106). A scripture from the original Ling-pao canon (ca. A.D. 400).

*T'ai-shang tung-hsüan ling-pao pen-hsing yin-yüan ching* (HY 1107). A scripture from the original Ling-pao canon (ca. A.D. 400).

*T'ai-shang tung-hsüan ling-pao san-yüan p'in-chieh kung-te ch'ing-chung ching* (HY 456). A scripture from the original Ling-pao canon (ca. A.D. 400).

*T'ai-shang tung-hsüan ling-pao shou-tu i* (HY 528). Compiled by Lu Hsiu-ching (406–March 31, 477) about A.D. 454.

*T'ai-shang t'ung-shen san-huang i* (HY 802). This text probably dates from the early T'ang dynasty.

*T'ang Yeh chen-jen chuan* (HY 778). The origin of this work is unknown. The Preface, dated 1241 and written by Ma Kuang-tsu (fl. 1226–1269), a governor of Kua-ts'ang, states that Ma received the text from Chang Tao-t'ung (fl. 1240), who was his cousin.

*Tao-chiao i-shu* (HY 1121). Compiled by Meng An-p'ai (fl. 684–704) around A.D. 700.

*Tao-chiao ling-yen chi* (HY 590). Compiled by Tu Kuang-t'ing (850?–933).

*Tao-men ting-chih* (HY 1214). Compiled by Lü Yüan-su (fl. 1188–1201) and edited and collated by Hu Hsiang-lung. Lü preface is dated A.D. 1188.

*T'ien-t'an Wang-wu shan sheng-chi chi* (HY 967). Compiled by Tu Kuang-t'ing (850?–933).

Tu Kuang-t'ing (850?–933). *Tung-t'ien fu-ti yüeh-tu ming-shan chi* (HY 599).

*Tung-chen t'ai-shang tzu-tu yen-kuang shen-yüan pien ching* (HY 1321). Completed prior to A.D. 577.

*Tung-hsüan ling-pao ch'ang-yeh chih fu chiu-yu yü-kuei ming-chen k'o* (HY 1400). A scripture from the original Ling-pao canon (ca. A.D. 400).

*Tung-hsüan ling-pao san-tung feng-tao k'o-chieh ying-shih* (HY 1117). Compiled by Chin-ming Ch'i-chen (fl. 545–554) around A.D. 550.

*Tung-hsüan ling-pao tzu-jan ch'üan i* (HY 522). Date unknown.

*Tung-hsüan ling-pao Yü-ching shan pu-hsü ching* (HY 1427). A scripture from the original Ling-pao canon (ca. A.D. 400).

*Wu-shang pi-yao* (HY 1130). Compiled under imperial auspices by a commission between 577 and 578.

*Yao-hsiu k'o-i chieh-lü ch'ao* (HY 463). Compiled by Chu Chün-hsü (alias Chu Fa-man, d. July 9, 720).

*Yu-lung chuan* (HY 773). Compiled by Hsieh Shou-hao (1131–1212) and submitted to the throne in 1191.

*Yuan-shih wu-liang tu-jen shang-p'in miao-ching ssu-chu* (HY 87). Compiled by Ch'en Ching-yuan. His preface is dated September 26, 1067.

*Yün-chi ch'i-ch'ien* (HY 1026). Compiled by Chang Chün-fang (fl. 1008–1029) and completed in A.D. 1028 or 1029.

## 2. Sources in Chinese and Japanese

*Ch'ang-an chih.* Compiled by Sung Min-ch'iu (1019–1079). A preface by Chao Yen-jo is dated March 12, 1076. In vol. 1 of *Sung-Yüan ti-fang chih ts'ung-shu.* Taipei, 1980.

Chang Cho (657–730). *Ch'ao-yeh ch'ien-tsai.* Completed sometime between 713 and 730. Ts'ung-shu chi-ch'eng. Shanghai, 1936.

Chang Tsun-liu. "Sui T'ang Wu-tai Fo-chiao nien-piao." In Fan Wen-lan, *T'ang-tai Fo-chiao.* Peking, 1979, pp. 91–310.

Ch'en Kuo-fu. "Nan-pei ch'ao T'ien-shih tao k'ao ch'ang-pien." In *Tao-tsang yüan-liu k'ao,* vol. 2, pp. 308–369.

———. *Tao-tsang yüan-liu k'ao.* 2d ed. 2 vols. Peking, 1963.

Cheng Ch'i (ca. 889–904). *K'ai-T'ien ch'uan-hsin chi.* In *T'ang-tai ts'ung-shu,* pp. 128–131. Taipei, 1968.

*Chin-shih hsü-pien.* Compiled by Lu Yao-yü. His preface is dated 1868. Appended to the *Chin-shih ts'ui-pien.*

*Chin-shih ts'ui-pien.* Compiled by Wang Ch'ang (1725–1806) and completed in 1805. Shanghai, 1921.

*Chiu T'ang shu.* Compiled by a commission under the direction of Liu Hsü (887–946) and submitted to the throne on July 12, 945. Peking, 1975.

*Chōan to Rakuyō, shiryō hen.* Compiled by Hiraoka Takeo. Kyoto, 1965.

*Ch'üan T'ang wen.* Compiled under imperial auspices by a commission under the direction of Tung Kao (1740–November 8, 1818). His preface is dated 1814. Taipei, 1961.

*Chuang Tzu chi-shih.* Assembled by Kuo Ch'ing-fan (1844–1896) and Wang Hsien-ch'ien (1842–1918). First printed in 1894. Peking, 1978.

*Chung-kuo li-tai chih-jan-hsiu t'u-lu.* Edited by Kao Han-yü. Hong Kong, 1986.

*Chung-kuo ta pai-k'o ch'üan-shu, Fang-chih.* Edited by Hu Ch'iao-mu. Peking, 1984.

Fa-lin (572–August 15, 640). *Pien-cheng lun.* Completed in 629 or shortly thereafter. In *Taishō shinshu Daizōkyō,* vol. 52, pp. 489–550. Tokyo, 1922–1936.

Fan Tsu-yü. *T'ang chien.* Peking, 1958.

*Fo-hsüeh ta-tz'u-tien.* Compiled by Ting Fu-pao from a Japanese dictionary of the same name compiled by Oda Tokumo. Taipei, 1969.

*Hsin T'ang shu.* Compiled by Ou-yang Hsiu (1007–1072) and others and submitted to the throne in 1060. Shanghai, 1975.

Kishibe Shigeo. *T'ang-tai yin-yüeh shih ti yen-chiu.* Translated by Liang Tsai-p'ing and Huang Chih-chiung. Taipei, 1973.

Ko Hung (283–343). *Pao-p'u Tzu.* The *nei-p'ien* in 20 ch. was completed in A.D. 317, and the *wai-p'ien* in 50 ch. sometime later. Collated and corrected by Sun Hsing-yen (1753–1818). His preface is dated 1813. Taipei, 1969.

*Ku-chin t'u-shu chi-ch'eng.* Begun by Ch'en Meng-lei (1651–d. ca. 1723), who finished the first manuscript in 1706. Reedited by a commission under the direction of Chiang T'ing-hsi (1669–1732) at imperial behest. First printed in 1728. Taipei, 1979.

Kusuyama Haruki. "Kajokō chu no seiritsu." In *Rōshi densetsu no kenkyū,* pp. 125–170. Tokyo, 1979.

———. "Kankoku ni okeru Rōshi to In Ki." In *Rōshi densetsu no kenkyū,* pp. 393–422.

———. "Taijo kongen shiroku ko." In *Dōkyō kenkyū ronshū, Yoshioka Yoshitoyo Festschrift,* pp. 457–476. Tokyo, 1977.

*Lao Lieh Chuang san-Tzu chih-chien shu-mu.* Compiled by Yen Ling-feng. Taipei, 1965.

*Lao Tzu pien-hua ching* (S. 2295). Reproduced in Anna Seidel, *La divinisation de Lao Tseu dans le Taoisme des Han,* pp. 131–136. Paris, 1969.

Li Hsien-chang. "Tao-chiao chiao-i ti k'ai-chan yü hsien-tai ti chiao." *Chūgoku gakushi* 5 (1969): 1–64.

Li Shang-yin (813?–858?). *Li I-shan shih-chi. Ssu-pu ts'ung-k'an.* Shanghai, 1919–1937.

*Lieh-hsien chuan chiao-cheng pen.* Attributed to Liu Hsiang (ca. 79–ca. 6 B.C.), but probably first written about A.D. 200; the text contains interpolations made in the third and fourth centuries A.D. Collated and annotated by Wang Chao-yüan (1763–1851). Her preface is dated March 12, 1804. In *Li-tai chen-hsien shih-chuan,* edited by Hsiao T'ien-shih. Taipei, 1970.

Liu Chih-wan. "Chung-kuo hsiu-chai k'ao." In *Chung-kuo min-chien hsin-yang lun-chi,* pp. 22–23. Taipei, 1974.

Liu Su (fl. 806–821). *Ta-T'ang hsin-yü.* Liu's preface is dated the first month (February 11 to March 12) of 807. Collated and punct. by Hsü Te-nan and Li Ting-hsia. Peking, 1984.

Ōfuchi Ninji. "Dōen shinju kyō no naiyō ni kansuru kenkyū." In *Dōkyō shi no kenkyū,* pp. 435–487. Tokyo, 1964.

———. "Dōen shinju kyō no seiritsu." In *Dōkyō shi no kenkyū,* pp. 435–487.

———. "Sankōbun yori Tōshinkyō e." In *Dōkyō shi no kenkyū,* pp. 277–297.

Ōmura Seigai. *Shina bijutsu shi, chōsō hen.* Tokyo, 1915.

*Pao-k'o lei-pien.* Compiled by an unknown author around 1279. *Ssu-pu ts'ung-k'an.* Shanghai, 1919–1937.

*Pen-ts'ao kang-mu.* Compiled by Li Shih-chen (1518–1593) and completed in 1596. Hong Kong, 1976.

*Pen-tsi king (Livre de terme originel).* Edited by Wu Chi-yu. Paris, 1960.

P'u-jen (pseud. for Wang Chia-yu). *Ti-wang sheng-huo.* Taipei, 1968.

Sato Tatsugen. *Chūgoku Bukkyō ni okeru kairitsu no kenkyū.* Tokyo, 1986.

*Shen-hsien chuan.* The original was compiled by Ko Hung, but the present version has been greatly altered by later hands. In *Li-tai chen-hsien shih-chuan.*

*Shih chi.* 130 ch. Compiled by Ssu-ma Ch'ien (145–86 B.C.), who began about 104 B.C. and had essentially finished by 91 B.C. Annotated by P'ei Yin (fl. 420–479) (the *Chi-chieh*), Ssu-ma Chen (fl. A.D. 713) (the *So-yin*), and by Chang Shou-chieh (fl. 713–742) (the *Cheng-i*). Original 1959. Peking, 1972.

*Sui shu.* Compiled by Wei Cheng (580–643) and others and completed in 636. Peking, 1973.

Sun K'o-k'uan. "T'ang-tai tao-chiao yü cheng-chih." In *Han-yüan Tao-lun,* pp. 132–137. Taipei, 1977.

Sung Ch'ang-pai (Ch'ing). *Liu-t'ing shih-hua.* Taipei, 1971.

*Ta T'ang chiao-ssu lu.* Compiled by Wang Ching (fl. 785–804) and completed in 793. In *Shih-yüan ts'ung-shu.* N.p., 1913–1917.

*Ta T'ang liu-tien.* Compiled under imperial auspices by a commission nominally under the direction of Li Lin-fu (d. December 22, 752) and completed in 738 or 739. Taipei, 1968.

*T'ai-p'ing huan-yü chi.* Compiled by Yüeh Shih (930–1007) and completed in 986. Taipei, 1963.

*T'ai-p'ing kuang-chi.* Compiled under imperial auspices by a commission directed by Li Fang (925–996); begun in March of 977 and completed in August of 978. Taipei, 1969.

*T'ang hui-yao.* Final compilation made by Wang P'u (932–982) and completed in 961. Taipei, 1968.

*T'ang liang-ching ch'eng-fang k'ao.* Compiled by Hsü Sung (1781–1848) and completed in 1810. Taipei, 1963.

*T'ang lü shu-i.* First compiled in 618, and revised in 624, 637, 651, and 653; the present edition represents that completed in 653 by a commission, under the direction of Chang-sun Wu-chi (d. 659), which also added the commentary. Taipei, 1969.

*T'ang ta chao-ling chi.* Compiled by Sung Min-ch'iu and completed in 1070. Taipei, 1978.

T'ang Yung-t'ung and T'ang I-chieh. "K'ou Ch'ien-chih ti chu-tso yü ssu-hsiang." *Li-shih yen-chiu* 5 (1961): 64–77.

*Tao-tsang tzu-mu yin-te.* Compiled by Weng Tu-chien. Taipei, 1966.

*Tonkō Dōkei, mokuroku hen.* Compiled by Ōfuchi Ninji. Tokyo, 1978.

*Tonkō Dōkei, zurokuhen.* Compiled by Ōfuchi Ninji. Tokyo, 1979.

Toyama Gunji. *Sokuten Bukō.* Tokyo, 1966.

*Ts'e-fu yüan-kuei.* Compiled under imperial auspices by a commission under the direction of Wang Ch'in-jo (962–1052) and Yang I (974–1020); begun in 1005 and submitted to the throne on September 20, 1013. Taipei, 1967.

*T'ung-chien chi-shih pen-mo.* Compiled by Yüan Shu (1131–1205). First printed in 1174. Peking, 1979.

*Tung-hsiao t'u-chih.* Compiled by Teng Mu (1247–1306) in 1302. Ts'ung-shu chi-ch'eng. Shanghai, 1935.

*T'ung-tien.* Compiled by Tu Yu (735–December 23, 812). Submitted to the throne between March 19 and March 26 of 803. Taipei, 1965.

*Tzu-chih t'ung-chien.* Compiled under imperial auspices by Ssu-ma Kuang (1019–1086) and others. Completed on January 1, 1085. Annotated by Hu San-hsing (1230–1287). His preface is dated December 14, 1285. Shanghai, 1976.

*Wang Mo-chieh ch'üan-chi chien-chu.* Annotated by Chao T'ien-ch'eng. His preface is dated February 26, 1736. Taipei, 1966.

Wang Shu-nu. *Chung-kuo ch'ang-chi shih.* Shanghai, 1935.

*Wen-hsien t'ung-k'ao.* Compiled by Ma Tuan-lin (1254–1325). First printed in 1339. Taipei, 1963.

Yamazaki Hiroshi. "Tōdai ni okeru sōni sorei no mondai." *Shina Bukkyō shiseki* 3, no. 1 (1939): 1–4.

Yang Lien-sheng. "*Lao-chün yin-sung chieh-ching* chiao-shih." *Chung-yang yen-chiu yüan Li-shih yü-yen yen-chiu-so chi k'an* 28, no. 1 (1956): 17–54.

Yoshioka Yoshitoyo. *Dōkyō keiten shiron.* Tokyo, 1955.

———. "*Saikairoku to Shigensō.*" *Taishō Daigaku kenkyū kiyō* 52 (1968): 283–301.

———. "Sandō hōdō kakai gihan no kenkyū." In *Dōkyō to Bukkyō,* vol. 3, pp. 75–160. Tokyo, 1976.

———. "Sandō hōdō kakai gihan no seiritsu ni tsuite." In *Dōkyō kenkyū,* vol. 1, pp. 5–108. Tokyo, 1965.

———. "Tonkō Taiheikyō ni tsuite." In *Dōkyō to Bukkyō,* vol. 2, pp. 9–114. Tokyo, 1970.

*Yü-hai.* Compiled by Wang Ying-lin (1223–1296). Taipei, 1964.

Yüeh Shih (930–1007). *Yang T'ai-chen wai-chuan.* Probably written after 986. In *K'ai-yüan T'ien-pao i-shih shih-chung,* edited by Ting Ju-ming, pp. 131–148. Shanghai, 1985.

## 3. Western-Language Sources

*Alchemy, Medicine and Religion in the China of A.D. 320.* Translated by James Ware. Boston, 1966.

Balazs, Stefan. "Beiträge zur Wirtschaftgeschichte der T'ang-Zeit," *Mitteilung des Seminars für Orientalische Sprachen* 36 (1933): 1–62.

Beck, B. J. Mansvelt. "The Date of the *Taiping jing.*" *T'oung Pao* 64, nos. 4–5 (1980): 163–164.

Benn, Charles. *Taoism as Ideology in the Reign of Emperor Hsüan-tsung (712–755).* Unpublished doctoral dissertation, University of Michigan, 1977.

Bokenkamp, Stephen. "Sources of the Ling-pao Scriptures." In *Tantric and Taoist Studies in Honour of R. A. Stein,* edited by Michel Strickmann, vol. 2. Brussels, 1982, pp. 434–486.

Boltz, Judith. *A Survey of Taoist Literature, Tenth to Seventeenth Centuries.* Berkeley, 1987.

*The Cambridge History of China.* Vol. 3, *Sui and T'ang China, 589–906,* part 1, edited by Denis Twitchett and John K. Fairbank. New York, 1979.

Chavannes, Edouard. "Le jet des dragons." In *Mémoirs concernant l'Asie Orientale,* vol. 3, pp. 51–220. Paris, 1919.

Ch'en, Kenneth. *Buddhism in China, a Historical Survey.* Princeton, 1964.

———. *The Chinese Transformation of Buddhism.* Princeton, 1973.

Chi Han. *Nan-fang ts'ao-mu chuang: A Fourth Century Flora of Southeast Asia.* Translated by Li Hui-lin. Hong Kong, 1979.

Ch'u T'ung-tsu. *Han Social Structure.* Seattle, 1972.

*The Complete Works of Chuang Tzu.* Translated by Burton Watson. New York, 1968.

Duyvendak, J. J. L. "The Dreams of Emperor Hsüan-tsung." In *India Antiqua,* pp. 102–108. Leiden, 1947.

*Ennin's Diary, the Record of a Pilgrim to China in Search of the Law.* Translated by Edwin O. Reischauer. New York, 1955.

*Facets of Taoism.* Edited by Anna Seidel and Holmes Welch. New Haven, 1979.

Fitzgerald, C. P. *The Empress Wu.* Melbourne, 1955.

Forte, Antonio. *Political Propaganda and Ideology in China at the End of the Seventh Century.* Naples, 1976.

Guisso, Richard. "The Reigns of Empress Wu, Chung-tsung and Jui-tsung (684–712)." In *The Cambridge History of China,* vol. 3, pp. 290–345.

———. *Wu Tse-t'ien and the Politics of Legitimation in T'ang China.* Bellingham, Washington, 1978.

Kaltenmark, Max. *Lao Tzu and Taoism.* Translated by Roger Greaves. Stanford, 1969.

———. "*Ling-pao:* note sur un terme du Taoisme religieux." In *Mélanges publié par l'Institut des Hautes Études Chinoises,* pp. 558–588. Paris, 1960.

Lagerway, John. *Taoist Ritual in Chinese History and Society.* New York, 1987.

———. *Wu-shang pi-yao, somme Taoiste du VIe siècle.* Paris, 1981.

Lai, Whalen. "The Earliest Folk Buddhist Religion in China." In *Buddhist and Taoist Practice in Medieval Chinese Society.* Vol. 2 of *Buddhist and Taoist Studies,* edited by David Chappell, pp. 16–32. Honolulu, 1987.

Levy, Howard. "How a Prince Became Emperor." *Sinologica* 6, no. 2 (1959): 101–119.

*Le Lie-sien tchouan.* Translated by Max Kaltenmark. Peking, 1953.

Lin Yu-tang. *Lady Wu, a Novel.* New York, 1965.

Maspero, Henri. *Taoism and Chinese Religion.* Translated by Frank Kierman. Amherst, Massachusetts, 1981.

Mather, Richard. "K'ou Ch'ien-chih and the Taoist Theocracy." In *Facets of Taoism,* pp. 103–122.

Needham, Joseph, and Lu Gwei-djen. *Science and Civilization in China.* Vol. 5, *Chemistry and Chemical Technology,* pt. 2. Cambridge, England, 1974.

Ōfuchi Ninji. "The Formation of the Taoist Canon." In *Facets of Taoism,* pp. 253–268.

———. "On *Ku Ling-pao ching.*" *Acta Asiatica* 27 (1974): 34–56.

Robinet, Isabelle. *La révélation du Shangqing dans l'histoire du Taoisme.* 2 vols. Paris, 1984.

des Rotours, Robert. "Les insignes en deux parties *(fou)* sous la dynastie des T'ang (618–907)." *T'oung Pao* 41, nos. 1–3 (1952): 1–148.

Saso, Michael. *The Teachings of Taoist Master Chuang.* New Haven, Connecticut, 1978.

Schafer, Edward. "The Capeline Cantos." *Asiatische Studien* 32 (1978): 5–65.

———. *The Golden Peaches of Samarkand.* Berkeley, 1963.

Schafer, Edward, and B. E. Wallacker. "Local Tribute Products of the T'ang Dynasty." *Journal of Oriental Studies* 4 (1957–1958): 213–248.

Seidel, Anna. *La divinisation de Lao Tseu dans le Taoisme des Han.* Paris, 1969.

———. "Imperial Treasures and Taoist Sacrements—Taoist Roots in the Apocrypha." In *Tantric and Taoist Studies in Honour of R. A. Stein,* edited by Michel Strickmann, vol. 3, pp. 305–352. Brussels, 1983.

Sivin, Nathan. *Chinese Alchemy, Preliminary Studies.* Cambridge, Massachusetts, 1968.

Soper, Alexander. *Literary Evidence for Early Buddhist Art in China.* Ascona, 1959.

Stein, Rolf. "Religious Taoism and Popular Religion from the Second to the Seventh Centuries." In *Facets of Taoism,* pp. 53–82.

Strickmann, Michel. "The Mao Shan Revelations, Taoism and the Aristocracy." *T'oung Pao* 63, no. 1 (1977): 1–64.

———. "On the Alchemy of T'ao Hung-ching." In *Facets of Taoism,* pp. 123–192.

———. *Le Taoisme du Mao chan, chronique d'une révélation.* Paris, 1981.

Stuart, G. A. *Chinese Materia Medica, the Vegetable Kingdom.* Taipei, 1979.

*The T'ang Code.* Translated by Wallace Johnson. Princeton, 1979.

"Une traduction juxtalinaire commente de la biographie officielle de l'Imperatrice Wou Tso-t'ien." Translated by Nghiem Toan and Louis Richard. *Bulletin de la Société des Études Indochinoises* 34, no. 2 (1959): 59–227.

*Traité des fonctionnaires et Traité de l'armée.* Translated by Robert des Rotours. 2 vols. San Francisco, 1974.

Twitchett, Denis, and Howard Wechsler. "Kao-tsung (reign 649–83) and the Empress Wu: The Inheritor and the Usurper." In *The Cambridge History of China,* vol. 3, pp. 242–289.

Wechsler, Howard. *The Mirror to the Son of Heaven, Wei Cheng at the Court of T'ang T'ai-tsung.* New Haven, 1974.

Weinstein, Stanley. "Imperial Patronage in T'ang Buddhism." In *Perspectives on the T'ang,* edited by Arthur Wright and Denis Twitchett. New Haven, 1973, pp. 239–264.

"The *Wei Shu* and *Sui Shu* on Taoism." Translated by James Ware. *Journal of the American Oriental Society* 53 (1933): 215–250.

Welch, Holmes. *The Practice of Chinese Buddhism, 1900–1950.* Cambridge, Massachusetts, 1967.

———. *Taoism, the Parting of the Way.* Boston, 1966.

Wheatley, Paul. *The Pivot of Four Quarters.* Edinburgh, 1971.

Zürcher, E. "Buddhist Influence on Early Taoism." *T'oung Pao* 66, nos. 1–3 (1980): 84–147.

# INDEX

Titles of texts from the *Tao-tsang* are indexed here by the numbers assigned them in the Harvard-Yenching index (e.g., HY 1). Refer to Appendix Three and the Bibliography to find the numbers.

Abbey of Refuge in Perfection. *See* Kuei-chen kuan
Abbot of the Supreme Purity Abbey, 1, 19, 115
ablutions, 39, 171 n. 2
accruing merit, 10, 12, 36, 37, 144, 158 n. 10, 163 n. 29
Activation of the Talismans for Ascending to Heaven and Reclining on Earth, 135
administrations (of princesses), 13, 159 n. 16
Akizuki Kan'ei, 177 n. 1
alchemy, 30, 60, 97, 169 n. 16, 184 n. 27
aloeswood, 29, 34, 144
altars, 20, 21, 99, 106, 109, 144, 164 n. 1, 166 n. 7, 167 n. 10
altars, Ling-pao: color scheme, 26, 27; fixtures and furniture, 27–32, 38, 69, 99; gates, 23–27, 29, 32, 38, 46, 107–109, 165 n. 5, 166 nn. 6, 7, and 8; size, 21–23; structure, 21, 23–24, 116
An Chin-ts'ang, 6, 155 n. 3
An-k'ang (Princess), 104
An-kuo kuan (abbey), 14
An-lo (Princess), 19, 163 n. 28
An Lu-shan, 16
Announcement of the Petition for the Enunciation of Merit, 134
annunciation, 44, 48–49, 51, 52, 54, 56, 122

Annunciation and Veneration, 131
apocrypha, 64, 174 n. 28
appanages, 13, 14, 15, 159 n. 16, 162 n. 23
articles of appeasement, 32, 116
asterisms, 52, 54
Attendants of the Incense, 41
Attendants of the Lanterns, 41
Attendants of the Scripture, 41
Attendants of the Seats, 172 n. 9
Audience with the Four Poles, 133
Audience with the Nine Heavens, 46, 127

banners. *See* pennons
bells, 40, 124, 126, 172 n. 5, 186 n. 1
Belt Talismans, 2, 57, 116
blossom poles, 21, 23–26, 107, 108, 116
Blue-Green Sovereign of the Eastern Region, 50, 53, 55, 57
Boards for the Five Preceptors, 133–134
Borneo camphor, 30
Bowing to the Capital, 122
Brahman Chanting, 135
Brahman ether, 61, 94
brocades, 27, 29, 31, 34, 38, 50, 116, 117, 118, 119, 120, 150, 168 n. 13, 169 n. 18
Buddhism (Buddhists), 10, 17, 18, 22, 25, 30, 56, 62, 66, 75, 94, 98, 104, 139, 140, 157 n. 9, 157–158 n. 10,

162 n. 27, 164 n. 2, 166 n. 7, 167 n. 8, 168 n. 12, 176 n. 48, 179–180 n. 7, 180 nn. 8 and 9, 186 n. 41

Buddhist precept (ordination) platforms, 22, 164–165 n. 2, 167 n. 8

bunting. *See* pennons

Bureaus of the Three Heavens, 134

bureaucratic titles and offices, 1, 6, 16–17, 155 n. 3, 162 n. 25

burning incense, 39–40, 171 n. 2

candles, 28, 119

canon cases, 31, 118

Canon of the Central Covenant, 1, 63, 116

Canon Preceptor of the Three Caverns, 20, 83, 142

Canon Preceptors, 40, 126, 141, 170 n. 34, 172 n. 5, 181 n. 14

canon wrappers, 31, 41, 50, 117, 169 n. 18

Cantors, 40, 56, 126, 172 n. 5

Capital Altar, 23, 46, 107, 109, 127, 128, 166 n. 5

cash, 33–34, 38, 117, 120

Casting of the Dragon Tablets, 35–36, 69–71, 136, 170 n. 31, 176–177 n. 56

Cavern Palaces, 143

Celestial Gate, 23, 107

Celestial Hall, 127

Celestial Intonations in the Golden Rules, 50

Celestial Master, 32, 64, 72, 76, 77, 94, 98, 134, 136, 140, 141, 143, 147, 148, 149, 171 n. 2, 172–173 n. 13, 173 n. 18, 176 n. 56, 178 n. 3, 180 nn. 8 and 9, 183 n. 20, 185 n. 41

Celestial Numinous Treasure Writ, 53

Celestial Portal, 126, 128

Celestial Texts, 49

Celestial Venerable of the Primordial Commencement, 49, 50, 61, 66, 94

Celestial Venerables, 27, 47, 48, 60, 61, 64, 125, 129–130

Celestial Writ of the Numinous Treasure, 59

celibacy, 9, 12, 76–77, 97–98, 179 n. 4, 181 n. 11, 186 n. 41

censer. *See* incense-braziers

Central Covenant, 44, 124

*Chai-chüeh,* 130

*Chai-i,* 86

Ch'an (Zen), 4

Chang Heng, 183 n. 20

Chang Hsüan-pien, 83

Chang Jen-sui, 83

Chang Kuo, 158 n. 13

Chang Lu, 183 n. 20

Ch'ang-lung (Jade-Perfected), 12–13

Ch'ang-tao kuan (abbey), 159 n. 17

Chang Tao-ling, 80, 136, 143, 180 n. 9, 183 n. 20

Chang Wan-fu, 1, 9, 12, 73, 78, 80–81, 82, 84–86, 87–90, 95, 97, 98, 163 n. 28, 164 n. 1, 170 n. 27, 177 n. 1, 178 nn. 2, 3, and 4, 179 nn. 5 and 6, 180 nn. 7, 8, and 9, 181 n. 14, 183 n. 23, 186 n. 1; life, 19–20; on altar fixtures, 27, 116–120, 167 n. 10; on altar furniture, 27–32, 116–120, 168 nn. 13 and 14; on incense, 30–31; on injunctions, 75–77; on pledges, 32–36, 170 n. 23; on the Princesses' altar, 21–23, 25–26, 37–38, 115–120, 166 n. 7; on the Princesses' ordination, 39, 42, 57, 58, 63, 66, 68, 69, 115, 120, 151, 172 nn. 10 and 13, 173 n. 15; works, 19–20, 137–151, 163 n. 28

chanting of the Gold Perfected's Petition of the Great Space, 46, 128

chanting the Hymn for the Salute to the Canon, 133, 176 n. 46

chanting the Hymn for Worship of the Injunctions, 135

chanting the Hymns for the Five Perfected, 122, 132

chanting the Invocation of the Guardian Powers and Gods, 129

chanting the Lyrics for Pacing the Void, 133

chanting the Lyrics on the Three Paths and Five Sufferings, 123, 134

chanting the Preface to the True Writs, 132

chanting the Stanzas for Wisdom, 123

Chao T'ien-ch'eng, 161 n. 21

Chappell, David, 180 n. 9

Chavannes, Edouard, 177 n. 56

*Chen-i tzu-jan ching chüeh,* 165 n. 3

Ch'en Kuo-fu, 173 n. 13
Chen-wen ch'ih-shu ching, 149
Chen-yüan Cloister, 164 n. 2
Chen-yüan kung (temple), 15
Cheng-i. See Celestial Master
Cheng-i chai i, 79
Cheng-i chen-chüan, 74
Cheng-i chieh wen, 74
Cheng-i ching, 78, 182 n. 19
Cheng-i fa-wen, 140, 178 n. 3, 180 n. 9
Cheng-i fa-wen k'o-chieh p'in, 148
Cheng-i fa-wen tu-lu tu-chih i, 147
Cheng-i meng-wei chih ching, 182 n. 19
Cheng-i meng-wei fu-lu, 79
Cheng-i meng-wei ti-tzu yüan-ming chen-jen, 78
Cheng-i meng-wei yüan-ming chen-jen, 78
Cheng-i pa-chieh wen, 74
Cheng-i wu-chieh, 178 n. 3
Ch'eng-t'ien Gate, 19
Cheng Yin, 91
ch'i (energy), 32, 38, 44, 47, 75, 97, 145, 146
Ch'i-pai-erh-shih men yao chieh lü chüeh wen, 140
Ch'i-shih-erh chieh, 76
Ch'i-shih-wu chiang-chün lu, 74, 147
Ch'iao-ling (tumulus), 14
Chieh-wen, 84
Ch'ien-erh-pai kuan i, 79
Ch'ien-erh-pai ta-chang, 78
Chih-chiao chai, 81, 182 n. 20
Chih-chiao ching, 183 n. 20
Chih-hui shih-chieh ti-tzu, 179 n. 4
Ch'ih-sung Tzu li, 182 n. 19
Chin-hsien. See Gold-Immortal
Chin-kang t'ung-tzu lu, 87
Chin-lu chien-wen (ching), 28, 137, 165 n. 3, 168 n. 12, 171 n. 4
Chin-ming Ch'i-chen, 63, 64, 65, 72, 73, 76-77, 78, 79, 80, 82, 87, 95, 96, 98, 167 n. 10, 168 n. 13, 169 n. 18, 172 n. 13, 175 n. 43, 177 n. 1, 178 nn. 3 and 4, 181 n. 14
Ch'ing-chen ti-tzu, 183 n. 25
Ch'ing-ch'eng (Mt.), 159 n. 17
Ch'ing-hsin ti-tzu, 74-75, 183 n. 25
Ch'ing-hua yüan-yang men, 108
Ching-t'u, 163 n. 29
Ch'ing-tu kuan (abbey), 20, 142, 146

Ch'ing-wei Heaven, 55, 132
Chiu-hsien fan-hsing men, 108
Chiu-huang chiao i, 147
Chiu-huang pao-lu, 95-96
Chiu-huang t'u, 90
Chiu-ling huang-chen men, 108
Chiu-t'ien fa-ping fu, 88
Chiu-t'ien pao-ching, 128
Chiu-t'ien yin, 90
Chu Ch'ang-chung, 58
Ch'u-chen chieh, 9, 76, 77, 180-181 n. 10, 181 n. 11
Ch'u-chen pa-shih-i chieh, 179 n. 4
ch'u-chia, ch'u-su, 9, 98
Ch'ü Keng-sheng, 58-59
Ch'u-kuo (Princess), 103
Chu-shih fu, 88
Ch'uan-i, 86
Chuang Tzu, 8, 97, 185 n. 40
Chung (Mt.), 53
Chung-tsung, 5, 6, 7, 10, 13, 19, 156 n. 5, 159 n. 16
cinnabar, 30, 169 n. 16
Cinnabar Ink Writ, 61, 62, 122
clerical hierarchy (orders), 3-4, 20, 64, 72-73, 78-98, 185 n. 41
Clerks of the Five Sovereigns' True Talismans, 57-59
cloves, 30
Commanding the Lesser Functionaries and Gods, 146
commentaries, 8, 73, 84-86
confession, 68, 102, 176 n. 56
confirmation, 11, 73, 76, 148, 179 n. 4
Confucian canon, 17
consecration, 47
conspiracy, 5-10, 16, 18-19, 155 n. 3
contracts, 79, 90, 96, 150, 173 n. 14, 176 n. 45
cordons, 21, 23-27, 108, 116, 164 n. 1
court politics, 5-10, 13-16, 18
Courtyard of Flowing Fire, 49
covenants, 3, 33, 36, 45, 60, 68, 69, 83, 100, 101, 131, 150, 151
cushions, 27, 69, 116
cutting of hair, 31, 36, 150

dance, 65, 145
Days of the Eight Segments, 174 nn. 24 and 30

Days of the Three Primes, 171 n. 2
Declaration of the Cinnabar Ink Writ,
60, 122, 132
demons, 48, 51, 52, 80, 82, 128, 129,
131, 174 n. 28
Department of Justice, 162 n. 25
destiny, 33, 35, 51, 59
Destiny Silk, 33, 37, 169 n. 21
dharani, 56
diplomacy, 10–11
Directors of the Retreat, 40–41, 172 n. 6
Discourse on the Doctrine and the
Transmission of the Ten Injunctions,
123
Discourse on the Interdictory Injunctions of the Primordial Commencement, 66, 133
Dispatching the Gods and the Perfected, 146
Dispatching the Memorial, 122, 131
Divine Diamond Kings, 31, 117, 119
Divine Staffs. *See* staffs
domestic animals, 57, 70, 127, 134
dragon plaques, 29, 35, 70, 116, 117,
150
dragon whisker, 27, 116, 167–168 n. 11
dragons, 51, 52, 150
drama, 99–100
Drum of the Law, 125
drums, 40, 81, 124, 131, 172 n. 5
Duke of the Great Bourne, 87

E-mei (Mt.), 91
Eastern Dipper, 70
Eastern Talismanic Mandate, 53
ecclesiastical titles, 72–73, 74, 76–77,
81, 82, 84–85, 87, 89, 92, 93, 95, 96,
101
Eight Difficulties, 127
eight directions (and their gods), 75,
180 n. 9
Eight Effulgent Spirits, 49, 55, 93, 112,
131, 174 n. 29
Eight Registers, 15
eight trigrams, 28, 109
elixirs, 30, 39, 91
Elysian Fields, 10, 145
Empress Wei, 8, 13
Empress Wu. *See* Wu Tse-t'ien

Empty Cavern, 49, 61
Ennin, 22, 164 n. 2, 167 n. 8
Enunciation of Merit and the Restoration of the Bureaucrats, 123
epiphanies, 15, 39, 68, 104–105, 120,
156 n. 8, 160 n. 20, 182 n. 19
*Erh-shih-ssu chih cheng-i ch'ao i*, 74
*Erh-shih-ssu sheng ching*, 149
Esoteric Intonations, 49, 56, 93, 95,
100, 113, 131
Esoteric Pronunciations of the Eight
Effulgent Spirits, 125
establishing the altar and its seats, 144
ethers, 47, 49, 51, 52, 53–54, 55, 59,
100, 110, 111, 113, 174 n. 30
eunuchs, 6, 16, 161 n. 22
Externalizing the Officials (Bureaucrats), 44, 121, 124, 130, 145

Fa-lin, 184 n. 30, 185 n. 36
*Fa-wen*, 79, 173 n. 13
Fan Yün-hsien, 155 n. 3
fasting, 39–40, 42, 91, 105, 129,
171 n. 2, 172 n. 12
Fitzgerald, C. P., 157 n. 10
Five Aromatics, 29–30, 39, 150,
171 n. 2
Five Demon Monarchs, 32, 112,
174 n. 28
five desires, 34, 75
Five Destinies, 127
five directions (and their gods), 29, 30–
31, 32, 45, 47, 48, 49, 50, 56, 58, 59,
60, 69, 116, 126, 128, 129, 130, 131,
132, 169 n. 20
Five Elders. *See* five directions
five elements or phases, 54, 165 n. 5
Five Marchmounts (and their gods), 23,
28, 34, 38, 60, 61, 69, 70, 94, 125,
129, 130, 143
Five Sovereigns. *See* five directions
Five Sovereigns of the Soil Administration, 70
five stars, 28, 129
Five (Ling-Pao) Talismans, 23, 31, 49,
52, 59, 62, 95, 100, 106, 111, 131,
149, 174 n. 26; transmission of, 52–54
five turbities, 75, 180 n. 8
flour coverings, 27, 116

Foundry of Cavern-Yang, 49
frankincense, 29
Fu I, 84

gage. *See* pledges
Gate of the Nine Heavens, 136
Gate of the Perfected, 26
ginkgo, 29, 57, 69
gold, 34, 38, 117, 150
Gold-Immortal (Princess), 1, 3, 4, 12,
    20, 73, 104, 106, 156 n. 8, 158 n. 10,
    159 n. 15; age, 154 n. 1; altar, 21–32;
    death, 14, 159 n. 17; early life, 5, 8–
    10; later life, 14; Ling-pao ordina-
    tion, 13, 20, 39–40, 41–42, 44, 45–
    46, 49, 61, 63, 65, 68, 69, 70, 73,
    102, 104, 106, 115, 120, 151,
    159 n. 15, 169 n. 21, 171 n. 36,
    172 n. 10, 186 n. 1; pledges, 32–38;
    Shang-ch'ing ordination, 4, 13, 95,
    106, 151, 159 n. 15; temple in her
    name, 12–14, 159 n. 15
gold knobs, 35–36, 69, 117, 150
Gold Register Retreat, 101–102,
    160 n. 19
gold tablets, 2, 49, 61
Golden Portal, 146
Governor for the Cinnabar Terrace and
    Jade Gate-Tower, 51
Governor for the Hall of the Eastern
    Blossom, 51
Governor for the Institute of the East-
    ern Mulberry, 51
Governor for the Primal Terrace, 50
Grand Canon Preceptor of the Three
    Caverns, 1, 16, 115
Grand Canon Preceptors, 66, 139
Grand (Third) Covenant, 181 n. 14
Grand Sovereigns of the Sources of the
    Twelve Rivers, 69
Grand-Worthy, 19
Grandee of Illustrious Noble Rank,
    Gold Signet and Purple Ribbon, 1,
    17, 115
The Great Confession, 134
Great Covenant (of the Numinous-
    Treasure), 44, 69, 135
Great Injunctions, Superior Grade, of
    Wisdom, 44, 66

Great Inner Palace, 2, 16, 19, 21, 116,
    163–164 n. 1

hagiographies, 84, 85, 96
Han-ku Pass, 86, 160 n. 20
hang-t'u, 21
Heavenly Treasure, 15, 160 n. 20
Heaven's Drum, 124
hell, 10, 28, 34, 57, 60, 70, 102, 123,
    127, 134, 144, 145, 158 n. 10,
    163 n. 29
Heng (Mt.), 15
*Heng-hang yü-nü chou yin-fa,* 82
Hidden Discourse of the Great
    Brahman, 56, 113, 138, 174 n. 31
Ho-ming (Mt.), 80
*Ho-shang Kung chen-jen chu,* 84
*Ho-t'u pao-lu,* 147
Hsi-ling chen-jen, 91
Hsi-ning (Gold-Immortal), 12–13
*Hsi-sheng ching,* 87
*Hsiang-erh chu,* 84
*Hsiang-erh erh-shih-ch'i chieh,* 85,
    183 n. 26
Hsien-i (Princess), 103
*Hsien-kuan ch'i-shih-wu chiang-chün lu,* 74,
    76
*Hsin chai,* 97
Hsin-ch'ang (Princess), 103
Hsin-yang (Princess), 103
Hsing-ch'ing Palace, 16
Hsü Ch'iao, 154 n. 1
Hsü Hui, 96
Hsü Mi, 96
*Hsüan-men ling-yen chi,* 138
*Hsüan-men ta-i,* 182 n. 19
*Hsüan-men ta-lun,* 186 n. 4
Hsüan-tsung, 5, 11, 14, 102, 105, 138,
    155 n. 2, 156 n. 8, 158 n. 13, 159 n. 17,
    160 n. 20, 161 n. 22, 162 n. 26; fall,
    16; and Jade-Perfected, 14–16; pal-
    ace coups, 8; and Yang Yu-huan, 11–
    12
Hsüan Yin-feng, 58
Hua-yang (Princess), 103
*Huang-jen san-i piao-wen,* 85
*Huang-lu chien-wen,* 42, 130, 165 n. 3,
    172 n. 12
*Huang-lu ching,* 24

*Huang-lu hsü-shih i,* 182 n. 19
*Huang-nü shen-fu,* 89
*Huang-shen ch'ih-chang,* 82
*Huang-shen yüeh-chang,* 86
*Huang-ti tan-shu nei-wen,* 88
Hung-tao kuan (abbey), 154 n. 1
hungry ghosts, 57, 70, 127, 134
HY 1, 19, 54, 56, 113, 137–138; internal divisions, 138
HY 22, 50, 52, 53, 110, 111, 114
HY 87, 138
HY 95, 137
HY 97, 56, 113
HY 177, 124, 139
HY 178, 75, 138–141
HY 335, 81
HY 352, 23, 26, 51, 52
HY 388, 53, 94, 111
HY 445, 126, 141
HY 457, 66
HY 459, 83
HY 463, 124
HY 464, 160 n. 19
HY 508, 22, 25, 28, 46, 107, 108, 142, 163 n. 29
HY 522, 43, 121–123
HY 525, 82
HY 526, 82
HY 527, 82
HY 528, 22, 26, 39, 79, 110, 121, 124–135, 136
HY 532, 65
HY 590, 82, 138
HY 640, 92
HY 664, 84
HY 666, 85
HY 682, 84
HY 787, 142–144
HY 802, 87–92
HY 1010, 96, 148
HY 1026, 85
HY 1106, 135
HY 1115, 18, 19, 138
HY 1117, 63, 64, 73, 87, 139, 140, 142, 144, 147, 149, 177 n. 1
HY 1130, 22, 23, 24, 25, 26, 29, 31, 37, 39, 61, 68, 75, 87, 109, 121, 125, 126, 127, 139, 140, 141, 166 nn. 7 and 8, 171 n. 1, 172 n. 11
HY 1193, 92

HY 1199, 64
HY 1202, 144
HY 1230, 95, 146–148
HY 1231, 20, 73, 88, 115–120, 135, 140, 141, 148–151, 177 n. 1
HY 1396, 54, 55, 112
HY 1400, 126
HY 1427, 65
Hymn for Returning the Injunctions, 135
Hymn for the Salute to the Canon, 65
Hymn for the Transmission of the Canon, 61
Hymn of the Perfected, T'ai-chi, 138
hymns, 49, 65, 68, 122

I-ch'ang (Princess), 104
*I chiang-chün lu,* 74, 76, 178 n. 4
*I-ch'ieh Tao-ching yin-i,* 18, 138
*I-ching,* 109
icons, 31–32, 64
illustrations, 22, 25, 42, 44, 81, 86, 90, 91, 93, 95, 96, 107–114, 144, 165 n. 3, 168 n. 13, 178 n. 2
Immortal Lads, 31, 65, 105, 117
immortality, 69–70, 97, 125, 127, 134, 146, 184 n. 30
immortals, 26, 34, 38, 50, 59, 70, 91, 97, 99, 101, 124, 127, 143, 186 n. 41
Imperial Successor, 5, 6
Incantation for Entering the Portal, 145
Incantation for Leaving the Portal, 146
incantations, 81–82, 96, 141
incense, 29–31, 37, 41, 47, 49, 68, 117, 121, 122, 124, 125, 129, 132, 136, 145, 146, 165 n. 2, 170 n. 26
incense-braziers (burners), 29–31, 41, 49, 117, 125, 168 n. 14
Initial Covenant, 42, 45, 121, 139
initiation, 9, 64, 73–78, 98, 101, 139, 140, 143, 146, 148, 150, 157 n. 8, 158 n. 11, 163 n. 29, 172 n. 13, 177 n. 1, 178 n. 3, 178–179 n. 4, 179 n. 6
Initiation Preceptor, 40, 127
injunctions, 2, 33, 34, 35, 42, 46, 64, 68, 73, 74, 75–76, 80, 83, 84, 85, 86, 89, 97, 98, 100, 101, 117, 139–141, 148, 170 n. 30, 172 n. 13, 173 n. 15, 176 n. 49, 177 n. 1, 178 n. 3, 179 n. 4,

180 n. 9, 181 n. 14, 183 nn. 25 and 26, 185 n. 41

Injunctions for Arresting the Six Emotions, 42–44, 67, 139; transmission of, 124

inksticks, 35, 117

Inner Altar, 23, 28, 29, 46, 49, 65, 108, 109, 124, 128

Inventory of Ling-pao Scriptures for the Middle Covenant, 63

Invocation for Entering the Portal, 46, 126

invocations, 2, 39, 45, 51, 52, 55, 56, 57, 58, 62, 63, 69, 78, 121, 122, 123, 124, 125, 126, 127, 129, 131, 136, 137, 145, 174 nn. 25 and 31

jade disks, 29, 116, 150

Jade Emperor, 125, 146

Jade Graphs (of the Esoteric Intonations), 42, 44, 45, 49, 55, 64, 113, 131, 132; transmission of, 54–56

Jade Instructions, 49, 51, 52, 61, 100, 112, 165 n. 3, 175 n. 36

Jade Instructions (in Red Graphs for the Eight Effulgent Spirits), 64, 132; transmission of, 54–55

Jade Lads, 56, 119, 125, 126, 130, 146

Jade Maids, 48, 51, 56, 57, 58, 65, 100, 105, 117, 119, 125, 126, 130, 146

Jade-Perfected (Princess), 1, 3, 4, 12, 20, 73, 104, 106, 156 nn. 8, 158 nn. 10 and 13, 159 n. 15; age, 154 n. 1; altar, 21–32; concern for justice, 14, 160 n. 18; death, 16; early life, 5, 8–10; estate, 15, 161 n. 21; and Hsüan-tsung, 14–16; later life, 14–16; Ling-pao ordination, 13, 20, 39–40, 41–42, 44, 45–46, 49, 61, 63, 65, 68, 69, 70, 73, 102, 104–105, 106, 115, 120, 151, 156 n. 8, 159 n. 15, 169 n. 21, 171 n. 36, 172 n. 10; liturgical services for the throne, 14–15, 160–161 n. 19; pledges, 32–38; Shang-ch'ing ordination, 4, 13, 95, 106, 151, 159 n. 15; temple in her name, 12–14, 159 n. 15

jade slats, 2, 49, 50, 122, 130, 132, 173 n. 19

Jade Taboos of the Five Demons, 54, 61, 100, 112, 132

*Jen-huang nei-wen,* 89

Ju Ch'ü-cheng, 58

Jui-tsung, 1, 10, 16, 17, 158 n. 8, 159 n. 15; censure of, 13, 38, 159 n. 16; construction of temples for his daughters, 12–14; daughters, 1, 9, 38, 104, 153 n. 1, 156 n. 7; and *Tao-te ching,* 8, 156 n. 6; victim of persecution, 5–8, 155 n. 3, 156 n. 5; wives, 5–6, 153 n. 1, 154–155 n. 2

*K'ai-yüan ching,* 149

K'ai-yüan kuan (abbey), 14, 83

K'ai-yüan Monastery, 164 n. 2

*Kao-hsüan ti-tzu,* 84

*Kao-shang (Lao Tzu nei-)chuan,* 85

*Kao-shang yü-ch'en feng-t'ai ch'ü-su shang-ching,* 150

Kao-tsung, 10, 105, 161 n. 20, 163 n. 1

karma, 102, 139

*Keng-ling (chiu-kuan) lu,* 74, 177 n. 2, 178 n. 4

kerchiefs, 29, 31, 35, 41, 117, 150, 168 n. 13

knives, 35, 43, 117, 170 n. 29

Ko Ch'ao-fu, 62, 78, 94, 97, 175 n. 41, 185 n. 36

Ko Hsüan, 53, 60, 61, 62, 87, 94, 99, 101, 175 n. 41, 184 n. 36

Ko Hung, 36, 60, 91, 170 n. 33, 175 n. 39

K'ou Ch'ien-chih, 98

*Kuan-ling nei-chuan,* 84

Kuei-chen kuan (abbey), 2, 9, 12, 21, 22, 26, 28, 41, 106, 116, 163 n. 1

Lady Liu, 5–6, 155 n. 2

Lady Tou, 5–6, 153 n. 1, 155 n. 2

Lady Yang, 10

Lagerway, John, 164 n. 2, 166 nn. 7 and 8

Lai Chün-ch'en, 6–7, 155 n. 3

lamp-trees, 27, 119

lanterns, 25, 28, 37, 41, 108, 119–120, 168 n. 12

*Lao-chün ch'uan-i chu-chüeh,* 147

*Lao-chün i-pai-pa-shih chieh,* 79

*Lao-chün liu-chia pi-fu,* 86

*Lao-chün nei-kuan ching,* 150
Lao Tzu (Deified), 15, 53, 68, 86, 104,
    105, 120, 125, 129, 143, 145, 160–
    161 n. 20, 162 n. 26, 180 n. 9,
    182 n. 19, 183 n. 27, 185 n. 41
*Lao Tzu chieh-chieh,* 85, 87
*Lao Tzu chin-niu ch'ing-ssu,* 83
*Lao Tzu ch'ing-ssu chin-niu ti-tzu,* 82
*Lao Tzu chung-ching,* 85
*Lao Tzu erh-shih-ch'i chieh,* 183 n. 26
*Lao Tzu Hsiang-erh chu chiao-chien,* 84
*Lao Tzu miao-chen ching,* 85
*Lao Tzu nei-chieh,* 85
*Lao Tzu san-pu shen-fu,* 79
Ledger of Destiny, 34
ledgers, 32, 33, 34, 35–36, 69, 174 n. 24
Li (royal house of the T'ang), 4, 6, 7,
    104
Li An-kuo, 19
Li Ch'i-chih, 138
Li Ch'ung-fu, 155 n. 4
Li Ch'ung-jun, 156 n. 4
Li Fu-kuo, 161 n. 22
Li I-hsin, 14
*Li-tsang ching,* 85
Li Wei, 160 n. 18
Li Wu-shang, 83
*Liang-ching hsin-chi,* 157 n. 10
Libationer for the Directorate of the
    Sons of State, 16–17, 162 n. 23
libationers, 98, 148, 185–186 n. 41
Lighting of the Censer, 31, 69, 121,
    124, 129, 136, 145
*Ling-hsien k'o-p'in,* 130
*Ling-kuan ch'i-shih-wu chiang-chün lu,* 74,
    76
Ling-pao, 54, 181 n. 14, 185 n. 41;
    canon, 1, 2, 3, 16, 23, 24, 25, 28, 29,
    31, 32, 33, 34, 35, 36, 38, 39, 42, 44,
    45, 50, 51, 53, 54, 56, 60, 61, 62, 64,
    65, 72, 77, 78, 83, 93, 94, 95, 96, 97,
    98, 100–101, 105, 126, 137, 139, 142,
    143, 147, 149, 151, 161 n. 23,
    165 n. 3, 171 n. 2, 173 n. 23, 175 n. 42,
    176 n. 56, 177 n. 1, 180 n. 7, 182 n. 20,
    184 n. 36, 187 n. 8; ordinations, 9, 12,
    13, 20, 22, 25, 26, 28, 33, 35, 39–71,
    98, 99, 100–101, 107, 109, 121–136,
    161 n. 23, 163 n. 29, 165 n. 3, 166 n. 7,
    169 n. 21, 171 nn. 1 and 3; retreats, 2,

3, 4, 48, 71, 92, 94, 101, 185 n. 36;
    transmission of the canon, 60–63,
    93–95
*Ling-pao ching,* 149
*Ling-pao ching-mu,* 62
*Ling-pao ch'u-meng pi-sai liu-ch'ing chieh
    wen,* 139
*Ling-pao chung-meng ching,* 93
*Ling-pao fu wu-ya li-ch'eng,* 175 n. 43
*Ling-pao san-yüan chai i,* 175 n. 43
*Ling-pao sheng-hsüan pu-hsü chang,* 139
*Ling-pao tzu-jan ching-ch'üan,* 93
*Ling-pao yü-tzu ching,* 137
Ling-t'ung chin-shang men, 108
liturgical vestments, 33, 46, 73, 126,
    143–144, 169 n. 21
Liu Chih-chi, 154 n. 2
Liu T'ung-sheng, 161 n. 21
*Lo shu,* 27, 147
long kneelings, 41, 122, 130, 131, 132
Lord Lao. *See* Lao Tzu
Lord Liu's Grotto, 91
Lord Wang, 91
Lou-kuan, 161 n. 21
Lu Hsiu-ching, 22, 23, 24, 26, 30, 32,
    39, 43, 44, 46, 48, 50, 51, 53, 54, 55,
    57, 61, 62, 63, 65, 68, 69, 72, 79, 81,
    91, 98, 99–100, 107, 121, 122, 124,
    126, 127, 128, 132, 133, 135, 142,
    161 n. 23, 165 n. 3, 166 nn. 5 and 7,
    167 n. 9, 171 n. 1, 173 nn. 16 and 22,
    174 nn. 24, 30, and 31, 175 n. 42,
    176 n. 46, 186 n. 1
Lu-sheng, 74, 75, 140, 178 n. 3
*Lu-sheng san-chieh wen,* 74
Lu-sheng ti-tzu, 179 n. 4
Lunar Gate, 107
Lung-ch'ang (Gold-Immortal), 12
Lyrics for Pacing the Void, 65, 176 n. 46

Ma-chi (Mt.), 60
Ma Yu-?, 83
Mao (Mt.), 72, 96
marchmounts. *See* Five Marchmounts
marriage, 9–12, 156 n. 8, 158 nn. 11 and
    13, 159 n. 15
Marvelous Canon of the Treasure Writs
    in Ten Sections, 60, 61
Master Hu, 15, 161 n. 20
mats, 27, 116, 167–168 n. 11

memorial paper, 35, 117
*Meng-wei fu,* 144
Middle Covenant, 66, 68, 181 n. 14
*Ming (-chen) k'o,* 28, 45, 165 n. 3,
   173 n. 17
Most Exalted Bureaus, 45
Most Exalted Lord of the Great Tao,
   50, 61, 94
motifs: on altar fixtures, 27, 28, 29, 31,
   116–120; in Ling-pao ordinations,
   46–48
Mou chih-ch'i cheng-i meng-wei ti-tzu,
   78
Mou chih-ch'i nan-kuan nü-kuan, 74
Mountain Interdictions, 106
Mountain of the Jade Capital, 65
music, 38, 43, 120, 186 n. 1
Mysterious Code, 50
Mysterious Metropolis, 59, 61, 65
Mysterious Petition of the Perfected
   Cavern, 51
Mysterious Terrace, 49, 61

Nan-sheng nü-sheng, 74
Nan-sheng ti-tzu, 179 n. 4
Needham, Joseph, 30
net, 32, 33, 38, 116, 117, 120, 150,
   169 n. 21
New Protocols Imperially Compiled,
   77, 161 n. 23, 172 nn. 11 and 12
Nine Heavens (and their gods), 34, 45,
   48, 49, 50, 51, 52, 57, 59, 127, 131,
   143
Nocturnal Annunciation (Revelation),
   13, 15, 20, 23, 28, 29, 32, 33, 34, 42,
   44, 45, 46, 49, 61, 66, 68, 69, 70,
   120, 121, 122, 123, 124, 126–135,
   142, 171 nn. 1 and 2, 172 n. 11
numerology, 27, 28, 29, 30, 32, 38,
   169 n. 20
numinous bureaucrats, 32, 33, 35,
   36–37, 48, 51, 70, 101, 112, 143,
   145
numinous mountains, 51, 56, 59, 125,
   128
Numinous Text of the Three Caverns in
   Purple Writ, 15
Numinous Treasure Writs. *See* Five
   Talismans
non-action, 8

oaths, 3, 31, 32, 33, 35, 36, 60, 66, 75,
   97, 100–101, 131, 150, 151, 179 n. 4,
   181 n. 11; transmission of, 67–68
Office of the Bureaucrats of the Shades,
   34, 37
Office of the Capital Spirits, 34, 37
officiants, 2–3, 16, 23, 25, 29, 31, 32,
   38, 72, 100, 101, 105, 107, 141–142,
   145–146, 168 n. 14, 170 n. 30,
   171 n. 4, 172 n. 9, 173 nn. 16 and 22,
   174 n. 30; at Ling-pao ordinations,
   39–71, 121–137
Ōfuchi Ninji, 165 n. 3, 175 n. 42,
   177 n. 1, 186 n. 4
One-Hundred and Eighty Injunctions
   of Lord Lao, 182 n. 18
One-Hundred and Eighty Injunctions
   of the Three Primes, 69, 135,
   176 n. 54
oral instructions, 82, 91, 96, 137,
   173 n. 22
oratories, 39, 125, 171 n. 2, 179 n. 4
ordained princesses, 102–104
ordinands, 2–3, 23, 24, 26, 29, 31, 32,
   33, 34, 35, 36, 72, 73, 78, 100, 101,
   105, 163 n. 29, 170 n. 28, 173 n. 22,
   176 n. 46, 179 n. 4; at Ling-pao ordinations, 39–71, 122, 124–136
Ordinands Read Their Own Covenants, 132

*Pa-ch'eng wu-sheng shih-san fu,* 88
*Pa-chieh (wen),* 75–76, 140, 178 n. 3,
   180 n. 9
*Pa-pai wen,* 140
*Pa-shih lu,* 88
*Pa-ti hsüan-pien ching,* 92
*Pa-ti ling-shu nei-wen,* 88
*Pa-ti miao-ching ching,* 92
*Pa-ti shen-hua ching,* 92
*Pai-pa-shih chieh chung-lü,* 80
*Pai-wu-shih chiang-chün lu,* 74, 76, 147,
   178–179 n. 4
Palace of Purple Subtlety (Tenuity), 49,
   51, 61
*P'an-tai,* 90
Pao (Mt.), 53
Pao Ching, 91
parishes, 32, 74–75, 141, 147, 179 n. 5
Pear Garden Troupe, 16, 161 n. 22

P'ei Fei-kung, 155 n. 3
Pei-mang (Mt.), 105
pennons, 27, 28, 108, 118–119,
167 n. 10
the Perfected, 2, 23, 24, 26, 29, 38, 53,
61, 62, 69, 94, 96, 97, 99, 101, 119,
125, 127, 143, 145, 166 n. 6, 186 nn.
41 and 2
Petitioning the Officials to Report the
Rite, 145
petitions, 79, 80, 82, 86
phoenix pinions, 27, 116, 167–168 n. 11
Pieh-chia, 156 n. 8
pilgrimage, 22, 46–47
Pillar of State, 1, 17, 115
P'ing-en (Princess), 103
placards, 23, 24, 26, 29, 107, 108, 109,
165 n. 5, 167 n. 9
pledges, 3, 4, 27, 32–38, 45, 63, 68, 70,
79, 91, 100, 117, 120, 123, 130, 150,
169 nn. 16, 19, and 21, 170 nn. 23,
26, 29, 30, and 34, 171 n. 35
Po Ho, 91
pongee, 33, 91, 117, 120
Preceptor of Ordination, 141
preceptors. See officiants
precepts. See injunctions
Primordial Commencement, 49, 50,
51, 59
Principality-Founding Duke, Ho-nei
Commandery, 1, 17, 115
Procedure for Establishing an Altar to
Perform the Su-lu Rite, 24
protocols, 2, 4, 12, 20, 74, 80, 82, 84,
86, 87, 92, 97, 99, 100, 171 nn. 35, 2,
and 3, 172 n. 11, 173 n. 14, 176 n. 56,
183 n. 20; altar fixtures and furniture,
27–32; for Ling-pao ordinations, 42–
71; ordination officiants, 40–41;
pledges, 32–37; schedules for ordination, 40; structure of altars, 22–26;
title-tablets, 25–26
P'u-hsia pan, 88
Pure Capital Abbey. See Ch'ing-tu
kuan
Purifying the Altar to Free It from
Defilement, 144–145
purple-gold, 21, 25–26, 167 n. 9
Putchuk, 30, 169 n. 15

Quiet Visualization of the Three Preceptors, 127

reading of the Covenant's Writ, 61
reading of the Petition on Yellow Silk,
44–45, 122, 124, 125, 171 n. 1
reading of the Slips, 69–70, 136
reading the Boards, 133–134
reading the Covenant's Writ, 132
reading the Memorial's Writ, 131
realgar, 30
Receiving the Canon, 123
Red Petition on Yellow Silk, 122
Red Script, 49, 50, 110, 112, 130
Red Sovereign (of the South), 53, 55
Regal Gate, 24, 69, 124, 136, 165 n. 5
Register Preceptor, 40, 127, 141
registers, 2, 11, 31, 39, 46, 51, 55, 64,
65, 69, 70, 73, 74, 75, 76–77, 79–81,
85, 86, 87, 88, 91, 92, 93, 95, 96, 97,
100, 101, 118, 127, 141, 145, 146–
147, 148, 176 n. 45, 177 n. 1, 177–
178 n. 2, 178 n. 3, 178–179 n. 4,
179 n. 5, 180 n. 9, 181 n. 14
registration, 75, 179 n. 5
reign of terror, 6–7, 14, 155 n. 3
Reischauer, Edwin, 164 n. 2
remission of sins, 70
rending the (Spontaneously Generated)
Tally, 1, 42–43, 67, 121–124,
173 n. 14
Rescript for Revering the Compact, 45,
125
Restoration of the Bureaucrats, 125,
134
Retreat for Clarifying Perfection, 102
Retreat of Eight Segments, 102
Retreat of Spontaneity, 102
retreat of thanksgiving for mercy, 69,
136
Retreat of the Gold Register, 15, 54,
174 n. 27
Retreat of the Three Primes, 102, 109,
166 n. 8
retreats, 27, 30, 32, 34, 62, 63, 65, 68,
73, 80, 82, 86, 87, 92, 94, 96–97, 98,
186 n. 4
Return to the Censer, 30, 69, 125, 134,
136, 146

revelation, 2, 3, 53, 61–62, 72, 80, 82, 86–87, 91, 94, 96, 99, 173 n. 23, 174 n. 26, 175 n. 41, 180 n. 9, 182 n. 19, 184 nn. 27, 30, and 36, 185 nn. 40 and 41
Rules of Deportment, 50

sacred mountains, 34, 38
Salute and Bows to the Ten Directions in Circuit, 123
Salute to the Original Preceptor, 133
Salute to the Three Preceptors, 133
salvation, 10, 12, 15, 37, 38, 56, 57, 61, 69–70, 81, 94, 101–102, 144, 163 n. 29, 167 n. 10, 178 n. 2
*San chiang-chün fu-lu,* 74, 178 n. 3
*San chiang-chün t'u,* 90
*San-chieh (wen),* 139, 179 n. 4, 180 n. 9
*San-chüeh wen,* 140
*San-huang chai-i,* 92
*San-huang ch'ao-i,* 92
*San-huang chen-hsing nei-hui pan,* 90
*San-huang chiu-t'ien chen-fu ch'i-ling,* 90
*San-huang ch'uan-pan,* 90
*San-huang ch'uan-shou i,* 92
*San-huang nei-chen hui,* 88
*San-huang nei-ching fu,* 88
*San-huang nei-wen,* 89, 149
*San-huang piao,* 90
*San-huang san-chieh wu-chieh pa-chieh wen,* 88
*San-huang san-i chen-hsing nei-hui pan,* 90
*San-huang t'ien-wen ta-tzu,* 89
*San-huang tzu-wu chai,* 184 n. 30
*San-huang wen,* 9, 16, 35, 36, 72, 76, 78, 94, 95, 98, 141, 142, 143, 148, 149, 161 n. 23, 166 n. 7, 177 n. 1, 181 n. 14, 184 n. 30; transmission of, 87–92
*San-huang yin,* 90
*San-huang yü-ch'üan,* 90
*San-i ti-tzu, Ch'ih-yang chen-jen,* 78
*San-kuei chieh,* 75, 76
*San-kuei wu-chieh,* 74
*San-pai-liu-shih chang,* 78
*San-pai ta-chang,* 79
*San-pu pa-ching tzu-jan chih-chen yü-lu,* 93
*San-t'ien chai,* 182 n. 20
*San-t'ien cheng-fa ch'u liu-t'ien yü-wen,* 149
San-tung chiang fa shih, 143

*San-wu ta-chai chih chüeh,* 82
*San-yao wen,* 140
sandalwood, 29, 118
Saso, Michael, 164 n. 1
satchels (bags, etc.), 31, 50, 57, 118
scripts (talismanic, etc.), 2, 25, 26, 50, 53, 54, 55, 56, 59, 107, 108, 112, 174 n. 24
Scriptural Preceptors, 33, 40, 127, 141
Sealing of the Staffs, 57–60, 132, 135
seals, 36, 90, 100
Seidel, Anna, 176 n. 45
Self- (or Spontaneously) Generated Tally of the Numinous-Treasure, 1, 42, 43, 115
Service for Stentorian Annunciation, 1, 17, 115
Service of the Grand Standard-Bearer, 6, 155 n. 3
seven luminaries, 28
seven-treasure, 27, 31, 34, 61, 117, 118, 119, 150, 168 n. 12
Seventy-Two Elysian Fields, 125
Shan-kuang Monastery, 167 n. 8
Shang-ch'ing, 169 n. 21, 170 nn. 26 and 29, 181 n. 14, 185 n. 40; canon, 4, 16, 20, 33, 34, 72, 78, 94, 95–96, 98, 99, 105, 106, 142, 143, 147–148, 149, 151, 161 n. 23, 177 n. 1, 185 n. 40, 187 n. 8; ordination, 20, 148, 166 n. 6; retreats, 185 n. 40; transmission of the canon, 95–97
*Shang-ch'ing ching,* 147–148
*Shang-ch'ing fa-lu,* 144
*Shang-ch'ing hsüan-tu ta-tung san-ching ti-tzu, Wu-shang san-tung fa-shih,* 96
*Shang-ch'ing pei-ti shen-chou wen,* 95
*Shang-ch'ing p'in ching fu,* 78
*Shang-ch'ing ta-tung chen-ching,* 96
*Shang-fa chiu-t'ien ling-wen,* 130
*Shang-huang pao-p'ien,* 173 n. 19
Shao-yang (Princess), 103
*Shen-chou ching,* 147, 181 n. 14; transmission of, 81–82
*Shen-chou ch'üan,* 81
*Shen-chou lu,* 81
*Shen-hsien chin-chou ching,* 81
Shen-pao chün, 91
shen-tsu ti-tzu, 41

*Sheng-chi ching,* 186 n. 4
*Sheng-hsüan ch'i-shih-erh tzu ta-lu (ch'üan),* 92
Sheng-hsüan fa-shih, 92
*Sheng-hsüan (nei-chiao) ching,* 142, 172 n. 6, 181 n. 14; transmission of, 92–93
Sheng-shan ssu (monastery), 17, 162 n. 23
*Sheng-t'ien ch'üan,* 90
*Shih chi,* 86
*Shih ch'i-hsin ju-tao san-kuei-chieh wen,* 139
*Shih chiang-chün fu-lu,* 74, 76, 178 nn. 2 and 3, 179 n. 4
*Shih-chieh ching,* 83
*Shih-chieh shih-ssu ch'ih-shen chieh,* 83
Shih Ch'ung-hsüan, 1, 3, 41, 42, 161–162 n. 23, 162 n. 26, 163 n. 28, 172 n. 10, 180 n. 10; life, 16–20; titles, 1, 16–18, 115, 162 n. 26
*Shih-erh k'o-ts'ung liu-ch'ing chieh,* 77
*Shih-san-chin wen,* 140
Shih-yang sheng-ch'i men, 108
Shou (Prince), 158 n. 12
Signet of the Five Elders, 57, 58
Signet of the Primordial Commencement, 56, 58
sila, 75, 140, 180 n. 9
singing the Formulae for the Celestial Venerables of the Ten Directions, 129
singing the Three Salutes, 76, 133
sitting in forgetfulness, 97
Six Heavens, 45, 50, 67, 80, 173 n. 18
Slip (Board) Writs (of the Eight Authorities), 49, 51, 63, 68, 70, 100, 114, 150, 175 n. 36; transmission of, 56–57, 171 n. 1
smearing blood on the lips, 31, 33, 36, 150, 170 n. 22
So Ch'ung-shu, 83
soil god, 164 n. 1
Solar Gate, 107
sorcery, 5, 154–155 n. 2
specters, 48, 49, 51, 52, 57, 60, 67, 80, 129
*Ssu-chi ming-k'o,* 60, 175 n. 37
Ssu-ma Ch'eng-chen, 15, 160 n. 19
Ssu-ma Ch'ien, 86
Ssu-ma Kuang, 154 n. 2, 159 n. 14

*Ssu-shen t'u,* 81
staffs, 2, 49, 63, 68, 95, 100, 114, 116, 130, 131, 171 n. 1, 175 n. 36; transmission of, 57–60
stale emanations, 45
statues, 27
Student of the Three Caverns, 20, 139, 141, 143, 144, 146
Students of the Register for the Five Thousand Words, 84
Students of True-Unity, 76
Su-ch'i and Su-lu. *See* Nocturnal Annunciation
Su Huai-ch'u, 138
Su-tsung, 16
Sun Yu-yüeh, 91
Sung (Mt.), 15, 91, 160 n. 20
Sung Wen-ming, 62, 175 n. 42
supernumerary offices, 17, 162 n. 24
Supreme Purity Abbey. *See* T'ai-ch'ing kuan
symbolism, 34, 35; alchemical, 30–31; of altars, 25, 38; of colors, 25–27, 29, 38, 169 n. 18; of light, 28, 29

Ta-ch'ih (Great Red) Heaven, 55, 112, 132
Ta-lo, 143
Ta-lo fei-fan men, 108
Ta-ming Palace, 160 n. 20, 163 n. 1
*Ta T'ang liu-tien,* 101
Ta-tung fa-shih, 144
*Ta-yu lu-t'u Jen-huang nei-wen,* 92
*Ta-yu lu-t'u Ti-huang nei-wen,* 92
*Ta-yu lu-t'u T'ien-huang nei-wen,* 91
table cloths, 33, 34, 38, 117
table settings, 29, 116
tables, 29, 31–32, 35, 49, 109, 118, 131, 168 n. 13, 169 n. 19
tablets, 79, 88, 90, 95, 96, 133
taboos, 88, 90, 112, 141–142, 146
T'ai (Mt.), 57, 59, 69, 177 n. 56
*T'ai-chen k'o,* 97, 124, 171 n. 2, 177–178 n. 2, 178 n. 3, 182 nn. 19 and 20
*T'ai-chen meng-chüeh,* 130
T'ai-chi Hall, 162 n. 27
*T'ai-chi pao-chüeh,* 137
*T'ai-chi tso-hsien kung Tao-te ching hsü,* 148–149
*T'ai-ch'ing chung-ching shen-tan fang,* 91

T'ai-ch'ing kuan (abbey), 18, 19, 139, 141, 143, 148, 162 n. 25, 162–163 n. 28, 163 n. 29, 172 n. 10
*T'ai-ch'ing yin-yang chieh,* 84
*T'ai-hsüan ching,* 87, 149
*T'ai-hsüan ho-t'u,* 95
*T'ai-i pa-t'ieh t'un-chia hsien-lu,* 85
Tai-kuo (Princess), 104, 187 n. 6
T'ai-p'ing (Princess), 6, 8, 12, 17, 18, 20, 102, 104, 157 n. 10, 158 n. 11, 163 n. 28; as abbess, 10–11; clique, 8, 17; Taoist ordination, 10–11
T'ai-p'ing kuan (abbey), 157–158 n. 10
*T'ai-p'ing tung-chi ching,* 182 n. 19
*T'ai-shang huang shih-lu,* 154 n. 2
*T'ai-shang kao-hsüan fa-shih,* 84
T'ai-shang Lao-chün (Lao Tzu Deified), 80
*T'ai-shang ling-pao tung-hsüan ching,* 78
*T'ai-shang ling-pao tung-hsüan ti-tzu,* 93
*T'ai-shang san-huang t'ien-wen,* 78
*T'ai-shang Tao-chün,* 82
*T'ai-shang ti-tzu,* 85, 139
*T'ai-shang tung-hsüan ling-pao chu-t'ien nei-yin lu,* 93
*T'ai-shang tung-hsüan ling-pao erh-shih-ssu sheng t'u,* 93
*T'ai-shang tung-hsüan ling-pao sheng-hsüan nei-chiao ching,* 92
*T'ai-shang tung-hsüan ling-pao yü-chüeh,* 22
*T'ai-shang yü-ching yin-chu,* 149
Talisman That Commands the Multitudes, 56
talismans, 2, 39, 42, 44, 57, 58, 59, 64, 68, 73, 80, 81, 86, 88, 89, 95, 100, 101, 114, 135, 144, 145, 174 n. 27, 176 n. 45, 178 n. 2, 180 n. 9
Talismans of the Six Chia Spirits, 106, 144
Talismans of the Three Sovereigns, 106, 144, 147
tallies, 35, 42–43, 73, 79, 81, 90, 92, 93, 94, 97, 122, 133, 150, 170 n. 30, 172–173 n. 13, 173 nn. 13 and 14, 176 n. 45
T'ang Chen-chieh, 83
T'ang measures, 164 n. 1
T'ang P'ing, 82
the T'ang's Taoist ideology, 10, 18,

104, 157 n. 9, 158 n. 10, 162 n. 26, 187 n. 6
Tao-hu teng, 168 n. 12
T'ao Hung-ching, 91, 92, 94, 96, 187 n. 9
*T'ao-kung ch'uan i,* 147, 187 n. 9
*Tao-men chi-yen chi,* 138
*Tao-men ta-lun,* 186 n. 4
tao-shih, 98, 186 n. 41
*Tao-te ching,* 8, 9, 11, 35, 72, 73, 78, 139, 141, 142, 143, 147, 148–149, 158 n. 10, 161 n. 23, 170 n. 28, 171 n. 35, 172 n. 11, 177 n. 1, 181 n. 14, 183 n. 23; transmission of, 82–87
*Tao-te tsun-ching Hsiang-erh chieh,* 183 n. 26
Taoist scriptures: bibliography for, 18, 162 n. 26; glossary to, 18, 162 n. 26
Te-fei, 153 n. 1
T'e-ying, 15–16
ten abominations, 5, 76, 180 n. 9
ten directions (and god), 25, 28, 34, 47, 56, 63, 123, 125, 129, 132, 133–134, 145, 146, 166 n. 7
Ten Heavens, 25
Ten Injunctions, 161 n. 23
ten virtues, 76, 180 n. 9
Terrestrial Portal, 23, 107, 124, 126, 128
Third Covenant, 135–136
thirty-eight officiants, 35, 40–41
Thirty-Six Heavens, 28, 124
Thirty-Two Heavens, 108, 126
thread, 34, 117, 150
Three Caverns, 16, 98, 148, 161–162 n. 23
Three Covenants, 42, 172–173 n. 13
Three Formulae of Refuge or Surrender, 75, 179 n. 7
Three Heavens, 80
Three Heavens' Most Exalted Writ of the Mountain Spirit, 57
Three Officials, 33, 37
Three Preceptors, 126
Three Realms, 125
Three Treasures, 66, 75, 179 n. 7
*Ti-huang chi-shu wen,* 89
*Ti-tzu feng-shih k'o-chieh wen,* 139
Tibetans, 10–11, 157 n. 10, 163 n. 28

*T'ien-huang nei-hsüeh wen,* 89
*T'ien-shui fei-teng fu,* 88
T'ien-t'ai (Mt.), 62, 94
*T'ien-tsun shih-chieh shih-ssu ch'ih-shen chieh,* 77
T'ien T'ung-hsiu, 160 n. 20
title-tablets, 21, 23–26, 116
transmission of Liturgical Positions (by Means of Slips), 68, 133
transmission of the Procedures, 68–69, 120, 135
transmission of the Slip-Board Writs, 132, 135
transmission of the Tally, 122
transmission of the True Writ Registers, 133
transmission of the True Writs, 132
transmission of the Writs for the Six Oaths, 133
Treasure Slats of the Supreme Sovereign, 45
Treasure Talismans. *See* Five Talismans
triratna, 66, 176 n. 48
trisarna, 139
True Talisman of the Five Sovereigns, 59
True-Unity Canon, 79–81
True Writ for the East, 110
True-Writ Registers, 2, 61, 65, 116, 123, 124; transmission of, 63–65, 171 n. 1
True Writs, 23, 31, 42, 44, 45, 53, 54, 56, 61, 65, 78, 100, 120, 125, 130, 131, 173 nn. 19, 22, and 23, 174 nn. 24 and 27; transmission of, 49–52, 171 n. 1
*Tsa-shuo,* 84
tsai-chia, 98
Ts'ai Wei, 154 n. 1, 156 n. 8, 160 n. 20
*Tse-t'ien shih-lu,* 154 n. 2
Tu Kuang-t'ing, 80, 82, 138, 160 n. 19, 182 n. 19
*T'u-t'an chai,* 81, 182–183 n. 20
Tu-yang Palace, 82
Tuan Wan-hsien, 19, 162 n. 27
Tun-huang (and manuscripts), 62, 83, 93, 175 n. 42, 177 n. 1, 183 nn. 22 and 25
*Tung-chen fa-shih,* 95
*Tung-hsi chin-wen,* 149

*Tung-hsi erh-chin fu,* 144, 147
*Tung-hsi liang-chin,* 88
Tung-hsüan. *See* Ling-pao
*Tung-hsüan ling-pao chai nei-shih hsin-yeh hsü,* 137
*T'ung-hsüan lun,* 62
Tung-ling kung (temple), 15
*Tung-shen* (and canon), 16, 33, 35, 37, 43, 76, 78, 89, 90, 91–92, 140, 147, 180 nn. 8 and 9, 184 n. 30
Tung-shen chai, 92
*Tung-shen san-tung yao-yen wu chieh shih-san chieh ch'i-pai erh-shih chieh men,* 89
*Tung-shen t'ai-ch'ing t'ai-chi kung ching,* 149
Tung-shen ti-tzu, 42, 87
Tung-yang t'ai-kuang men, 108
T'ung-yin chin-ch'üeh men, 108
*Tung-yüan ling-pao shih-pu ching hsü,* 137
*Tung-yüan shen-chou ching,* 141
*Tung-yüan shen-chou ta-tsung san-mei fa-shih hsiao-chao chen-jen,* 81
Turks, 7
twenty-eight asterisms, 28
twenty-four astral deities, 55
Twenty-Four Celestial Master Parishes, 125
twenty-four life vapors, 34
twenty-four segmental energies, 28, 32, 129
twenty-four spirits, 49, 55
*Tzu-chih t'ung-chien k'ao-i,* 154 n. 2
*Tzu-hsü lu,* 86
*Tzu-jan ch'üan,* 94, 172 n. 13
*Tzu-kung i-tu ta-lu,* 86

Uighur khan, 103

Venerable Canon in Thirty-Six Sections, 66, 75, 139
visitation boards (tablets), 47, 129, 133
Visiting the Preceptor and Submitting the Statement, 41, 42, 121
visualizations, 2, 31, 39, 47, 48, 56, 57, 58, 63, 64, 79, 97, 100, 105, 123, 126, 127, 129, 130, 141, 142, 145, 179 n. 4
vows, 9, 10, 11, 34, 36, 38, 46, 61, 68, 100–101, 163 n. 29, 169 n. 19, 179 n. 4, 180 n. 8

Wan-an (Princess), 103
Wan-sheng Ordination Platform,
    165 n. 2
Wang Fang-p'ing, 91
Wang Pao, 91
Wang Shou-tao, 161 n. 21
Wang Tsuan, 82
Wang Wei, 15
Wang-wu (Mt.), 15, 160 n. 20
Wang Yü-chen, 83
Water Sovereign of the Eastern Ocean,
    51, 52
Water Sovereign of the Nine Adminis-
    trations, 69
Wei Cheng, 14
Wei-kuo kuan (abbey), 163 n. 28
Wei Shu, 157 n. 10
Wei T'ao, 160 n. 19
Wei Ts'ou, 162 n. 25
Wei T'uan-erh, 5–6, 7, 154 n. 2
Wei Yüan-chung, 154 n. 2
Wen-an (Princess), 103
writs, 2, 41, 46, 51, 52, 72, 73, 74, 80,
    83, 85, 88, 89, 91, 92, 93, 95, 96,
    100, 114, 144, 145, 174 nn. 30 and
    31, 176 n. 45; Ling-pao transmission
    of, 48–60
Writ for the Six Oaths, 67–68
Writ of the Covenant, 128
writing brushes, 35, 117
Wu-chieh (wen), 75, 140, 179 n. 4,
    180 n. 9, 181 n. 11, 183 n. 25, 184 n. 27
Wu-ch'ien wen, 86
Wu-ch'ien-wen ch'ao-i, 84
Wu-fa, 95, 106, 147, 187 n. 9
Wu-fu, 144, 147
Wu-fu ch'uan-pan, 95
Wu-fu hsü, 95
Wu-shang chen-jen chuan, 84
Wu-shang shih chieh, 76
Wu-shang tung-hsüan fa-shih, 93
Wu-shang tung-shen fa-shih, 89
Wu-t'ai (Mt.), 164 n. 2
Wu-ti (r. 561–578), 77, 161 n. 23,
    171 n. 1, 172 nn. 11 and 12

Wu Tse-t'ien, 9, 10, 12, 13, 17,
    157 n. 9, 158 n. 10; overthrow of, 7;
    political influence of, 7; treatment of
    the T'ang, 5–7, 155 n. 3; usurpation,
    5
Wu Yen-chi, 156 n. 4
Wu-yüeh chen-hsing t'u, 36, 91, 95, 106,
    144, 147, 149
Wu-yüeh kung-yang t'u, 95

Yang Hsi, 96, 99, 186 n. 2
Yang-t'ai kuan (abbey), 14
Yang Yü-huan (Yang Kuei-fei), 12,
    158 n. 12
Yeh Fa-shan, 9, 17, 154 n. 1, 156 n. 8
Yellow Register Retreat, 22, 24, 26, 28,
    102, 106, 108, 109, 166 n. 7
Yellow Silk Petition, 130, 131, 172–
    173 n. 13
Yen Lü-ming, 83
Yin Hsi, 84, 86, 160 n. 20, 183 n. 27
Yin-i, 137–138
Yin-sheng kuang-ling men, 108
Yoshioka Yoshitoyo, 138, 162 n. 26,
    163 n. 29, 177 n. 1
Yü (the Great), 53, 174 n. 26
Yü (Mt.), 62, 94
Yü-chen. See Jade-Perfected
Yü-chen kuan (abbey), 16
Yü-li ching, 85, 87
Yü-lu chai, 185 n. 36
Yü-tzu shang-ching, 149
Yü-wen Jung, 160 n. 18
Yü-yü Heaven, 55, 132
Yüan-huang kao-ch'en men, 108
Yüan-shih ling-ts'e, 93
Yüan-shih tung-hsüan ling-pao ch'ih-shu
    chen-wen lu, 93
Yüan-shih wu-lao ch'ih-shu yü-p'ien chen-
    wen, 130
Yüan-tu kuan (abbey), 14, 163 n. 29
Yung-an (Princess), 103
Yung-chia (Princess), 103
Yung-mu (Princess), 102
Yung-t'ai (Princess), 7, 9, 156 n. 4

# ABOUT THE AUTHOR

**Charles Benn** received his Ph.D. in Chinese history from the University of Michigan. His field of specialization is the history of Taoism. His article "Religious Aspects of Hsüan-tsung's Taoist Ideology" appeared in *Buddhist and Taoist Practice in Medieval Chinese Society* (1987). Currently, he is working on a number of projects including a translation of a collection of devotional accounts of Taoist miracles in the T'ang dynasty and a history of banquets during the reign of Emperor Chung-tsung (A.D. 705–710). Dr. Benn is an instructor of Chinese religion at the University of Hawaii.

# ASIAN STUDIES AT HAWAII

No. 1   *Bibliography of English Language Sources on Human Ecology, Eastern Malaysia and Brunei.* Compiled by Conrad P. Cotter with the assistance of Shiro Saito. 1965. Two Parts. (Available only from Paragon Book Gallery, New York.)

No. 2   *Economic Factors in Southeast Asian Social Change.* Edited by Robert Van Niel. 1968. Out of print.

No. 3   *East Asian Occasional Papers (1).* Edited by Harry J. Lamley. 1969. Out of print.

No. 4   *East Asian Occasional Papers (2).* Edited by Harry J. Lamley. 1970.

No. 5   *A Survey of Historical Source Materials in Java and Manila.* Robert Van Niel. 1971.

No. 6   *Educational Theory in the People's Republic of China: The Report of Ch'ien Chung-Jui.* Translated by John N. Hawkins. 1971. Out of print.

No. 7   *Hai Jui Dismissed from Office.* Wu Han. Translated by C. C. Huang. 1972. Out of print.

No. 8   *Aspects of Vietnamese History.* Edited by Walter F. Vella. 1973. Out of print.

No. 9   *Southeast Asian Literatures in Translation: A Preliminary Bibliography.* Philip N. Jenner. 1973. Out of print.

No. 10  *Textiles of the Indonesian Archipelago.* Garrett and Bronwen Solyom. 1973. Out of print.

No. 11  *British Policy and the Nationalist Movement in Burma, 1917–1937.* Albert D. Moscotti, 1974. Out of print.

No. 12  *Aspects of Bengali History and Society.* Edited by Rachel Van M. Baumer. 1975.

No. 13  *Nanyang Perspective: Chinese Students in Multiracial Singapore.* Andrew W. Lind. 1974.

No. 14  *Political Change in the Philippines: Studies of Local Politics preceding Martial Law.* Edited by Benedict J. Kerkvliet. 1974. Out of print.

No. 15  *Essays on South India.* Edited by Burton Stein. 1976.

No. 16  *The* Caurāsī Pad *of Śrī Hit Harivaṁś.* Charles S. J. White. 1977.

No. 17  *An American Teacher in Early Meiji Japan.* Edward R. Beauchamp. 1976. Out of print.

No. 18  *Buddhist and Taoist Studies I.* Edited by Michael Saso and David W. Chappell. 1977.

No. 19  *Sumatran Contributions of the Development of Indonesian Literature, 1920–1942.* Alberta Joy Freidus. 1977.

No. 20  *Insulinde: Selected Translations from Dutch Writers of Three Centuries on the Indonesian Archipelago.* Edited by Cornelia N. Moore. 1978.

No. 21  *Regents, Reformers, and Revolutionaries: Indonesian Voices of Colonial Days, Selected Historical Readings, 1899–1949.* Translated, edited, and annotated by Greta O. Wilson. 1978.

No. 22  *The Politics of Inequality: Competition and Control in an Indian Village.* Miriam Sharma. 1978.

No. 23  *Brokers of Morality: Thai Ethnic Adaptation in a Rural Malaysian Setting.* Louis Golomb. 1979. Out of print.

No. 24  *Tales of Japanese Justice.* Ihara Saikaku. Translated by Thomas M. Kondo and Alfred H. Marks. 1980. Out of print.

No. 25  *Mandarins, Gunboats, and Power Politics: Owen Nickerson Denny and the International Rivalries in Korea.* Robert R. Swartout, Jr. 1980.

No. 26  *Nichiren: Selected Writings.* Laurel Rasplica Rodd. 1980. Out of print.

No. 27  *Ethnic Groups and Social Change in a Chinese Market Town.* C. Fred Blake. 1980.

No. 28  *The Evolution of Hindu Ethical Ideals.* S. Cromwell Crawford. 1982. Out of print.

No. 29  *Experimental Essays on Chuang-tzu.* Edited by Victor H. Mair. 1983.

No. 30  *Songs of Nepal.* Siegfried Lienhard. 1984.

No. 31  *The Origins of Japan's Modern Forests: The Case of Akita.* Conrad Totman. 1985.

No. 32  *Thailand in Transition: The Role of Oppositional Forces.* Ross Prizzia. 1985.

No. 33  *Law and the State in Traditional East Asia: Six Studies on the Sources of East Asian Law.* Edited by Brian E. McKnight. 1987.

No. 34  *Buddhist and Taoist Practice in Medieval Chinese Society: Buddhist and Taoist Studies II.* Edited by David W. Chappell. 1987.

No. 35  *An American Scientist in Early Meiji Japan: The Autobiographical Notes of Thomas C. Mendenhall.* Edited by Richard Rubinger. 1989.

No. 36  *A History of Indian Buddhism: From Śākyamuni to Early Mahāyāna.* Hirakawa Akira. Translated and edited by Paul Groner. 1990.

No. 37  *Ilocano Irrigation: The Corporate Resolution.* Henry T. Lewis. 1991.

Orders for Asian Studies at Hawaii publications should be directed to the University of Hawaii Press, Order Department, 2840 Kolowalu Street, Honolulu, Hawaii 96822. Present standing orders will continue to be filled without special notification.